DREAMS, WAKING THOUGHTS AND INCIDENTS

Mr. Gemmett has also edited Beckford's
BIOGRAPHICAL MEMOIRS OF EXTRAORDINARY
PAINTERS

DREAMS, WAKING THOUGHTS AND INCIDENTS

by
William Beckford of Fonthill

Edited
with An Introduction and Notes
by

ROBERT J. GEMMETT

Rutherford • Madison • Teaneck
FAIRLEIGH DICKINSON UNIVERSITY PRESS

Associated University Presses, Inc.
Cranbury, New Jersey 08512

ISBN: 0-8386-7648-0
Printed in the United States of America

For
Stephen and Scott

Contents

Contents

List of Illustrations

Foreword

This edition of *Dreams, Waking Thoughts and Incidents* is practically a verbatim reprint of the suppressed edition of 1783. Beckford never wanted the book to be widely distributed, and he destroyed almost 500 copies by fire to prevent this from happening. Fortunately, a few volumes survived the holocaust and still exist today. The one used for the present work is currently on deposit in the Beinecke Rare Book and Manuscript Library. Its early owner was Beckford's solicitor, Richard Samuel White.

There are some changes in this new edition: the original eighteenth-century spellings have been retained, but a few obvious typographical errors have been corrected; the long "s" has been dropped; missing quotation marks have been supplied for passages of direct speech; and titles of works have been italicized as have the foreign words and phrases. Beckford incorporated fourteen notes in the original text, and his name appears in this edition after each to distinguish them from others added by this editor. The new footnotes are biographical and identificatory, or of a general explanatory nature. The Latin and Italian literary quotations in the text have been translated and their sources located. For the reader who may be interested in learning how Beckford altered *Dreams* for publication in 1834 as the first volume of *Italy; with Sketches of Spain and Portugal,* an appendix has been prepared which outlines the principal variations between the two texts.

In the process of preparing this work for publication, I was aided by the generosity of several people: Diana Steel and Drs. Joseph Jenks and Joseph Siracusa of SUNY at Brockport provided considerable assistance with the translations; Debra Kowlakowski doggedly prepared the typescript of the appendix from

11

my sometimes mystifying handwriting; J. C. Maxwell saved me from embarrassment by identifying the source of one of Beckford's Latin quotations; two Beckford scholars, Guy Chapman and André Parreaux, were very kind in their willingness to answer my queries about *Dreams;* and Wilmarth Lewis graciously permitted me to photograph for this volume two prints from his impressive collection housed in the Lewis Walpole Library in Farmington, Connecticut. To all of the above I am very grateful.

I wish also to express my appreciation to the Beinecke Library for permission to use the copy of *Dreams* in their possession and for the right to quote from unpublished material in the Beckford Collection.

I am especially indebted to my wife, Kendra, for her constant encouragement and for her unfailing support during this project.

Introduction

  A handsome quarto volume, consisting of a collection of letters
from the Low Countries and Italy in 1780-82, and an account
of the Grand Chartreuse in 1778, *Dreams, Waking Thoughts and
Incidents* was published in 1783 but suppressed before distribution and relegated to a state of limbo for over fifty years. It was
allowed to appear in 1834, after numerous alterations, as the
first volume of *Italy; with Sketches of Spain and Portugal*. The
decision to sell *Dreams* in an expurgated form was Beckford's. He
revised heavily as he read through one of the few surviving copies,
touching page after page with a careful editor's hand. In the end
most of the changes were omissions: he pared the text of *Dreams*
closer to the bone and in the process changed its character. He
cut away the personal allusions and the anecdotes that might in
any way make the persistent rumors about his homosexual nature
more credible; he slashed passages brimming with sentimentality;
he eliminated the dream machinery along with the excessive flights
of imagination; the art criticism, which bulked large in the book,
he qualified and made less rhapsodic. In short, he gave the book
a general toning down in an obvious effort to avoid extravagance
of any kind. The result was that the 1834 volume became cooler
in tone, more classical in character, exhibiting greater restraint of
imagination and propriety of expression and a more formal decorum throughout. The work of 1783, on the other hand, was
freer, more spontaneous, and more passionate. *Italy* reflected the
seventy-three-year-old man whose youthful ardor had cooled, whose
tastes and spirit had tempered with age. *Dreams* reflected the
young Beckford, spoiled, undisciplined, eager to display his artistic sensibilities, an artist so absorbed with his own image that
he easily became one of the sublime solipsists of his age.

13

I

A story of tortured youth provides the background for *Dreams*. The son of a wealthy merchant and prominent Member of Parliament (twice Lord Mayor), Beckford, almost from the day of his birth in 1760, was condemned to match his father's talents in the political and economic spheres of English society. The enforced competition was harmful to the growing boy, whose sensitive nature ill-prepared him for these tasks. The early death of his father complicated matters by putting him in the control of his mother, an autocratic woman, fiercely possessive of her son's affection and even more obsessed than her husband with the preparations for his career. A strong influence on his life, she instilled in him her own Calvinistic sense of fate and sin, which pervaded so much of what Beckford later wrote, and she turned his attention to a study of his own ancestry, which increased his self-centeredness and bred in him a vanity of birth that he never lost. When it came time to send him away to school where he might have developed more normally among boys his age, Mrs. Beckford refused to allow it, educating him instead at home, where he was constantly subjected to the pressures of a family council composed of dowager aunts and people removed from his generation. It was a stifling atmosphere, which made him lonely and secretive, prone to moods of extreme depression and to long periods of exaggerated introspection.

The private education did little to make his existence bearable; it was rigidly classical in orientation, with the objective being "to look upon taste and sentiment as acquisitions of less importance, than the right use of reason."[1] Beckford was precociously intelligent, but he was also intensely emotional and willful by nature—a mercurial personality. In time the severity of the educational program chaffed "so warm an imagination," and he developed an addiction to the more volatile imaginative literature of the day, particularly the *Arabian Nights* and its imitations, after which the "classics fell flat upon his mind." There was food for daydream in the colorful tales he pored over in the isolation of his chambers, an outlet to escape the heavy demands at home. Attempts were made to curb this unclassical interest. On one occasion, the guardian tutor, the Reverend John Lettice, forced the boy to burn a "splendid heap of oriental drawings, etc." but the

1. John Lettice to W. Pitt, December 11, 1773, *Correspondence of William Pitt, Earl of Chatham,* ed. W. S. Taylor and J. H. Pringle (London, 1840), IV, 315.

repressive effort failed partly because of one tutor, Alexander Cozens, who consistently encouraged Beckford's exotic tastes and escapist longings. A widely traveled water-colorist, he stimulated the boy's lively imagination with extravagant stories from his past. He also taught Beckford much of what he knew about the graphic arts in the 1770s, the depth of which would soon become apparent in his student's first published work, *Biographical Memoirs of Extraordinary Painters.* Under Cozens, Beckford developed his pictorial sense of the natural landscape and a highly picturesque literary style. Once aware of the strength of this early influence, it is no surprise that readers of *Dreams* have found in the extensive descriptions analogies to various principles and techniques of painting.

Beckford came to know the intoxication of travel as early as 1777, when he was sent with Lettice to Switzerland to complete his education. It was an important year. He was emancipated for the first time from the claustrophobia of his home life, and he began the writing that prepared him for *Dreams.* Stimulated to creative activity, he was rarely without pen, constructing prose descriptions of spectacular Alpine scenery or confessional reveries for the eyes of Cozens back in England. During his year's stay, he produced *The Long Story* (published as *The Vision* in 1930) and *An Excursion to the Grande Chartreuse,* two remarkable compositions for a boy of seventeen. *Grande Chartreuse,* which was later appended to and published with *Dreams,* exhibited the author's poetic sensibility and love of picturesque scenery, though it tended to be excessively stiff and formal. More characteristic of his later work was *The Long Story,* which displayed the romantic subject matter of dream fantasy—Promethean landscapes, love of voluptuous seclusion and prelapsarian innocence—all in seemingly incongruous combination with the precise, chiseled language of a classicist. *Dreams* itself has been described as a book in which "the characteristic moods of romanticism are set forth in a prose that has not yet yielded its classical restraint to the turgidity that followed the romantic triumph."[2]

Following his return to England in 1778 and for the next few years prior to the composition of *Dreams,* Beckford found himself pulled in different directions by a variety of emotional conflicts. During a tour of England in 1779, he met and developed almost instantly a "strange wayward passion" for William Courtenay, the feminine eleven-year-old son of Lord Courtenay of Powderham

2. "Vathek's Grand Tour," *TLS,* May 3, 1928, p. 331.

Castle. "I grew sensible," he wrote later, "there was a pleasure in loving something besides oneself and felt there would be more luxury in dying for him than living for the rest of the universe."[3] Shortly thereafter Beckford became acquainted with Louisa Beckford, the wife of his cousin Peter, and began an affair with her that flamed into passion by the end of his European tour in the spring of 1781. To these complex relationships were added the troubling responsibilities connected with his wealth and social position. His only relief was the escapism of self-induced visionary states in which he increasingly indulged during the months immediately preceding his departure for the Continent. "Visions play around me," he wrote of himself, "and at some solemn moments I am cast into prophetic Trances. Lost in Dreams and magic slumbers my Hours glide swiftly away. I have none to awaken me—none to sympathize with my feelings. Those I love are absent. Thus desolate and abandoned I seek refuge in aerial conversations and talk with spirits whose voices are murmuring in the Gales."[4]

The ten-month Grand Tour of Europe, which provided material for most of the letters in *Dreams,* became for Beckford a period of deep self-analysis interfused with dark moments of despair. If the family council at Fonthill believed that this tour would somehow cure the vagaries of his personality, they were seriously mistaken. It simply added to his panoply of disorders. On 19 June 1780, he set out from Margate with the ubiquitous Lettice and embarked on the first portion of the journey, moving at a rapid pace through the Low Countries, where he grew "as scurrilous as Dr. Smollet" in his complaints about Dutch and Flemish taste. But when he reached Venice in August some new poison entered his system. Sometime during his month-long stay he got caught up in the decadence of Venetian high society, largely through the help of the adventuress Madame de Rosenberg, and her *cavaliere servente,* Count Benincasa; before long he became involved in a homosexual entanglement with a young member of the aristocratic Vendramin family which left him in a feverish and agitated state. Years later he attempted to explain the relationship in discreet terms as "a passion of the mind—resembling those generous attachments we venerate in ancient history, and holy writ—what David felt towards the brother of his heart, the

---

3. W. B. to Charlotte Courtenay, 22 February 1781, Guy Chapman, *Beckford* (London: Rupert Hart-Davis, 1952), p. 82.

4. W. B. to Louisa Beckford, January 1780, Lewis Melville, *The Life and Letters of William Beckford of Fonthill* (London: William Heinemann, 1910), p. 78.

son of Saul."[5] But the immediate impact on him was traumatic. For the rest of the tour his mind was haunted by one object: "One image alone possesses me and pursues me in a terrible way. In vain do I throw myself into Society—this image forever starts up before me. In vain do I try to come up to the great expectations formed of me—my words are cut short and I am halted in mid-career. This unique object is all I hope for—and I am dead to everything else."[6]

By the time Beckford reached Naples in November he had worked himself into such an overwrought state of mind that he could no longer contain his feelings. He unloaded all his emotional freight upon the shoulders of a new friend and confidante, Lady Hamilton, the first wife of Sir William Hamilton, the English ambassador to the Court of Naples. Beckford stayed with the Hamiltons for a month, during which time Lady Hamilton acted as a positive and fortifying influence, disapproving completely of his Venetian affair and making him aware of the dangers he might be led into if he continued. With her aid he made an effort to discipline himself, though reasonable behavior was a struggle for him to sustain. When he left Naples in the first week of December, Lady Hamilton attempted to continue her influence through a series of letters in which she urged him to remember the "harsh truths" she had forced him to face. But he was on his way to Venice again, to Vendramin and the "pestilential air" Lady Hamilton had urged him to avoid. "Resist nobly a sentiment that in your soul you cannot approve," she pleaded, "and which if indulged must end in your misery and in the destruction of a mother who dotes on you."[7] In Venice at the end of December, Beckford wrote assurances that he would not yield to the "insinuating whisper of a soft but criminal delight,"[8] and she answered with a letter imploring him to continue the resistance: "Every day you will find the struggle less—the important struggle! What is it for? No less than *honor, reputation* and all that an honest and noble Soul holds most dear, while Infamy, eternal infamy (my soul freezes while I write the word), attends the giving way to the soft alluring of a criminal passion."[9] Apparently Beckford surmounted the temptation because by 10

5. A footnote to a copy letter done in 1838. See Chapman, p. 69

6. W.B. To Count Benincasa, 21 October 1780, Boyd Alexander, *England's Wealthiest Son* (London: Centaur Press, 1962), p. 76.

7. 11 December [1780], J. W. Oliver, *The Life of William Beckford* (London: Oxford University Press, 1932), p. 52.

8. 29 December 1780, Oliver, p. 54.

9. 9 January 1781, *Ibid.*, p. 55.

January 1781 he had abandoned his "Venetial state" and with it his "fatal connection."

If leaving Venice raised Beckford's spirits, the relief was short-lived. Once out of Italy the proximity of England and the unwelcome responsibilities it held for him loomed large in his mind. By early February he was in Paris where he deliberately lingered for two months trying to forget the "sullen realities" of business and politics, including the Chancery proceedings against a bastard brother for which he would have to prepare before his twenty-first birthday in September, or risk losing control of some profitable sugar estates in Jamaica. The prospect of immersing himself in such affairs terrified and depressed him. "Don't call me *illustre ami*, and *homme unique*," he would later plead, "I'm still in my cradle! Spare the delicacy of my infantile ears. Leave me to scamper on verdant banks—all too ready, alas, to crumble, but rainbow-tinted and flower-strewn."[10] He finally returned to England on 14 April, but just before he departed from Paris he wrote to his friend Lady Hamilton the following confession: "I fear I shall never be . . . good for anything in this world, but composing airs, building towers, forming gardens, collecting old Japan, and writing a journey to China or the moon."[11] These were defensive and apologetic words, but they were remarkably prophetic. For the next few years, Beckford began fulfilling part of that prophecy by committing himself to writing instead of politics. He would, in fact, never become the civic-minded gentleman the family wished him to be. *Dreams* would be one of a long line of diversions that would help him to realize a different kind of destiny.

II

During the Grand Tour Beckford kept with him a number of notebooks in which he made abbreviated day-to-day entries. These manuscript notes, only a small portion of which survive,[12] were "very inefficient in themselves" ("Left Florence—a sober Autumnal Eve:—Thunder storm—Ruins of Castles in a Vale—shrouded by poplars—with faded yellow leaves"), but they served as useful skeleton material for most of the letters in *Dreams*, with memory

10. W. B. to Countess Rosenberg, 7 October 1781, Alexander, p. 14.

11. 2 April 1781, Melville, p. 105.

12. Only one notebook has been found; it runs from the 26th to the 31st of October 1780. See Guy Chapman and John Hodgkin, *A Bibliography of William Beckford of Fonthill* (London: Constable and Co., 1930), p. 11.

and imagination supplying whatever material was wanting.[13]
When the process of transformation was completed, it was not to
be an ordinary book of travel filled simply with the "facts" of
the journey but as much a visionary pilgrimage revealing occa-
sionally the inner world of the author's own soul. The personal
anguish investing his life at the time of composition was generally
masked and kept under control, but the root of the book's constant wavering between reality and fantasy combined with the
persistent invocations of Morpheus was inevitably Beckford's ag-
gravated psyche. "Shall I tell you my dreams?" became the opening
words of the volume. "To give an account of my time, is doing,
I assure you, but little better. Never did there exist a more ideal
being. A frequent mist hovers before my eyes, and through its
medium, I see objects so faint and hazy, that both their colours
and forms are apt to delude me. This is a rare confession, say the
wise, for a traveller to make; pretty accounts will such a one give
of outlandish countries: his correspondents must reap great benefit, no doubt, from such purblind observations:—But . . . with my
visionary way of gazing, I am perfectly pleased."

Although Beckford could have begun transforming his diary
notes into finished letters sometime during his extended stay in
Paris in 1781, he more likely did not begin serious work on *Dreams*
until after his arrival in London on 20 April. It is clear, at any
rate, that the work was well underway by 31 August 1781, when
he wrote to Lettice: "I am impatient to have you look over my
Italian Journey and will do my best to make it worth looking
at."[14] It is also evident that this effort was not a literary exercise
carried out merely to please a tutor, but a serious work for publication and one that they had already discussed. "You know I have
my heart set upon the success of my book," he wrote in the same
letter, "and shall not at all relish its being only praised as a lively,
picturesque excursion." At this early stage Beckford had also
given some thought to the composition of Letter XXVII, a long,
reflective essay on the political, economic, and artistic characteristics of the principal European countries he had seen. The decision
to include a letter of this kind seems to have been the outcome
of a certain self-consciousness about the potentially "luxuriant
and sentimental" nature of the travelogue. Speaking metaphori-

---

13. Cyrus Redding, *Memoirs of William Beckford of Fonthill* (London: Charles
Skeet, 1859), II, 310. While in Rome Beckford did write a few of the letters in
full and later incorporated them into the book with only slight alterations.
14. Melville, p. 109.

cally, he indicated to Lettice what role the reflective letter would serve in the book: "Unless there is a good solid trunk that cuts fair and sound in the grain I would not give a farthing for leaves and flowers, so I propose being wise and solemn in the Letter of reflections."

Most of the letters were written up, though perhaps not in final form, by the Christmas season of 1781, when Beckford met the Reverend Samuel Henley, formerly a professor at William and Mary College, Virginia, who because of the Revolution had returned to England where he served as a schoolmaster, private tutor, and, significantly, as editor of Henry Swinburne's *Travels in the Two Sicilies.* Henley's Oriental interests and his willingness to take on certain literary tasks undoubtedly recommended him to Beckford's attention. Before they parted, Henley had agreed to edit *Dreams* and to act as a professional go-between when it came time to approach a London publisher. The Reverend Lettice had occupied a similar role when Beckford's first book, *Biographical Memoirs of Extraordinary Painters,* was being readied for the press a year and a half earlier.[15] The guardian tutor might have continued had it not been for the Christmas meeting with Henley. Thereafter Lettice's role as literary assistant diminished to providing aid with the preparation of a fair-copy manuscript, while Henley's took on increasing significance.

Beckford was in constant communication with Henley in 1782-83 during the completion of the travel book. Numerous letters were exchanged; and a number of meetings between the two men were held to discuss editorial matters in detail. "There will be no proceeding in our work," Beckford wrote in January 1782, "without long consultations."[16] One concrete result of this collaboration was the inclusion of the episode of the two Neopolitan lovers in Letter XXIII which Beckford began writing at Henley's urging. On Wednesday, 16 January 1782, Henley wrote the following to Beckford: "The situation of your mind at the time of your writing excited in me all the energy of sympathy. I have something to communicate analogous to what you perhaps refer to—but of this more on Saturday [19 January] when I hope to see you."[17] The proposed visit took place and on Monday, 21 January, Beckford

15. See the introduction to my edition of *Extraordinary Painters* (Rutherford: Fairleigh Dickinson University Press, 1969), pp. 16–18.

16. Alfred Morrison, *Collection of Autograph Letters and Historical Documents,* Second Series (Privately printed, 1893), I, 183.

17. Oliver, p. 95.

wrote to his colleague: "The spirit has moved me this eve; and shut up in my apartment as you advised, I have given way to fancies and inspirations. What will be the consequence of this mood I am not bold enough to determine."[18] The consequence of this "romantic" mood on the 21st has often been identified as the composition of *Vathek,* but Henley's reply makes it clear that Beckford was referring to the episode in Letter XXIII of *Dreams*:

> I am not surprised to find that the Spirit hath moved you. I knew the moment of inspiration would come, and beheld the Power herself descending, surrounded by an effulgence of glory. A splendor of golden radiance kindled beneath her foot steps, and the fiery track that marked her way thro clouds of the saddest purple is still glowing from earth to heaven. Such was my vision! I conversed too, with your crone, visited the top of the chasm into which the unhappy fair one fell: noted the ivory that surrounded the sarcophagus which her lover was exploring; and beheld the earth still fresh, from whence the loosened crag broke beneath his weight.—But truce to visions! I shall wait with the most anxious impatience till I learn the story from yourself.[19]

The above letter is undated, but as a reply to Beckford's letter of 21 January it is reasonable to conclude that Henley had written it before the end of the month. The letter concludes with a further reference to *Dreams,* specifically Letter XIX, containing the description of Valombrosa, and *An Excursion to the Grande Chartreuse,* which Beckford had already decided to incorporate as part of *Dreams.* Henley was busily engaged with both pieces:

> The evening I returned I neither gave sleep to my eyes nor slumber to my eyelids till I had carefully transcribed Valombrosa, and transferred the remaining corrections to the Grande Chartreuse. I shall think every hour a century till I receive and we have prepared the whole.

On 29 January Beckford drafted another letter to Henley. This time he explained that his inspirations concerning the "wild and terrible story of unbridled passion" had reached the point of being set down on paper. Using the language of the tale itself ("I tremble to relate what has happened"), Beckford wrote: "You are answerable for having set me to work upon a story so horrid that I tremble whilst relating it, & have not a nerve in my frame

---

18. *Morrison Collection,* I, 183.
19. Oliver, p. 96.

but vibrates like an aspen."[20] Further words of encouragement came quickly from Henley:

> My soul rejoices to know that your imagination hath been wrapped in the thickest gloom: never is the lightning so glorious as when it flashes from the darkest clouds.
> I will gladly answer for all the horrible imaginings that may have been suggested by my surly spirit, though the murder which so shakes your state of mind were more than fantastical.[21]

Two months passed before Beckford completed the episode. He then wrote Henley on 25 April that the "story is finished," and, referring to the conclusion of Letter XXIII, added that he had brought himself "home pretty decently to Naples."[22]

By the middle of May Beckford was off on his second journey to Naples, the occasion for the seven additional letters he later included in the volume. Still pressed by the prospect of assuming the responsibilities of manhood in public life and continually badgered by his family, he sought once again the congenial society of Sir William and Lady Hamilton. "I really am not able to blaze at present in the political Hemisphere," he wrote to Lady Hamilton. "Twelve months of leisure and tranquility may prepare me for as many years of Torment and Illustration."[23] He set out for Dover on the 16th, traveling in sumptuous style with postilions, a charge of servants, and spare horses. Lettice accompanied him along with a physician, Dr. Ehrhart, a musician, John Burton, and the water-colorist John Robert Cozens, son of Alexander, who had agreed to sketch whatever scenery caught his employer's eye. He followed the same route as on the previous journey. He drove through Ostend and Brussels to Cologne, a rough, tiring passage over some difficult roads, and then on to Augsburg, Innsbruck, and Padua, reaching this last city on 11 or 12 June. Resting in Padua, after maintaining a grueling pace of travel, he ran into his old friends Madame de Rosenberg and Count Benincasa, and indulged the delights of their hospitality.[24] All was not play, how-

---

20. *Morrison Collection*, I, 183.
21. Oliver, p. 98.
22. *Morrison Collection*, I, 183.
23. Melville, p. 148.
24. There is some evidence available which reveals that while in Padua Count Benincasa was given access to some unpublished material of Beckford's. Since we know that it was in epistolary form, it is possible that the material was a manuscript version of *Dreams*. What is clear from a letter written by Reverend Lettice to Benincasa on 29 and 30 July from Naples is that during the stay in Padua Beckford, Lettice, and the Count had talked about a plan leading to the publi-

ever. *Dreams* was very much on his mind, but he still had not completed the long "Letter of reflections" which he wanted to serve as the conclusion to the first twenty-six letters of the book. By 18 June he had made significant progress, telling Henley in a letter that the "strange Letter for the conclusion" was "far advanced."[25] When a letter from Henley arrived a few days later, pressing him to complete the remaining material and notifying him that Cipriani had completed two drawings for the travel letters, Beckford responded optimistically about bringing the work to an end. "I beg you will see Cipriani paid," he wrote on 29 June, and then added: "I hope . . . you will have patience a fortnight longer when I shall have finished the conclusive Epistle."[26]

Beckford might have completed the task as planned had it not been for a severe fever, which immobilized him shortly after his arrival in Naples on 8 July. It kept him bedridden, or at least weak, for the rest of the month. August at the Hamilton country house in Portici might have been better, but Lady Hamilton came down with a serious illness which may help to explain the further delay. He made an attempt to finish the letter, for on 20 August he wrote to Henley: "I have been spinning out my conclusive letter, & I flatter myself you will not dislike my web. As I bring it along with me, we cannot publish till after Xmas, the best mo-

---

cation of a collection of Beckford's "letters." Benincasa's role is not clearly defined in the letter, but it would most probably be as translator. He would later do this kind of work for M. de Rosenberg, and it would not make much sense to consult him about an English edition of any of Beckford's works, let alone *Dreams*. This could mean, as Guy Chapman has already suggested, an Italian edition of *Dreams*, or perhaps the publication of a portion of the book in Italian. (No such publication has yet been found.) The possibility that the "publication in question" refers to another series of Beckford letters cannot be ruled out, however, especially in view of the fact that Lettice's letter describes the work as containing expressions "infinitely beyond the most violent language of ordinary passions," which is not an apt characterization of *Dreams* as we know it today. A third possibility is that the final, published version of *Dreams* was considerably altered from the original manuscript. At any rate, on 20 July Count Benincasa drafted a letter to Lettice in which he proposed "two plans" for the "publication in question." Lettice's reply is printed in Chapman's *Beckford*, pp. 137–138.

25. Melville, p. 153.
26. *Ibid.*, p. 157. In his unpublished notes on *Dreams*, now at the Bodleian, John Hodgkin wrote that he believed the "conclusive Epistle" referred to "either Letter VI, dated Rome 30 June 1782, second trip to Italy or Letter VII, dated Naples July 8th, 1782." It seems unlikely, however, that at this stage Beckford had it in mind to include any account of his second tour in *Dreams* and, assuming that he did, that he even knew what the conclusive epistle for the second tour would be.

ment, too, I believe."[27] Before the end of the month, however, Lady Hamilton died of a "bilious fever," a blow for Beckford considering the quality of their relationship. Within a matter of days he experienced another setback with the death of one of his traveling companions, John Burton, his favorite harpsichord player.[28] On 10 September he understandably left Naples for home. Not until Paris is *Dreams* mentioned again. By this time (28 October) the final letter was "almost finished."

By the winter of 1782–3 the final preparations for the publication of *Dreams* were underway. There were some last-minute revisions to be made, and Henley was close at hand to provide whatever aid Beckford desired. The decision was made to incorporate the seven letters of 1782 to complete the volume. On 15 January 1783 Beckford complained to Henley that "Mr. L[ettice]'s abominable amanuensis [had] committed a thousand errors in the concluding letter."[29] The following month he was still consulting with Henley about the book: "We must look over the last letter, so don't forget to bring it with you."[30] Very soon after their meeting on Saturday, 16 February, the book must have been in the press with everything done to make certain it would fulfill the original expectations of its ambitious author. Cipriani's representations of the abject female in the episode of Letter XXIII and St. Bruno in *An Excursion to the Grande Chartreuse* had been engraved by Bartolozzi in the previous year and were finally published by J. Johnson and P. Elmsly of London on "Mar. 10, 1783." By the end of March or the first part of April *Dreams* had been bound and was ready for distribution. Then came the unexpected decision: Beckford wrote Henley on 15 April 1783 that the production of the travel book would have to cease and his solicitor, Thomas Wildman, would pay for whatever expenses were incurred:

> I have been considering & reconsidering, & *cannot* reconcile myself in the least with the idea of committing my *Dreams* to the wide world. Therefore must beg you will stop advertisements, entries, &c., at

27. *Morrison Collection,* I, 186.

28. According to an entry in Thomas Jones's diary, dated September 1782, Burton died "during the Delirium of a Fever, and execrating in a most shocking manner, the Person who was . . . instrumental . . . in bringing him into this deplorable Situation." See *Memoirs of Thomas Jones,* Walpole Society, XXXII (London: Oliver Burridge, 1951), 114. Most reference works give 1785 as the year of Burton's death.

29. *Morrison Collection,* I, 188.

30. *Ibid.,* I, 189.

Stationers' Hall, &c., &c. Don't imagine I shall change my mind any more. This determination is as fixed as the Sun. As for the copies? I will have them locked up like my title-deeds, not one shall transpire, so Hamilton must go without his *large paper* for some years to come.

I have desired Mr. Wildman to settle everything concerning expences. Seeing you upon my return from F. becomes now more necessary than ever. Give me that satisfaction, & believe me most.[31]

This letter was followed by another to Henley fifteen days later in which Beckford complained about not having received the copies that J. Johnson had printed:

Mr. Johnson has not yet delivered up the copies, to my great surprise, & I have desired Mr. Wildman to renew his application. I must entreat you will take care that none transpire. . . . Don't forget the original copy & the letters from Lucca and Padua."[32]

Why did Beckford decide suddenly to suppress a book he once was so eager to publish? Part of the explanation lies in the fact that family pressure made it intolerable for him to do otherwise. This is evident from subsequent correspondence, particularly a letter to Henley in November 1783. "How can I endure my book of *Dreams*," Beckford lamented, "when I reflect what *disagreeable waking* thoughts it has occasioned us? If you have a mind to reconcile me to it, let me be assured you are not less my affectionate friend than when you silenced the hiss of serpents at Fonthill. Neither Orlando nor Brandimart were ever more tormented by demons and spectres in an enchanted castle than William Beckford in his own hall by his nearest relations."[33] The specific objections the family had to the book are not really clear, but Beckford's biographers have offered several possible explanations. Such an effusive travelogue, it is usually said, could seriously compromise the author's Parliamentary career. The display of "lively imagination" and "quickness of sensibility . . . so opposite to common modes of thinking," wrote Cyrus Redding, could "prejudice him in the House of Commons, and make ministers imagine he was not capable of solid business."[34] Another theory is that the family sought to dissuade him from publishing the book because "beneath all its veneer of fine language there was a moral rottenness" that presumably would lend credence to the ugly rumors that were circulating about Beckford's questionable

31. *Ibid.*, I, 189.
32. *Ibid.*, I, 189.
33. *Ibid.*, I, 189.
34. Redding, I, 138.

relationship with William Courtenay.[35] Still another theory is that Beckford consented to "abandon everything that was equivocal in his life" once he agreed to a family-arranged marriage, a decision that was made about the time *Dreams* was to appear. In this case, getting rid of a book "charged with all the dangerous tendencies his mother had feared" would serve as "one symbol of the sincerity of his intentions."[36] One final theory, and perhaps the most plausible, is that once the book was distributed the severe criticisms of the Dutch that filled its early pages would offend many prominent political figures, particularly at a time when the English government was attempting to maintain good relations with that country.[37]

Whatever the precise reason, Beckford consented to the sacrifice and removed the whole edition—said to total 500 copies—from the publisher's hands.[38] Once in his possession, Beckford destroyed all of the copies by fire save a small number which he kept at Fonthill to display to friends and interested visitors. He was never secretive about its existence, and on occasion distributed copies to a few fortunate individuals. Among these were his bookseller, George Clarke, his solicitor, Richard Samuel White, and Louise Necker, known later as Madame de Stael, who expressed enthusiasm for the book in a letter to the author:

> I have not as yet finished the extraordinary work which you had the kindness to entrust to me, Monsieur. It is difficult to tear myself away from it, for you travel so rapidly from idea to idea, from scene to scene, that it is impossible to find a moment's pause between one sensation and another. You dream when you have nothing to describe. Imagination, which invents or represents objects, has never been given more freedom. Nature has a great hold on you. Your soul is carried away by all that surrounds it. You should never forget the places that you have seen, for each one of them has evoked thoughts that can never be erased. Your manner of depicting

35. Chapman, *Beckford,* p. 153. To substantiate this view Chapman cites elsewhere the following comment which Beckford wrote on a letter sent to him by his attorney, Thomas Wildman, dated 14 April 1789: "The only method of interfering effectually would be to produce the wretched book in open daylight, and to such an exposition I am certain L. C. (whom I take to be Lord Courtenay, i.e., William, who had recently succeeded to the title) would never consent." *Bibliography,* p. 13.

36. Oliver, p. 129.

37. This theory is supported by a Beckford letter to Lettice, dated 3 March 1787, containing the comment: "I cannot permit the mutilation of the book. . . . Not a word of the first letter can I spare. . . . I cannot agree to expunging the strokes I have launched at the Dutch and Flemings." See Chapman, *Bibliography,* p. 13.

38. Redding, I, 138.

has often made me laugh, but I believe that you never realized how spirited you were, for you speak your natural language, while we, at the same time, find you to be extraordinary. I do very much like the origin you attribute to the Flemish. As for you, Monsieur, it is on Mount Etna that I will search for yours, and I shall hasten to see if you speak of that volcano with gratitude. Please accept, Monsieur, and rest assured of, these sincere sentiments with which I have the honor of remaining your humble and very obedient servant.[39]

How many copies actually survived the holocaust is difficult to determine. George Clarke, a recipient of a Large Paper version, claimed that all but four were destroyed and listed the names of the owners in his copy:

1	Mr. Beckford	The whole of the impression with
2	Samuel Rogers	the exception of these four copies
3	Earl Spencer	were purposely destroyed at Font-
This copy		hill in 1801.

G. Clarke

Unfortunately Clarke's statement cannot be accepted without reserve. First of all, five copies of *Dreams,* not four, are known to exist today. They have been located in the following places:

Large Paper:
1. British Museum. Previous owner unknown. Bound in olive calf with black leather label and marbled edges.
2. The Bodleian Library. George Clarke's copy. Later owned by John Hodgkin. Bound as (1).
3. Beckford Papers copy. Cased in marbled boards, cloth spine without label. Plates are missing.

Ordinary:
1. Beckford Papers copy. Cased as Large Paper (3). Plates are missing.
2. Beinecke Library (on deposit). Originally Richard Samuel White's copy, Beckford's solicitor during the early 1800s. Later owned by Michael Sadleir. Bound in black half calf with gilt edges.

In other words, assuming that the British Museum copy was once in the hands of Samuel Rogers or Earl Spencer, Clarke's statement fails to include the second copy among the Beckford Papers and the one owned by Richard Samuel White.

Still other considerations cast doubts on Clarke's figure. No copy of *Dreams* ever turned up at the sales of Samuel Rogers's library in 1856 and 1868, nor for that matter has one been found among Earl Spencer's books currently housed in the John Rylands

---

39. Paris, 1784. Original French text in Oliver, pp. 185–86.

Library in Manchester, England.[40] There is no doubt from a number of passages in Rogers's *Italy* (1830) that the poet had read *Dreams,* but he might have done so, as John Mitford recorded, by examining the "manuscript" (or printed text?) of the work during his visit to Fonthill in 1817, without having owned a copy himself.[41] Finally, there is the problem of the date of burning, which Clarke gives as 1801. This date we know is clearly wrong since as early as 1793 most of the issue had been destroyed. During that year Henri Meister had visited Fonthill, read the book, and noted at the time that Beckford had already "committed the whole edition to the flames."[42]

Chapman raised the possibility in 1930 that Clarke was referring to Large Paper copies only. This would seem to corroborate the figure of "half-a-dozen," given by Beckford's friend and biographer Cyrus Redding.[43] But even if the conjectures were true, it does not account for Louise Necker's copy, which would bring the total to seven—unless, of course, she returned her copy to Beckford. It is also quite possible that more than seven were retained by Beckford, for it would be very strange if he did not present copies to his collaborators, John Lettice and Samuel Henley. Nor should we overlook the likelihood that another recipient was Alexander Cozens, the man to whom most of the letters in the book seem to be directed.[44]

While *Dreams* remained unavailable to the public eye for many years following its suppression, it enjoyed a kind of notoriety among a select group of writers: Thomas Moore, Samuel Rogers, and John Mitford. Beckford considered putting it out in companionship with a volume of his Spanish-Portuguese letters as early as 1818. In that year he asked Rogers to encourage Moore to visit Fonthill in order to discuss the possibility of preparing the book for the press. Rogers dutifully communicated the offer to Moore; he even suggested that Beckford might give him "some-

40. Chapman, *Bibliography*, pp. 16–17.
41. Mitford's unpublished notes (1844–1849) on Beckford in the British Museum. See Add. MSS. 32.566, f. 35.
42. *Letters Written during a Residence in England* (London: Longman, 1799), p. 307.
43. Redding, I, 138.
44. The "you" in the book is quite obviously a painter: "those happy isles which you are so fond of painting"; "just such as you have created to complete a prospect." There is also the matter of a significant parallel between "Your friend H." in Letter XXV of *Dreams* from Rome and a letter to Cozens referring to "your Friend H. at Rome." For the letter see Melville, p. 95.

thing magnificent for it—a thousand pounds, perhaps."[45] But Moore quickly declined, saying he had no taste for having his name forever coupled with Beckford's. It is usually said that Moore, though he disdained the idea of being Beckford's *"sub,"* did not hesitate thereafter to borrow from the unpublished travel notes for parts of his poem "Rhymes on the Road" and for one of his songs in *Irish Melodies*.[46] But resemblances normally cited between Moore's work and *Dreams* are too slight to classify safely as "borrowings." "How Dear to Me the Hour!", the Irish melody that contains material supposedly taken from the Letter III of *Dreams,* was published in 1808, making the plagiarism theory even more implausible. There is no external evidence, further-more, to support the view that Moore ever saw Beckford's unpub-lished travels and particularly not so early as 1808. Much of what he knew about Beckford's writings came to him by way of Rogers, who did not visit Fonthill until the fall of 1817.[47] Rogers, on the other hand, did use material from *Dreams* for a few passages in his poem *Italy,* but, contrary to Beckford's biographers, he did ac-knowledge it in the notes appended to the first edition.[48]

Dreams finally appeared in 1834, after extensive revisions by its author, as volume one of *Italy; with Sketches of Spain and Por-tugal.* With editions printed in London, Paris, and Philadelphia, *Italy* was reviewed at length in leading literary journals, and almost without exception with unqualified enthusiasm. By now *Vathek* had made Beckford's name known in literary circles, but

45. *Memoirs, Journal, and Correspondence of Thomas Moore,* ed. Lord John Russell (London: Longman, 1853), II, 193.

46. John Gibson Lockhart, "Italy; with Sketches of Spain and Portugal," Rev. art., *Quarterly Review,* LI (June, 1834), 428; W. L. N., "Beckford's Letters," *Notes & Queries,* IV, 2nd Series (July 4, 1857), 14–15.

47. On the 17th of October Beckford enticed Rogers to Fonthill with the following interesting note: "If Mr. Rogers continues to feel any inclination to hear the secrets of the prison-house of Eblis unfolded, he may perhaps be inspired to appoint a day and a night for the purpose. Nothing would afford the Abbot of Fonthill higher gratification." R. Ellis Roberts, *Samuel Rogers and his Circle* (New York: E. P. Dutton, 1910), p. 102.

48. "For this thought I am indebted to some unpublished travels by the author of *Vathek.*" See *Italy, A Poem* (London, 1830), p. 252. Beckford was aware of the use of *Dreams* by Rogers and alluded to it in the opening lines of his preface to the 1834 edition. He had also made a similar charge approximately seven months earlier in an unpublished letter, dated 24 November 1833, to the book-seller, George Clarke: "Whoever deals for the *Dreams* etc. will have a pleasant book, and no compilation, the original of many copies, affording excellent sport for anti-plagiarists." Letters of William Beckford to His Bookseller. Manuscript copies made in 1894 for Richard Bentley, III, f. 440. Beinecke Rare Book and Manuscript Library, Yale University.

Italy established him as a travel writer of unsurpassed talent. "He is a poet, and a great one too," observed John Gibson Lockhart, "though we know not that he ever wrote a line of verse. His rapture amidst the sublime scenery of mountains and forests . . . is that of a spirit cast originally in one of nature's finest moulds; and he fixes it in language which can scarcely be praised beyond its deserts—simple, massive, nervous, apparently little laboured, yet revealing, in its effect, the perfection of art. Some immortal passages in Gray's letters and Byron's diaries, are the only things, in our tongue, that seem to us to come near the profound melancholy, blended with a picturesque description at once true and startling. . . . We risk nothing in predicting that Mr. Beckford's Travels will henceforth be classed among the most elegant productions of modern literature: they will be forthwith translated into every language of the Continent—and will keep his name alive, centuries after all the brass and marble he ever piled together have ceased to vibrate with the echoes of *Modenhas*."[49]

III

Further editions of *Italy* were issued during the remaining years of Beckford's life, while *Dreams* continued to gather dust among his private papers. Forty-six years after his death, however, Richard Garnett, the keeper of printed books at the British Museum, decided, after reading the library's copy, that its literary merit warranted public attention. He therefore published an article in the *Universal Review* introducing *Dreams* as the "production of a man of genius with a foot in either world, an incarnation . . . of the spirit of the eighteenth century writing in the yet unrecognized dawn of the nineteenth, flushed by emotions which he does not understand, and depicting the old courtly order of Europe on the eve of its dissolution."[50] Garnett felt *Dreams* compared favorably with Goethe's letters from Italy, which, "if infinitely more precious as material for the history of culture, scarcely rival Beckford's in graphic power, and are less vividly characteristic of the writer." He also sensed a strong affinity with Lord Beaconsfield's letters: "In both we have the same intoxication with the wine of youth, the same joy in travel and adventure, the same love for the gorgeous and fantastic, the same *outrecuidance*,

---

49. *Quarterly Review*, LI (June, 1834), 429, 456.
50. "Beckford's *Dreams*," *Universal Review*, VIII (September, 1890), 112. See also pp. 113–14. This description of Beckford first appeared in Garnett's article on the author in the *D.N.B.*

verging on insolence." In sum, Garnett was sufficiently impressed to want to see the text upon which *Italy* was based restored to its original integrity and in print again. ("It will . . . demonstrate that his literary reputation ought not to rest entirely upon *Vathek.*") Consequently, at Garnett's suggestion, G. T. Bettany reprinted it (omitting Letter XXVII) in 1891, along with *Vathek, Sketches of Spain and Portugal, and Recollections of Alcobaça and Batalha* as part of the Minerva Library series.

Cramming four Beckford works into one volume seems to have done little to draw particular attention to *Dreams;* not surprisingly it continued to live in obscurity. Almost nothing was written about it until 1926, when H. B. Grimsditch did a survey of Beckford's minor works in *The London Mercury.* As a travel author he found Beckford "open to all impressions," able to sustain a "running fire of spirited and humorous (or pathetic) commentary on pictures, architecture, scenery, religion, character, historical and literary associations and politics."[51] His style "has a flow, a virility and an unaffected candour that makes one wish he had collected less and written more." Comparing *Dreams* and *Italy,* Grimsditch preferred the precision of the revised work to the prolixity of the original. "Too often we have to eat large slabs of indigestible pudding in order to find the rings and sixpenny pieces concealed in the mixture." Two years after these comments were made *The Travel-Diaries of William Beckford of Fonthill,* edited by Guy Chapman, were published, with *Dreams* occupying the first volume. A reviewer in the London *Times Literary Supplement* pronounced it "one of the minor masterpieces of English travel literature,"[52] and later added: "In a century of great travel-letters . . . these have a very good claim to be considered the greatest."[53] Chapman himself expressed some reservations about the book—"Too often it betrays the young man vain of his taste and erudition"—but at the same time he was drawn to its youthful quality: "It has fire and enthusiasm and the wonder of the innocent eye."[54] More recently, André Parreaux indicated, in assessing the differences between the two versions of the book, a stronger liking for the "chef-d'oeuvre de la jeunesse," preferring the poetry, spontaneity and exuberant spirit of *Dreams* to the cool detach-

---

51. "William Beckford's Minor Works," *The London Mercury,* XIV (1926), 604.
52. *TLS,* May 3, 1928, p. 331.
53. "The Caliph of Fonthill," *TLS,* November 3, 1932, p. 798.
54. "Beckford the Caliph: A Traveller of Two Worlds, Passion and Fantasy," *TLS,* May 6, 1944, p. 222.

ment, equilibrium, and general inhibited character of *Italy*.[55] And Geoffrey Bullough, after concluding that the editorial revisions made "the later book . . . better than the suppressed one," hastened to add that in the history of English literature *Dreams* was a valuable document: "In its fluent expression of a personality exploiting its sensibility to the full it provides a striking example of Rousseauan romanticism," and proof of the power "of unbridled mental associations."[56]

To the extent that interest in Beckford's life and writings is sustained in the future, and the recent publication of new editions of his works as well as the appearance of previously unpublished journals and correspondence seem to assure it, *Dreams* will be looked upon as an important source of information about the author, especially since, in its unbuttoned fullness, it is a more open book than *Italy*. *Dreams* has a confessional character that wholesale deletions have for the most part erased in the revised work; it is laced with passages that possess the intimate tone of a private letter, which often has the effect of making the reader feel he is eavesdropping on confidences designed only for the eyes of a kindred spirit. The young Beckford comes into clearer view during these moments, and usually he reveals his feelings of isolation, his boredom, his basic restlessness. Enough has been said in biographical terms about the origin of his emotional turmoil and its particular intensity during the period of the book's composition. The apprehension he felt over the threats to his love of freedom and childish irresponsibility finds expression, even if only veiled, in various parts of *Dreams*. It can be detected in the escapist preoccupation with dreams and private fantasies, in the passages devoted to the pursuit of protective closure, in the evocation of paradisaical playgrounds, and in the kind of solipsistic longing evoked in his description of the fanciful globe he wished to construct beneath the dome of St. Peter's:

> We would have all the space to ourselves, and to such creatures too as resemble us. The windows I should shade with transparent curtains of yellow silk, to admit the glow of perpetual summer. Lanterns, as many as you please, of all forms and sizes; they would remind us of China, and, depending from the roofs of the palace, bring before us that of the emperor Ki, which was twice as large as St. Peter's . . . and lighted alone by tapers; for his imperial majesty, being tired of the

---

55. "Beckford en Italie Rêve et Voyage au XVIIIᵉ siècle," *Revue de Littérature Comparée*, XXXIII (1959), 326–327.

56. "Beckford's Early Travels and his 'Dream of Delusion,'" *William Beckford of Fonthill, Bicentenary Essays*, ed. Fatma Mahmoud (Cairo, 1960), p. 50.

sun, would absolutely have a new firmament of his own creation, and an artificial day. Was it not a rare fantastic idea? For my part, I should like of all things to immure myself, after his example, with those I love; forget the divisions of time, have a moon at command, and a theatrical sun to rise and set, at pleasure.

Aside from the psychological interest, *Dreams* remains one of the best illustrations of "literary picturesque" that was produced in the declining years of the eighteenth century. Among his devotees, Beckford's descriptive powers have always been identified as his major strength as a writer; they are fond of citing the graphic richness of the halls of Eblis in *Vathek,* where the carefully drawn descriptions flicker before the eye of the reader in the manner of an exotic motion picture. *Dreams* exhibits the same interest in visual imagery and pictorial composition, the character of which is best understood in terms of the aesthetics of William Gilpin, a theorist who defined "the picturesque" as "that peculiar kind of beauty, which is agreeable in a picture."[57] Chapman once complained that some of the descriptive passages in *Dreams* were "not a little stiff and formal," that sometimes a "figure seems arrested in its pose as in a painting."[58] But this characteristic—the analogy between prose description and painting—is an essential feature in Beckford's writing; it simply illustrates his training as an artistically conditioned observer. Almost from the date of his relationship with Cozens, and as a consequence of his training in the pictorial arts under this tutor, Beckford was in the habit of making observations about the world around him as if he were examining a painting in one of the galleries at Fonthill. The young writer's letters to the water-colorist, especially those from Switzerland in 1777 and 1778, provide additional evidence of his ability to structure a view, to reconstruct in prose his general impression of a scene with all the elements required to fill and frame a picture. When he came to write *Dreams,* therefore, he purposely aimed for pictorial effect, just as he did later in *Vathek.* Page after page of *Dreams* displays an eye eager for color, lights and shades, surface textures, distant lines, perspectives, and picturelike views. Beckford's picturesque orientation also explains why he reveals in *Dreams* his partiality for seeing objects in the "dubious, visionary light" of dusk, and why in the fashion of the picturesque theorists he is consistently drawn to the paintable

57. *An Essay upon Prints* (London, 1768), p. 2.
58. "Memoir of William Beckford," *The Travel-Diaries of William Beckford of Fonthill* (Cambridge, Eng.: Constable, 1928), I, lvii.

qualities of rough, rugged surfaces and irregular lines. Nor is it a coincidence that his own descriptions are frequently keyed to the works of famous painters, so that irregular hills, clumps of cypress and pastoral cottages become the ingredients for a scene that "Zuccarelli loved to paint," or rocks and grottoes, "half lost in thickets from which rise craggy pinnacles crowned by mouldering towers" constitute "just such scenery as Polemburg and Peter de Laer introduce in their paintings." Beckford cultivated seeing as if it were an art form, and he used the painter's guide book to learn how to see.

When pictorial accent is combined with poetic sensibility, *Dreams* achieves a distinctive character that finds few parallels in the history of travel literature. If Beckford has the facility for portraying with accuracy the genuine aspect of things, he is also capable of conveying how they make him feel. There are times in the book when he does not stop with a mere literal transcription of objective reality, but goes beyond to render the mood and feeling associated with it. There is a sense, therefore, in which some of Beckford's pictures become "equally objective and subjective . . . brilliantly clear in outline . . . yet steeped in the rich hues of his own peculiar feeling."[59] His sunsets, in particular, partake of this combination of pictorial and emotional values. Whether the closing scenes of day are described in terms of a final blush of crimson in a darkening sky, or in terms of the last sunbeams purpling the sails of ships at rest in the harbor, or in terms of a glow lingering on the verge of a landscape, which slowly fades into a variety of warm hues, and then into a deeper, more melancholy blue—these scenes take their meaning from the feeling observer, a man who is obviously touched by what he sees. The same is true of the following scene among the cliffs of Tyrol:

> A goat-track . . . conducted me, on the brink of the foaming waters, to the very depths of the cliff, whence issues a stream which, dashing impetuously down, strikes against a ledge of grey rock, and sprinkles the impending thicket with dew. Big drops hung on every spray, and glittered on the leaves partially gilt by the rays of the declining sun, whose mellow hues softened the summits of the cliffs, and diffused a repose, a divine calm, over this deep retirement, which inclined me to imagine it the extremity of the earth, and the portal of some other region of existence; some happy world beyond the dark groves of pines, the caves and awful mountains.

On these occasions, Beckford seems no longer concerned simply

---

59. Richard Garnett, *D.N.B.*, II, 84.

with the artistic analysis of pictorial effects. Color and form here have been surpassed, and observation has been enriched and vivified by the power of emotion.

As a traveler Beckford seems ever willing to allow experiences to operate on him, to remain freely exposed and open to the influence of whatever comes his way. In Mannheim, he indulges the repose of a cool garden where exotic birds sing, a tall poplar quivers in the wind, and jets of water rise above the foliage to spangle brilliantly in the sun; in Venice, at dusk, his careful eye catches the innumerable tapers glimmering through the awnings of windows, the variety of shadowy figures "shooting by in their gondolas," and the play of lantern lights upon the water; in Arqua, he makes a pilgrimage to Petrarch's house, sits in the poet's chair, and indulges a "train of pensive sentiments and soft impressions." "Who could sit in Petrarch's chair," he asks, "void of some effect?"; in Florence, he visits the art gallery and runs "childishly by the ample ranks of sculptures, like a butterfly in a pasture, that skims before it fixes, over ten thousand flowers." The effect of this sensitivity on the reader is cumulative and is reinforced throughout by means of deliberately contrasting scenes, moving "from the dark cathedral to the bright casino, from gay society to, 'wild spots where the arbutus flourishes;' and from the noisy mart to the lonely seashore."[60]

Dreams, in short, is a remarkable achievement for a young man of twenty-two, a testimony to literary powers that, unfortunately, were never to be fully realized. He wrote much between 1777 and 1787: an assortment of unpublished translations and Oriental pieces, *The Long Story, Biographical Memoirs of Extraordinary Painters, Vathek,* and the *Episodes of Vathek* in addition to *Dreams.* But the fertile years, it seems, passed away even more swiftly than the tower of Fonthill Abbey. Except for two light burlesques in 1796–97 and a book of travel in 1835, Beckford's literary muse seldom stirred after the age of twenty-seven. Thereafter he dissipated his creative energy in ways that never seemed wholly satisfying to him: in more travel, in collecting rare old books and paintings, and in his devotion to building and landscaping at Fonthill and Lansdown. As early as 1793 Henri Meister perceived in Beckford a vitiated talent, spoiled by wealth and fortune, excessively given to the odd and the whimsical. Swinburne in 1876, looking back over Beckford's life, spied the same canker of

---

60. H. T. Tuckerman, "William Beckford and the Literature of Travel," *Southern Literary Messenger,* XVI (January, 1850), 14.

unfulfillment. The melancholia and consuming malaise, the bitterness and cold cynicism so often seen in Beckford's character may well have been the products of an ever deepening belief that he had aborted his genius and trifled away his existence, and that he had in the end fulfilled the sad prophecy of his youth.

ROBERT J. GEMMETT
Brockport, N.Y.

DREAMS,
WAKING THOUGHTS
AND INCIDENTS

DREAMS,

WAKING THOUGHTS,

AND

INCIDENTS;

IN A

SERIES OF LETTERS,

FROM

VARIOUS PARTS OF EUROPE.

LONDON:

PRINTED FOR J. JOHNSON, ST. PAUL'S CHURCH YARD;

AND P. ELMSLY, IN THE STRAND,

M.DCC.LXXXIII.

A Summary of the Contents

41

Page

ADDITIONAL LETTERS.

DREAMS,
WAKING THOUGHTS
AND INCIDENTS

Letter I.

June 19, 1780.

Shall I tell you my dreams?—To give an account of my time, is doing, I assure you, but little better. Never did there exist a more ideal being. A frequent mist hovers before my eyes, and, through its medium, I see objects so faint and hazy, that both their colours and forms are apt to delude me. This is a rare confession, say the wise, for a traveller to make; pretty accounts will such a one give of outlandish countries: his correspondents must reap great benefit, no doubt, from such purblind observations:—But stop, my good friends; patience a moment!—I really have not the vanity of pretending to make a single remark, during the whole of my journey: if ―――― be contented with my visionary way of gazing, I am perfectly pleased; and shall write away as freely as Mr. A, Mr. B, Mr. C, and a million others, whose letters are the admiration of the politest circles.

All through Kent did I dose as usual; now and then I opened my eyes to take in an idea or two of the green, woody country through which I was passing; then closed them again; transported myself back to my native hills; thought I led a choir of those I loved best through their shades; and was happy in the arms of illusion. The sun sat before I recovered my senses enough to discover plainly the variegated slopes near Canterbury, waving with slender birch-trees, and gilt with a profusion of broom. I thought myself still in my beloved solitude, but missed the companions of my slumbers. Where are they?—Behind yon blue hills, perhaps, or t'other side of that thick forest. My fancy was travelling after these deserters, till we reached the town; vile enough o'conscience, and fit only to be past in one's sleep. The moment after I got out of the carriage, brought me to the cathedral; an old haunt of mine. I had always venerated its lofty pillars, dim ailes, and mysterious arches. Last night they were more solemn than ever, and echoed no other sound than my steps. I strayed about the choir and chapels, till they grew so dark and dismal, that I was half inclined to be frightened; looked over my shoulder; thought of spectres that have an awkward trick of syllabling men's names in dreary places; and fancied a sepulchral voice exclaiming: "Worship my toe at Ghent, my ribs at Florence; my skull at Bologna, Sienna, and Rome. Beware how you neglect this order; for my bones, as well as my spirit, have the miraculous property of being here, there, and every where." These injunctions, you may suppose, were received in a becoming manner, and noted all down in my pocket-book by inspiration (for I could not see) and, hurrying into the open air, I was whirled away in the dark to Margate. Don't ask what were my dreams thither:—nothing but horrors, deep-vaulted tombs, and pale, though lovely figures extended upon them; shrill blasts that sung in my ears, and filled me with sadness, and the recollection of happy hours, fleeted away, perhaps, for ever! I was not sorry, when the bustle of our coming-in dispelled these phantoms. The change, however, in point of scenery was not calculated to dissipate my gloom; for the first object in this world that presented itself, was a vast expanse of sea, just visible by the gleamings of the moon, bathed in watery clouds; a chill air ruffled the waves. I went to shiver a few melancholy moments on the shore. How often did I try to wish away the reality of my separation from those I love, and attempt to persuade myself it was but a dream!

This morning I found myself more chearfully disposed, by the queer Dutch faces with short pipes and ginger-bread complexions, that came smirking and scraping to get us on board their respective vessels; but, as I had a ship engaged for me before, their invitations were all in vain. The wind blows fair; and, should it continue of the same mind a few hours longer, we shall have no cause to complain of our passage. Adieu! Think of me sometimes. If you write immediately, I shall receive your letter at the Hague.

It is a bright sunny evening: the sea reflects a thousand glorious colours, and, in a minute or two, I shall be gliding on its surface.

Letter II.

T'other minute I was in Greece, gathering the bloom of Hymettus; but now I am landed in Flanders, smoked with tobacco, and half poisoned with garlick. Were I to remain ten days at Ostend, I should scarcely have one delightful vision; 'tis so unclassic a place! Nothing but preposterous Flemish roofs disgust your eyes when you cast them upwards: swaggering Dutchmen and mungrel barbers are the first objects they meet with below. I should esteem myself in luck, were the woes of this sea-port confined only to two senses; but, alas; the apartment above my head proves a squalling brattery; and the sounds which proceed from it are so loud and frequent, that a person might think himself in limbo, without any extravagance. Am I not an object of pity, when I tell you, that I was tormented yesterday by a similar cause? But I know not how it is; your violent complainers are the least apt to excite compassion. I believe, notwithstanding, if another rising generation should lodge above me at the next inn, I shall grow as scurrilous as Dr. Smollet, and be dignified with the appellation of the Younger Smelfungus. Well, let those make out my diploma that will, I am determined to vent my spleen; and, like Lucifer, unable to enjoy comfort myself, teaze others with the detail of my vexations. You must know then, since I am resolved to grumble, that, tired with my passage, I went to the Capuchin church, a large solemn building, in search of silence and solitude; but here again was I disappointed: half a dozen squeaking fiddles fugued and flourished away in the galleries, as many paralytic monks gabbled before the altars, whilst a whole posse of devotees, wrapped in long white hoods and flannels, were sweltering on either side. Such piety in warm weather was no very fragrant circumstance; so I sought the open air again as fast

as I was able. The serenity of the evening, joined to the desire
I had of casting another glance over the ocean, tempted me to
the ramparts. There, at least, thought I to myself, I may range
undisturbed, and talk with my old friends the breezes, and
address my discourse to the waves, and be as romantic and whimsical as I please; but it happened, that I had scarcely begun my
apostrophe, before out flaunted a whole rank of officers, with
ladies, and abbés, and puppy dogs, singing, and flirting, and
making such a hubbub, that I had not one peaceful moment to
observe the bright tints of the western horizon, or enjoy the
series of antique ideas with which a calm sun-set never fails to
inspire me. Finding therefore no quiet abroad, I returned to my
inn, and should have gone immediately to bed, in hopes of
relapsing again into the bosom of dreams and delusions, but the
limbo, I mentioned before, grew so very outrageous, that I was
obliged to postpone my rest till sugar-plumbs and nursery-
eloquence had hushed it to repose. At length peace was restored,
and about eleven o'clock I fell into a slumber, during which the
most lovely Sicilian prospects filled the eye of my fancy. I anticipated all the classic scenes of that famous island, and forgot
every sorrow in the meadows of Enna. Next morning, awakened
by the sun-beams, I arose quite refreshed with the agreeable impressions of my dream, and filled with presages of future happiness in the climes which had inspired them. No other ideas but
such as Trinacria and Naples suggested, haunted me whilst travelling to Ghent. I neither heard the vile Flemish dialect which
was talking around me, nor noticed the formal avenues and
marshy country which we passed. When we stopped to change
horses, I closed my eyes upon the whole scene, and was transported immediately to some Grecian solitude, where Theocritus
and his shepherds were filling the air with melody. To one so
far gone in poetic antiquity, Ghent is not the most likely place
to recall his attention; and, I know nothing more about it, than
that it is a large, ill-paved, dismal-looking city, with a decent
proportion of convents and chapels, stuffed with monuments,
brazen gates, and glittering marbles. In the great church were
two or three pictures by Rubens, mechanically, excellent; but
these realities were not designed in so graceful a manner as to
divert my attention from the mere descriptions Pausanias gives
us of the works of Grecian artists, and I would at any time
fall asleep in a Flemish cathedral, for a vision of the temple of
Olympian Jupiter. But I think I hear, at this moment, some

grave and respectable personage chiding me for such levities, and saying—"Really, Sir, you had better stay at home, and dream in your great chair, than give yourself the trouble of going post through Europe, in search of inspiring places to fall asleep. If Flanders and Holland are to be dreamed over at this rate, you had better take ship at once, and dose all the way to Italy."— Upon my word, I should not have much objection to that scheme; and, if some cabalist would but transport me in an instant to the summit of Ætna, any body might slop through the Low Countries that pleased. Being, however, so far advanced, there was no retracting; and, as it is now three or four years since I have almost abandoned the hopes of discovering a necromancer, I resolved to journey along with quiet and content for my companions. These two comfortable deities have, I believe, taken Flanders under their especial protection; every step one advances discovering some new proof of their influence. The neatness of the houses, and the universal cleanliness of the villages, shew plainly that their inhabitants live in ease and good-humour. All is still and peaceful in these fertile lowlands: the eye meets nothing but round unmeaning faces at every door, and harmless stupidity smiling at every window. The beasts, as placid as their masters, graze on without any disturbance; and I don't recollect to have heard one grunting swine, or snarling mastiff, during my whole progress. Before every town is a wealthy dunghill, not at all offensive, because but seldom disturbed; and there they bask in the sun, and wallow at their ease, till the hour of death and bacon arrives, when capacious paunches await them. If I may judge from the healthy looks and reposed complexions of the Flemings, they have every reason to expect a peaceful tomb.

But it is high time to leave our swinish moralities behind us, and jog on towards Antwerp. More rich pastures, more ample fields of grain, more flourishing willows!—A boundless plain before this city, dotted with cows and flowers, from whence its spires and quaint roofs are seen to advantage! The pale colours of the sky, and a few gleams of watery sunshine, gave a true Flemish cast to the scenery, and every thing appeared so consistent, that I had not a shadow of pretense to think myself asleep. After crossing a broad, noble river, edged on one side by beds of oziers, beautifully green, and on the other by gates and turrets, preposterously ugly, we came through several streets of lofty houses to our inn. Its situation in the Place de Mer, a vast open space, surrounded by buildings above buildings, and roof above roof, has something striking and singular. A tall gilt crucifix of bronze, sculptured by some famous artist,[1] adds to its splendor; and the tops of some tufted trees, seen above a line of magnificent hotels, have no bad effect in the perspective. It was almost dusk when we arrived, and, as I am very partial to seeing new objects by this dubious, visionary light, I went immediately a rambling. Not a sound disturbed my meditations: there were no groups of squabbling children or talkative old women. The whole town seemed retired into their inmost chambers; and I kept winding and turning about, from street to street, and from alley to alley, without meeting a single inhabitant. Now and then, indeed, one or two women in long cloaks and mantles glided about at a distance; but their dress was so shroud-like, and their whole appearance so ghostly, I was more than half afraid to accost them. As the night approached, the ranges of buildings grew more and more dim, and the silence which reigned amongst them more aweful. The canals, which in some places intersect the streets, were likewise in perfect solitude, and there was just light sufficient for me to observe on the still waters the reflexion of the structures above them. Except two or three tapers glimmering through the casements, no one circumstance indicated human existence. I might, without being thought very romantic, have imagined myself in the city of petrified people, which Arabian fabulists are so fond of describing. Were any one to ask my advice upon the subject of retirement, I should tell him: By all means repair to Antwerp. No village amongst the Alps, or hermitage upon Mount Lebanon, is less disturbed: you may pass your days in this great city, without being the least conscious of its sixty thousand inhabitants, unless you visit the churches: There, indeed, are to be heard a few devout whispers, and sometimes, to be sure, the bells make a little chiming; but, walk about, as I do, in the twilights of midsummer, and, be assured, your ears will be free from all molestation. You can have no idea how many strange amusing fancies played around me, whilst I wandered along; nor, how delighted I was with the novelty of my situation. But a few days ago, thought I, within myself, I was in the midst of all the tumult and uproar of London:[2] now, as if by some magic influence, I

1. Beckford identified this artist in the 1834 edition as "Cortels of Malines."
2. The Gordon "No Popery" riots led by Lord George Gordon throughout the city of London during the opening days of June 1780. Roman Catholic chapels were destroyed, Newgate was set on fire, the Bank of England was attacked, and over 450 people were killed or wounded before the violence was subdued.

am transported to a city, equally remarkable for streets and edifices; but whose inhabitants seem cast into a profound repose. What a pity, that we cannot borrow some small share of this soporific disposition! It would temper that restless spirit, which throws us sometimes into such dreadful convulsions. However, let us not be too precipitate in desiring so dead a calm; the time may arrive, when, like Antwerp, we may sink into the arms of forgetfulness; when a fine verdure may carpet our exchange, and passengers traverse the Strand, without any danger of being smothered in crowds, or lost in the confusion of carriages. Reflecting, in this manner, upon the silence of the place, contrasted with the important bustle which formerly rendered it so famous, I insensibly drew near to the cathedral, and found myself, before I was aware, under its stupendous tower. It is difficult to conceive an object more solemn or imposing than this edifice, at the hour I first beheld it. Dark shades hindered my examining the lower galleries or windows; their elaborate carved work was invisible: nothing but huge masses of building met my sight, and the tower, shooting up four hundred and sixty-six feet into the air, received an additional importance from the gloom which prevailed below. The sky being perfectly clear, several stars twinkled through the mosaic of the spire, and added not a little to its enchanted effect. I longed to ascend it that instant, to stretch myself out upon its very summit, and calculate, from so sublime an elevation, the influence of the planets. Whilst I was indulging my astrological reveries, a ponderous bell struck ten, and such a peal of chimes succeeded, as shook the whole edifice, notwithstanding its bulk, and drove me away in a hurry. No mob obstructed my passage, and I ran through a succession of streets, free and unmolested, as if I had been skimming along over the downs of Wiltshire. My servants', conversing before the hotel, were the only voices which the great Place de Mer echoed. This universal stillness was the more pleasing, when I looked back upon those scenes of horror and outcry, which filled London but a week or two ago, when danger was not confined to night only, and the environs of the capital, but haunted our streets at midday. Here, I could wander over an entire city; stray by the port, and venture through the most obscure alleys, without a single apprehension; without beholding a sky red and portentous with the light of fires, or hearing the confused and terrifying murmur of shouts and groans, mingled with the reports of artillery. I can assure you, I think myself very fortunate to have escaped the possibility of another such week of desolation, and to be peaceably roosted at Antwerp. Were I not still fatigued with my heavy progress through sands and quagmires, I should descant a little longer upon the blessings of so quiet a metropolis: but it is growing late, and I must retire to enjoy it.

Letter III.

My windows look full upon the Place de Mer, and the sun, beaming through their white curtains, awoke me from a dream of Arabian happiness. Imagination had procured herself a tent on the mountains of Sanaa, covered with coffee-trees in bloom. She was presenting me the essence of their flowers, and was just telling me, that you possessed a pavilion on a neighbouring hill, when the sunshine dispelled the vision; and, opening my eyes, I found myself pent in by Flemish spires and buildings; no hills, no verdure, no aromatic breezes, no hopes of being in your vicinity: all were vanished with the shadows of fancy, and I was left alone to deplore your absence. But I think it rather selfish to wish you here; for what pleasure could pacing from one dull church to another, afford a person of your turn? I don't believe you would catch a taste for blubbering Magdalens and coarse Madonnas, by lolling in Rubens' chair; nor do I believe a view of the Ostades and Snyders, so liberally scattered in every collection, would greatly improve your pencil. After breakfast this morning, I began my pilgrimage to all those illustrious cabinets. First, I went to Monsieur Van Lencren's, who possesses a suite of apartments, lined, from the base to the cornice, with the rarest productions of the Flemish School.

Heavens forbid I should enter into a detail of their niceties! I might as well count the dew-drops upon any of Van Huysem's flower-pieces, or the pimples on their possessor's countenance; a very good sort of man, indeed; but, from whom I was not at all sorry to be delivered. My joy was, however, of short duration, as a few minutes brought me into the court-yard of the Chanoin

61

Knyfe's habitation; a snug abode, well furnished with easy chairs and orthodox couches. After viewing the rooms on the first floor, we mounted a gentle staircase, and entered an anti-chamber, which those who delight in the imitations of art, rather than of nature; in the likenesses of joint stools, and the portraits of tankards; would esteem most capitally adorned: but, it must be confessed, that, amongst these uninteresting performances, are dispersed a few striking Berghems, and agreeable Polemburgs. In the gallery adjoining, two or three Rosa de Tivolis merit observation; and a large Teniers, representing a St. Anthony surrounded by a malicious fry of imps and leering devilesses, is well calculated to display the whimsical buffoonery of a Dutch imagination. I was observing this strange medley, when the Canon made his appearance; and a most prepossessing figure he has, according to Flemish ideas. In my humble opinion, his Reverence looked a little muddled, or so; and to be sure the description I afterwards heard of his style of living, favours not a little my surmises. This worthy dignitary, what with his private fortune, and the good things of the church, enjoys a revenue of about five thousand pounds sterling, which he contrives to get rid of, in the joys of the table, and the encouragement of the pencil. His servants, perhaps, assist not a little in the expenditure of so comfortable an income; the Canon being upon a very social footing with them all. At four o'clock in the afternoon, a select party attend him in his coach to an ale-house, about a league from the city; where a table, well spread with jugs of beer and handsome cheeses, waits their arrival. After enjoying this rural fare, the same equipage conducts them back again, by all accounts, much faster than they came; which may well be conceived, as the coachman is one of the brightest wits of the entertainment. My compliments, alas! were not much relished, you may suppose, by this jovial personage. I said a few favourable words of Polemburg, and offered up a small tribute of praise to the memory of Berghem; but, as I could not prevail upon Mynheer Knyfe to expand, I made one of my best bows, and left him to the enjoyment of his domestic felicity. In my way home, I looked into another cabinet, the greatest ornament of which was a most sublime thistle by Snyders, of the heroic size, and so faithfully imitated, that I dare say no ass could see it unmoved. At length, it was lawful to return home; and, as I positively refused visiting any more cabinets in the afternoon, I sent for a harpsichord of Rucker, and played myself quite out of the Netherlands. It was late before I finished

my musical excursion, and I took advantage of this dusky moment
to revisit the cathedral. A flight of starlings was fluttering about
the pinnacles of the tower; their faint chirpings were the only
sounds that broke the stillness of the air. Not a human form
appeared at any of the windows around; no footsteps were audible
in the opening before the grand entrance; and, during the half
hour I spent in walking to and fro beneath the spire, one solitary
Franciscan was the only creature that accosted me. From him I
learnt, that a grand service was to be performed next day, in
honour of Saint John the Baptist, and the best music in Flanders
would be called forth upon the occasion. As I had seen cabinets
enough to form some slight judgment of Flemish painting, I
determined to stay one day longer at Antwerp, to hear a little
how its inhabitants were disposed to harmony. Having taken this
resolution, I formed an acquaintance with Mynheer Vander
Bosch, the first organist of the place, who very obligingly permitted me to sit next him in his gallery, during the celebration
of high mass. The service ended, I strayed about the ailes, and
examined the innumerable chapels which decorate them, whilst
Mynheer Vander Bosch thundered and lightened away upon a
huge organ with fifty stops. When the first flashes of execution
were a little subsided, I took an opportunity of surveying the
celebrated descent from the cross, which has ever been esteemed
one of Rubens's *chef d'œuvres,* and for which, they say, old Lewis
Baboon[3] offered no less a sum than forty thousand florins. The
principal figure has, doubtless, a very meritorious paleness, and
looks as dead, as an artist could desire; the rest of the group have
been so liberally praised, that there is no occasion to add another
tittle of commendation. A swinging St. Christopher, fording a
brook with a child on his shoulders, cannot fail of attracting
your attention. This colossal personage is painted on the folding
doors, which defend the capital performance just mentioned, from
vulgar eyes; and, here, Rubens, has selected a very proper subject
to display the gigantic coarseness of his pencil. Had this powerful
artist confined his strength to the representation of agonizing
thieves, and sturdy Barabbasses, nobody would have been readier
than your humble servant, to offer incense at his shrine; but,
when I find him lost in the flounces of the Virgin's drapery, or

---

3. John Arbuthnot's appellation for King Louis XIV of France. In a collection
of humorous allegories entitled *The History of John Bull* (1712), Arbuthnot
advocated the end of the war with France, designating the various parties concerned
as John Bull (England), Nicholas Frog (the Dutch), Lord Strutt (Phillip of
Spain), and Lewis Baboon (Louis XIV).

bewildered in the graces of St. Catherine's smile, pardon me, if I withhold my adoration. After I had most dutifully observed all the Rubenses in the church, I walked half over Antwerp in search of St. John's relics, which were moving about in procession; but an heretical wind having extinguished all their tapers, and discomposed the canopy over the Bon Dieu, I cannot say much for the grandeur of the spectacle. If my eyes were not greatly regaled by the Saint's magnificence, my ears were greatly affected in the evening, by the music which sang forth his praises. The cathedral was crouded with devotees, and perfumed with incense. Several of its marble altars gleamed with the reflection of lamps, and, all together, the spectacle was new and imposing. I knelt very piously in one of the ailes, whilst a symphony, in the best style of Corelli,[4] performed with taste and feeling, transported me to Italian climates; and I was quite vexed, when a cessation dissolved the charm, to think that I had still so many tramontane regions to pass, before I could in effect reach that classic country, where my spirit had so long taken up its abode. Finding it was in vain to wish, or expect any preternatural interposition, and perceiving no conscious angel, or Loretto-vehicle, waiting in some dark consecrated corner to bear me away, I humbly returned to my hotel in the Place de Mer, and soothed myself with some terrestrial harmony; till, my eyes growing heavy, I fell fast asleep, and entered the empire of dreams, according to custom, by its ivory portal. What past in those shadowy realms is too "thin and unsubstantial" to be committed to paper. The very breath of waking mortals would dissipate all the train, and drive them eternally away; give me leave, therefore, to omit the relation of my visionary travels, and have the patience to pursue a sketch of my real ones, from Antwerp to the Hague.

Monday, June 26, we are again upon the pavé, rattling and jumbling along, between clipped hedges and blighted avenues. The plagues of Egypt have been renewed, one might almost imagine, in this country, by the appearance of the oak-trees: not a leaf have the insects spared. After having had the displeasure of seeing no other objects, for several hours, but these blasted rows, the scene changed to vast tracts of level country, buried in sand, and smothered with heath; the particular character of which I had but too good an opportunity of intimately knowing, as a tortoise might have kept pace with us, without being once

---

4. Arcangelo Corelli (1653–1713), an Italian composer and violinist.

out of breath. Towards evening, we entered the dominions of the United Provinces, and had all the glory of canals, trackshuyts, and windmills, before us. The minute neatness of the villages, their red roofs, and the lively green of the willows which shade them, corresponded with the ideas I had formed of Chinese prospects; a resemblance, which was not diminished, upon viewing, on every side, the level scenery of enamelled meadows, with stripes of clear water across them, and innumerable barges gliding busily along. Nothing could be finer than the weather; it improved each moment, as if propitious to my exotic fancies; and, at sun-set, not one single cloud obscured the horizon. Several storks were parading by the water-side amongst flags and osiers; and, as far as the eye could reach, large herds of beautifully spotted cattle were enjoying the plenty of their pastures. I was perfectly in the environs of Canton, or Ning-Po, till we reached Meerdyke. You know fumigations are always the current recipe in romance to break an enchantment: as soon, therefore, as I left my carriage, and entered my inn, the clouds of tobacco, which filled every one of its apartments, dispersed my Chinese imaginations, and reduced me in an instant to Holland. Why should I enlarge upon my adventures at Meerdyke? 'tis but a very scurvy topic. To tell you, that its inhabitants are the most uncouth bipeds in the universe, would be nothing very new, or entertaining; so, let me at once pass over the village, leave Rotterdam, and even Delft, that great parent of pottery, and transport you with a wave of my pen to the Hague.

As the evening was rather warm, I immediately walked out to enjoy the shade of the long avenue which leads to Scheveling. It was fresh and pleasant enough, but I breathed none of those genuine, woody perfumes, which exhale from the depths of forests, and which allure my imagination at once to the haunts of Pan and the good old Sylvanus. However, I was far from displeased with my ramble; and, consoling myself with the hopes of shortly reposing in the sylvan labyrinths of Nemi, I proceeded to the village on the sea-coast, which terminates the perspective. Almost every cottage-door being open to catch the air, I had an opportunity of looking into their neat apartments. Tables, shelves, earthen-ware, all glisten with cleanliness: the country people were drinking tea after the fatigues of the day, and talking over its bargains and contrivances. I left them, to walk on the beach; and was so charmed with the vast azure expense of ocean which opened suddenly upon me, that I remained there a full half hour.

More than two hundred vessels of different sizes were in sight,—
the last sun-beams purpling their sails, and casting a path of
innumerable brilliants athwart the waves. What would I not have
given to follow this shining track! It might have conducted me,
straight to those fortunate western climates, those happy isles,
which you are so fond of painting, and I of dreaming about. But,
unluckily, this passage was the only one my neighbours the Dutch
were ignorant of. To be sure, they have islands rich in spices,
and blessed with the sun's particular attention, but which their
government, I am apt to imagine, renders by no means fortunate.
Abandoning therefore all hopes, at present, of this adventurous
voyage, I returned towards the Hague; and, in my way home,
looked into a country-house of the late Count Bentinck,[5] with
parterres, and bosquets, by no means resembling (one should
conjecture) the gardens of the Hesperides. But, considering that
the whole group of trees, terraces, and verdure were in a manner
created out of hills of sand, the place may claim some portion
of merit. The walks and alleys have all that stiffness and for-
mality our ancestors admired; but the intermediate spaces, being
dotted with clumps, and sprinkled with flowers, are imagined in
Holland to be in the English stile. An Englishman ought certainly to behold it with partial eyes; since every possible attempt
has been made to twist it into the taste of his country. I need
not say how liberally I bestowed my encomiums on Count B.'s
tasteful intentions; nor, how happy I was, when I had duly ser-
pentized over his garden, to find myself once more in the grand
avenue. All the way home, I reflected upon the œconomical disposition of the Dutch, who raise gardens from heaps of sand, and
cities out of the bosom of the waters. I had still a further proof
of this thrifty turn, since the first object I met, was an unwieldy
fellow, (not able, or unwilling, perhaps, to afford horses) airing
his carcase in a one-dog chair! The poor animal puffed and panted;
Mynheer smoked, and gaped around him with the most blessed
indifference!

---

5. Presumably Christian Frederick Anthony, Count Bentinck de Varel (1734–
1768), grandson of the first Earl of Portland and a Captain in the British Navy.
He had been a resident in The Hague before his death.

Letter IV.

I dedicated the morning to the Prince of Orange's cabinet of paintings, and curiosities both natural and artificial. Amongst the pictures which amused me the most, is a St. Anthony by Hell-fire Brughel; who has shewn himself right worthy of the title; for a more diabolical variety of imps never entered the human imagination. Brughel has made his saint take refuge in a ditch filled with harpies, and creeping things innumerable, whose malice, one should think, would have lost Job himself the reputation of patience. Castles of steel and fiery turrets glare on every side, from whence issue a band of junior devils; these seem highly entertained with pinking poor St. Anthony, and whispering, I warrant ye, filthy tales in his ear. Nothing can be more rueful than the patient's countenance; more forlorn than his beard; more pious than his eye, which forms a strong contrast to the pert winks and insidious glances of his persecutors; some of whom, I need not mention, are evidently of the female kind. But, really, I am quite ashamed of having detained you, in such bad company, so long; and, had I a moment to spare, you should be introduced to a better set in this gallery, where some of the most exquisite Berghems and Wouvermans I ever beheld, would delight you for hours. I don't think you would look much at the Polemburgs; there are but two, and one of them is very far from capital: in short, I am in a great hurry, so pardon me, Carlo Cignani! if I don't do justice to your merit; and excuse me, Potter! if I pass by your herds without leaving a tribute of admiration. Mynheer Van Something is as eager to precipitate my motions, as I was to get out of the damps and perplexities of Soorflect, yesterday evening; so, mounting a very indifferent stair-case, he led me into a suite of garret-like apartments; which, considering the meanness of their exterior, I was rather surprized to find stored with some of the most valuable productions of the Indies. Gold cups enriched with gems, models of Chinese palaces in ivory, glittering armour of Hindostan, and japan caskets, filled every corner of this awkward treasury. What, of all its valuable baubles, pleased me the most, was a large coffer of some precious wood, containing enamelled flasks of oriental essences, enough to perfume a zennana; and so fragrant, that I thought the Mogul himself a Dutchman, for lavishing them upon this inelegant nation. If disagreeable fumes, as I mentioned before, dissolve enchantments, such aromatic oils have doubtless the power of raising them; for, whilst I scented their fragrance, scarcely could any thing have persuaded me that I was not in the wardrobe of Hecuba,

"where treasur'd odours breath'd a costly scent."

I saw, or seemed to see, the arched apartments, the procession of venerable matrons, the consecrated vestments, the very temple began to rise upon my sight; when a Dutch porpoise, approaching to make me a low bow, his complaisance was full as notorious as Satan's, when, according to Catholic legends, he took leave of Calvin, or Dr. Faustus. No spell can resist a fumigation of this nature; away fled palace, Hecuba, matrons, temple, &c. I looked up, and lo! I was in a garret. As poetry is but too often connected with this lofty situation, you won't wonder much at my flight. Being a little recovered from it, I tottered down the stair-case, entered the cabinet of natural history, and was soon restored to my sober senses. A grave hippopotamos contributed a good deal to their re-establishment. The butterflies, I must needs confess, were very near leading me another dance; I thought of their native hills, and beloved flowers of Haynang and Nan-Hoa[6]; but the jargon which was prating all around me prevented the excursion, and I summoned a decent share of attention for that ample chamber, which has been appropriated to bottled snakes and pickled fœtuses. After having enjoyed the same spectacle in the British Museum, no very new or singular objects can be selected in this. One of the rarest articles it contains, is the representation in wax of a human head, most dextrously flayed indeed! Rapturous encomiums have been bestowed by amateurs on this performance. A German professor could hardly believe it artificial; and,

_____

6. Hills in the neighborhood of Quang-Tong. [Beckford's note.]

prompted by the love of truth, set his teeth in this delicious morsel, to be convinced of its reality. My faith was less hazardously established, and I moved off, under the conviction, that art had never produced any thing more horridly natural. It was one o'clock before I got through the mineral kingdom, and another hour passed, before I could quit, with decorum, the regions of stuffed birds and marine productions. At length my departure was allowable, and I went to dine at Sir Joseph Yorke's,[7] with all nations and languages. The Hague is the place in the world for a motley assembly; and, in some humours, I think such the most agreeable. After coffee, I strayed to the great wood; which, considering that it almost touches the town with its boughs, is wonderfully forest-like. Not a branch being ever permitted to be lopped, the oaks and beeches retain their natural luxuriances, and form some of the most picturesque groups conceivable. In some places, their straight boles rise sixty feet, without a bough; in others, they are bent fantastically over the alleys; which turn and wind about, just as a painter could desire. I followed them with eagerness and curiosity; sometimes deviating from my path amongst tufts of fern and herbage. In these cool retreats, I could not believe myself near canals and wind-mills: the Dutch formalities were all forgotten, whilst contemplating the broad masses of foliage above, and the wild flowers and grasses below. Several hares and rabbits passed me as I sat; and the birds were chirping their evening song. Their preservation does credit to the police of the country, which is so exact and well regulated, as to suffer no outrage within the precincts of this extensive wood, the depth and thickness of which, seem calculated to favour half the sins of a capital.

Relying upon this comfortable security, I lingered unmolested amongst the beeches, till the ruddy gold of the setting sun ceased to glow on their foliage; then, taking the nearest path, I suffered myself, though not without regret, to be conducted out of this fresh sylvan scene, to the dusty, pompous parterres of the Greffier Fagel.[8] Every flower, that wealth can purchase, diffuses its perfume on one side; whilst every stench, a canal can exhale, poisons the air on the other. These sluggish puddles defy all the power of the United Provinces, and retain the freedom of stinking in spite of their endeavours: but, perhaps, I am too bold in my as-

---

7. Joseph Yorke (1724–1792), sometimes called "Colonel Yorke," had resided in The Hague since 1751 as a British diplomat and was elevated to the status of Ambassador in 1761.

8. Hendrik Fagel (1706–1790), Secretary of State for the States General.

sertion; for I have no authority to mention any attempts to purify these noxious pools. Who knows but their odour is congenial to a Dutch constitution? One should be inclined to this supposition, by the numerous banquetting-rooms, and pleasure-houses, which hang directly above their surface, and seem calculated on purpose to enjoy them. If frogs were not excluded from the magistrature of their country (and I cannot but think it a little hard that they are) one should not wonder at this choice. Such burgomasters might erect their pavilions in such situations. But, after all, I am not greatly surprized at the fishiness of their scite, since very slight authority would persuade me there was a period when Holland was all water, and the ancestors of the present inhabitants fish. A certain oysterishness of eye, and flabbiness of complexion, are almost proofs sufficient of this aquatic descent; and, pray tell me, for what purpose are such galligaskins, as the Dutch burthen themselves with, contrived, but to tuck up a flouncing tail, and cloak the deformity of their dolphin-like terminations? Having done penance, for some time, in the damp alleys which line the borders of these lazy waters, I was led through corkscrew hand-walks, to a vast flat, sparingly scattered over with vegetation. To puzzle myself in such a labyrinth there was no temptation; so, taking advantage of the lateness of the hour, and muttering a few complimentary promises of returning at the first opportunity, I escaped the ennui of this extensive scrubbery, and got home, with the determination of being wiser and less curious, if ever my stars should bring me again to the Hague. To-morrow I bid it adieu; and, if the horses but second my endeavours, shall be delivered in a few days from the complicated plagues of the United Provinces.

Letter V.

The sky was clear and blue when we left the Hague, and we travelled along a shady road for about an hour, then down sunk the carriage into a sand-bed; and I, availing myself of the peaceful rate we dragged at, fell into a profound repose. How long it lasted is not material; but when I awoke, we were rumbling through Leyden. There is no need to write a syllable in honour of this illustrious city: its praises have already been sung and said by fifty professors, who have declaimed in its university, and smoked in its gardens; so let us get out of it as fast as we can, and breathe the cool air of the wood near Haerlem; where we arrived just as day declined. Hay was making in the fields, and perfumed the country far and wide, with its reviving fragrance. I promised myself a pleasant walk in the groves, took up Gesner,[9] and began to have pretty pastoral ideas; but when I approached the nymphs that were dispersed on the meads, and saw faces that would have dishonoured a flounder, and heard accents that would have confounded a hog, all my dislike to the walking fish of the Low Countries returned. I let fall the garlands I had wreathed for the shepherds; we jumped into the carriage, and were driven off to the town. Every avenue to it swarmed with people, whose bustle and agitation seemed to announce that something extraordinary was going forwards. Upon enquiry, I found it was the great fair-time at Haerlem; and, before we had advanced much further, our carriage was surrounded by idlers and gingerbread-eaters of all denominations. Passing the gate, we came to a cluster of little illuminated booths beneath a grove, glittering with toys and

---

9. Solomon Gessner (1730–1788), German writer, author of *The Death of Abel and Idylls.*

looking-glasses. It was not without difficulty that we reached our
inn; and then, the plague was to procure chambers: at last we
were accommodated, and the first moment I could call my own
has been dedicated to you. You won't be surprized at the nonsense
I have written, since I tell you the scene of riot and uproar from
whence it bears date. At this very moment, the confused murmur
of voices and music stops all regular proceedings: old women and
children tattling; apes, bears, and shew-boxes under the windows;
the devil to pay in the inn; French rattling, English swearing,
outrageous Italians, frisking minstrels; *tambours de basque* at
every corner; myself distracted; a confounded squabble of cooks
and haranguing German couriers just arrived, their masters following open mouthed; nothing to eat, the steam of ham and
flesh-pots all the while provoking their appetite; Mynheers very
busy with the realities, and smoking as deliberately, as if in a
solitary lust-huys over the laziest canal in the Netherlands; squeaking chamber-maids in the galleries above, and prudish dames
below, half inclined to receive the golden solicitations of certain
beauties for admittance; but positively refusing them, the moment
some creditable personage appears: eleven o'clock strikes; half the
lights in the fair are extinguished; scruples grow less and less
delicate; mammon prevails, darkness and complaisance succeed.
Good night: may you sleep better than I shall!

Letter VI.

Well, thank Heaven! Amsterdam is behind us: how I got thither
signifies not one farthing; 'twas all along a canal, as usual. The
weather was hot enough to broil an inhabitant of Bengal, and the
odours, exhaling from every quarter, sufficiently powerful to regale
the nose of a Hottentot. Under these agreeable circumstances, we
entered the great city. The Stadt-huys being the only cool place
it contained, I repaired thither, as fast as the heat permitted, and
walked in a lofty marble hall magnificently covered, till the dinner was ready at the inn. That dispatched, we set off for Utrecht.
Both sides of the way are lined with the country houses and gardens of opulent citizens, as fine as gilt statues and clipped hedges
can make them. Their number is quite astonishing: from Amsterdam to Utrecht, full thirty miles, we beheld no other objects than
endless avenues, and stiff parterres, scrawled and flourished in
patterns, like the embroidery of an old maid's work-bag. Notwithstanding this formal taste, I could not help admiring the neatness
and arrangement of every inclosure, enlivened by a profusion of
flowers, and decked with arbours, beneath which, a vast number
of round, unmeaning faces were solacing themselves, after the
heat of the day. Each lust-huys we passed, contained some comfortable party, dozing over their pipes, or angling in the muddy
fishponds below. Scarce an avenue but swarmed with female
josses; little squat pug-dogs waddling at their sides, the attributes,
I suppose, of these fair divinities:—But let us leave them to loiter
thus amiably in their Ælysian groves, and arrive at Utrecht; which,
as nothing very remarkable claimed my attention, I hastily quitted,
to visit a Moravian establishment at Siest, in its neighbourhood.
The chapel, a large house late the habitation of Count Zinzen-

dorf,[10] and a range of apartments filled with the holy fraternity, are totally wrapped in dark groves, overgrown with weeds, amongst which some damsels were straggling, under the immediate protection of their pious brethren. Traversing the woods, we found ourselves in a large court built round with brick edifices, the grass plats in a deplorable way, and one ragged goat, their only inhabitant, on a little expiatory scheme, perhaps, for the failings of the fraternity. I left this poor animal to ruminate in solitude, and followed my guide into a series of shops furnished with gewgaws and trinkets, said to be manufactured by the female part of the society. Much cannot be boasted of their handy-works: I expressed a wish to see some of these industrious fair ones; but, upon receiving no answer, found this was a subject *of which there was no discourse*. Consoling myself as well as I was able, I put myself under the guidance of another slovenly disciple, who shewed me the chapel, and harangued, very pathetically, upon celestial love. In my way thither, I caught a distant glimpse of some pretty sempstresses, warbling melodious hymns, as they sat needling and thimbling at their windows above. I had a great inclination to have approached this busy group, but a roll of the brother's eye corrected me. Reflecting upon my unworthiness, I retired from the consecrated buildings, and was driven back to Utrecht, not a little amused with my expedition. If you are as well disposed to be pleased as I was, I shall esteem myself very lucky, and not repent sending you so incorrect a narrative. I really have not time to look it over, and am growing so drowsy, that you will, I hope, pardon all its errors, when you consider that my pen writes in its sleep.

---

10. Nikolaus Ludwig Zinzendorf (1700–1760), German religious leader, founder of the Herrnhut community.

Letter VII.

From Utrecht to Bois le Duc nothing but sand and heath; no inspiration, no whispering foliage, not even a grasshopper, to put one in mind of Eclogues and Theocritus.—"But, why did you not fall into one of your beloved slumbers, and dream of poetic mountains? This was the very country to shut one's eyes upon, without disparagement."—Why so I did, but the postillions and boatmen obliged me to open them, as soon as they were closed. Four times was I shoved, out of my visions, into leaky boats, and towed across as many idle rivers. I thought there was no end of these tiresome transits; and, when I reached my journey's end, was so compleatly jaded, that I almost believed Charon would be the next aquatic I should have to deal with.—The fair light of the morning (Tuesday July 4th) was scarcely sufficient to raise my spirits, and I had left Bois le Duc a good way in arrears, before I was thoroughly convinced of my existence; when I looked through the blinds of the carriage, and saw nothing but barren plains and mournful willows, banks clad with rushes, and heifers so black and dismal, that Proserpine herself would have given them up to Hecate. I was near believing myself in the neighbourhood of a certain evil place, where I should be punished for all my croakings. We travelled at this rate, I dare say, fifteen miles, without seeing a single shed: at last, one or two miserable cottages appeared, darkened by heath, and stuck in a sand-pit; from whence issued a half-starved generation, that pursued us a long while with their piteous wailings. The heavy roads and ugly prospects, together with the petulant clamours of my petitioners, made me quite uncharitable. I was in a dark, remorseless mood, which lasted me till we reached Brée, a shabby decayed town, encompassed by walls and ruined turrets. Having nothing to do, I straggled about them, till night shaded the dreary prospects, and gave me an opportunity of imagining them, if I pleased, noble and majestic. Several of these waining edifices were invested with thick ivy: the evening was chill, and I crept under their covert. Two or three brother owls were before me, but politely gave up their pretensions to the spot, and, as soon as I appeared, with a rueful whoop, flitted away to some deeper retirement. I had scarcely began to mope in tranquillity, before a rapid shower trickled amongst the clusters above me, and forced me to abandon my haunt. Returning in the midst of it to my inn, I hurried to bed; and was soon lulled asleep by the storm. A dream bore me off to Persepolis; and led me, thro' vast subterraneous treasures, to a hall, where Solomon, methought, was holding forth upon their vanity.[11] I was upon the very point of securing a part of this immense wealth, and fancied myself writing down the sage prophet's advice, how to make use of it, when a loud vociferation in the street, and the bell of a neighbouring chapel, dispersed the vision. Starting up, I threw open the windows, and found it was eight o'clock, (Wednesday July 5,) and had hardly rubbed my eyes, before beggars came limping from every quarter. I knew their plaguy voices but too well; and, that the same hubbub had broken my slumbers, and driven me from wisdom and riches to the regions of ignorance and poverty. The halt, the lame, and the blind, being restored, by the miracle of a few stivers, to their functions, we breakfasted in peace, and, gaining the carriage, waded through sandy deserts to Maestricht: our view however was considerably improved, for a league round the town, and presented some hills and pleasant valleys, smiling with crops of grain: here and there, green meadows, spread over with hay, varied the prospect, which the chirping of birds (the first I had heard for many a tedious day) amongst the barley, rendered me so chearful, that I began, like them, my exultations, and was equally thoughtless and serene. I need scarcely tell you, that, leaving the coach, I pursued a deep furrow between two extensive corn-fields, and reposed upon a bank of flowers, the golden ears waving above my head, and entirely bounding my prospect. Here I lay, in peace and sunshine, a few happy moments; contemplating the blue sky, and fancying myself restored to the valley at F,[12]

---

11. An allusion to the Caliph Vathek's voyage to the ruins of Istakhar (Persepolis), where he found Soliman Ben Daoud in a subterranean "hall of great extent . . . covered with a lofty dome, around which appeared fifty portals of bronze, secured with as many fastenings of iron."

12. I.e. Fonthill.

where I have past so many happy hours, shut out from the world, and concealed in the bosom of harvests. It was then I first grew so fond of dreaming; and no wonder, since I have frequently imagined, that Ceres did not disdain to inspire my slumbers; but, half concealed, half visible, would tell me amusing stories of her reapers; and, sometimes more seriously inclined, recite the affecting tale of her misfortunes. At mid-day, when all was still, and a warm haze seemed to repose on the face of the landscape, I have often fancied this celestial voice bewailing Proserpine, in the most pathetic accents. From these sacred moments, I resolved to offer sacrifice in the fields of Enna; to explore their fragrant recesses, and experience whether the Divinity would not manifest herself to me in her favorite domain. It was this vow, which tempted me from my native valleys. Its execution, therefore, being my principal aim, I deserted my solitary bank, and proceeded on my journey. Maestricht abounds in Gothic churches, but contains no temple to Ceres. I was not sorry to quit it, after spending an hour unavoidably within its walls. Our road was conducted up a considerable eminence, from the summit of which we discovered a range of woody steeps, extending for leagues; beneath lay a winding valley, richly variegated, and lighted up by the Maese. The evening sun, scarcely gleaming through hazy clouds, cast a pale, tender hue upon the landscape, and the copses, still dewy with a shower that had lately fallen, diffused the most grateful fragrance. Flocks of sheep hung browsing on the acclivities, whilst a numerous herd were dispersed along the river's side. I staid so long, enjoying this pastoral scene, that we did not arrive at Liege, till the night was advanced, and the moon risen. Her interesting gleams were thrown away upon this ill-built, crowded city; and I grieved, that gates and fortifications prevented my breathing the fresh air of the surrounding mountains.

Next morning (July 6th) a zigzag road brought us, after many descents and rises, to Spá. The approach, through a rocky vale, is not totally devoid of picturesque merit; and, as I met no cabriolets or tituppings on the *chausée,* I concluded, that the waters were not as yet much visited; and, that I should have their romantic environs pretty much to myself. But, alas, how widely was I deceived! The moment we entered, up flew a dozen sashes. Chevaliers de St. Louis, meagre Marquises, and ladies of the scarlet order of Babylon, all poked their heads out. In a few minutes, half the town was in motion; taylors, confectioners, and barbers, thrusting bills into our hands, with manifold grimaces and contortions.

Then succeeded a *grand entré* of *valets de place,* who were hardly dismissed before the lodging-letters arrived, followed by some-body with a list of *les seigneurs* & dames, as long as a Welsh pedi-gree. Half an hour was wasted in speeches and recommendations; another passed, before we could snatch a morsel of refreshment; they then finding I was neither inclined to go to the ball, nor enter the land where Pharoah reigneth, peace was restored, a few feeble bows were scraped, and I found myself in perfect solitude. Taking advantage of this quiet moment, I stole out of town, and followed a path cut in the rocks, which brought me to a young wood of oaks on their summits. Luckily, I met no saunterer: the gay vagabonds, it seems, were all at the assembly, as happy as billiards and chit-chat could make them. It was not an evening to tempt such folks abroad. The air was cool, and the sky lowering, a melancholy cloud shaded the wild hills and irregular woods at a distance. There was something so importunate in their appearance, that I could not help asking their name, and was told they were skirts of the forest of Ardenne, amongst whose enchanted labyrinths the heroes of Boyardo and Ariosto roved formerly in quest of adventures. I felt myself singularly affected whilst gazing upon a wood so celebrated in romance for feats of the highest chivalry; and, Don Quixote like, would have explored its recesses in search of that memorable Fountain of Hatred, which (if you recollect the story) was raised by Merlin to free illustrious knights and damsels from the torments of rejected love. So far was I advanced in these romantic fancies, that, forgetting the lateness of the hour, I wandered on, expecting to reach the fountain at every step; but at length it grew so dusky, that, unable to trace back my way amongst the thickets, in vain I strayed through intricate copses, till the clouds began to disperse, and the moon appeared. Being so placed as to receive the full play of silver radiance, to my no small surprize, I beheld a precipice immediately beneath my feet. The chasm was deep and awful; something like the entrance of a grot discovered itself below; and, if I had not been already disappointed on the score of the fount, I won't answer but that I should have flung myself adventurously down, and tried, whether I might not have seen such wonders as appeared to Bradamante, when cast by Pinnabel, rather unpolitely, into Merlin's cave. But, no propitious light beaming from the cavity, I concluded times were changed; and, searching about me, found at last a shelving steep, which it was just possible to descend without goats heels, and that's all. In my way home I passed the redoute; and, seeing a vast glare of lustres in its apartments, I ran upstairs, and found the gamblers, all eager at storming the Pharoah Bank: a young Englishman of distinction, seemed the most likely to raise the siege, which increased every instant in turbulence; but, not feeling the least inclination to protract, or to shorten its fate, I left the knights to their adventures, and returned, ingloriously, to my inn.

All languages are chattering at the Table d'Hôte, and all sorts of business transacted under my very windows. The racket and perfume of this place make me resolve to get out of it to-morrow; as that is the case, you won't hear from me till I reach Munich. Adieu! May we meet in our dreams by the fountain of Merlin, and from thence take out flight with Astolpho to the moon; for I shrewdly suspect the best part of our senses are bottled up there; and then, you know, it will be a delightful novelty to wake with a clear understanding.

"Indeed, Sir, no *Monsieur comme il faut,* ever left Spá in such dudgeon before, unless jilted by a Polish princess, or stripped by an itinerant Count. You have neither breakfasted at the Vauxhall, nor attended the Spectacle, nor tasted the waters. Had you but taken one sip, your ill-humour would have all trickled away, and you would have felt both your heels and your elbows quite alive, in the evening."—Granted, but, pray tell your postillions to drive off as fast as their horses will carry them. Away we went to Aix-la-Chapelle, about ten at night, and saw the mouldring turrets of that once illustrious capital, by the help of a candle and lantern. An old woman asked our names (for not a single soldier appeared) and, traversing a number of superannuated streets, without perceiving the least trace of Charlemain or his Paladins, we procured comfortable, though not magnificent apartments, and slept most unheroically sound, till it was time to set forwards for Dusseldorp.

(July 8th.) As we were driven out of town, I caught a glimpse of a grove, hemmed in by dingy buildings, where a few water-drinkers were sauntering along, to the sound of some rueful french-horns: the wan, greenish light, admitted through the foliage, made them look like unhappy souls, condemned to an eternal lounge for having trifled away their existence. It was not with much regret, that I left such a party behind; and, after experiencing the vicissitudes of good roads and rumbling pavements, found myself, towards the close of evening, upon the banks of the Rhine. Many wild ideas thronged into my mind, the moment I beheld this celebrated river. I thought of the vast regions through which it flows, and suffered my imagination to expatiate as far as its source. A red, variegated sky reflected from the stream, the woods trembling on its banks, and the spires of Nuys rising beyond them, helped to amuse my fancy. Not being able to brook the confinement of the carriage, I left it to come over at its leisure; and, stepping into a boat, rowed along, at first, by the quivering oziers: then, launching out into the midst of the waters, I glided a few moments with the current, and, resting on my oars, listened to the hum of voices afar off, while several little skiffs, like canoes, glanced before my sight; concerning which, distance and the twilight allowed me to make a thousand fantastic conjectures. When I had sufficiently indulged these extravagant reveries, I began to cross over the river in good earnest; and, being landed on its opposite margin, travelled forwards to the town. Nothing but the famous gallery of paintings, could invite strangers to stay a moment within its walls; more crooked streets, more indifferent houses, one seldom meets with: except soldiers, not a living creature moving about them; and, at night, a compleat regiment of bugs "marked me for their own." Thus I lay, at once, both the seat of war, and the victim of these detestable animals, till early in the morning, (Sunday, July 9) when Morpheus, compassionating my sufferings, opened the ivory gates of his empire, and freed his votary from the most unconscionable vermin, that ever nastiness engendered. In humble prose, I fell fast asleep; and remained quiet, in defiance of my adversaries, till it was time to survey the cabinet. This collection is displayed in five large galleries, and contains some valuable productions of the Italian school; but the room most boasted of, is that which Rubens has filled, with, no less than three, enormous representations of the last day; where an innumerable host of sinners are exhibited, as striving in vain to avoid the tangles of the devil's tail. The woes of several fat, luxurious souls, are rendered in the highest gusto. Satan's dispute with some brawny concubines, whom he is lugging off in spite of all their resistance, cannot be too much admired by those who approve this class of subjects, and think such strange embroglios in the least calculated to raise a sublime, or a religious, idea. For my own part, I turned from them with disgust, and hastened to contemplate a holy family by Camillo Procaccini, in another apartment. The brightest imagination can never conceive any figure more graceful than that of the young Jesus; and if ever I beheld an inspired countenance, or celestial features, it was here: but to attempt conveying in words, what colours alone can express, would be only reversing the absurdity of many a master in the gallery, who aims to represent those ideas by colours, which language alone is able to describe. Should you admit this opinion, you won't be surprized at my passing such a multitude of renowned pictures unnoticed, nor, at my bringing you out of the cabinet, without deluging ten pages with criticisms in the style of the ingenious Lady M.[13] As I had spent so much time in gazing at Camillo's divinity, the day was too far advanced to think of travelling to Cologne; I was, therefore, obliged to put myself, once more, under the dominion of the most inveterate bugs in the universe. This government, like many others, made but an indifferent use of its power, and the subject, suffering accordingly, was extremely rejoiced at flying from his persecutors to Cologne (July 10th). Clouds of dust hindered my making any remarks on the exterior of this celebrated city; but, if its appearance be not more beautiful from without, than from within, I defy Mr. Salmon[14] himself, to launch forth very warmly in its praise.—But, of what avail are stately palaces, broad streets, or airy markets, to a town which can boast of such a treasure, as the bodies of those three wise sovereigns, who were star-led to Bethlehem? Is not this circumstance enough to procure it every respect? I really believe so, from the pious and dignified contentment of its inhabitants. They care not a hair of an ass's ear, whether their houses be gloomy, and ill contrived; their pavement over-grown with weeds, and their shops with filthiness; provided the carcases of Gaspar, Melchior, and Balthazar might be preserved with proper decorum. Nothing, to be sure, can be richer, than the shrine which contains these precious relics. I payed my devotions before it, the moment I arrived; this step was inevitable; had I omitted it, not a soul in Cologne but would have cursed me for a Pagan. Do you not wonder at hearing of these venerable bodies, so far from their native country? I thought them snug in some Arabian pyramid, ten feet deep in spice; but, you see, one can never tell what is to become of one, a few ages hence. Who knows but the emperor of Morocco may be canonized some future day in Lapland? I asked, of course, how, in the name of miracles, they came hither? but found no

---

13. Lady Anna Miller (1741–1781), verse-writer, whose *Poetical Amusements at a Villa Near Bath* (1775) was described by Horace Walpole as "a bouquet of artificial flowers, and ten degrees duller than a magazine." Presumably Beckford had her travel book in mind: *Letters from Italy, describing the Manners, Customs, Antiquities, Paintings, etc. of the Country in 1770–1* (1776).

14. Thomas Salmon (1679–1767), historian and geographer, author of *The Universal Traveller* (1752–3) and *The Present State of all Nations* (1744–46). In the 1834 edition Beckford identifies Salmon as "the most courteous compiler of geographical dictionaries."

story of a supernatural conveyance. It seems, the holy Empress Helena,[15] as great a collectress of relics as the D——s of P.[16] is of prophane curiosities, first routed them out; then, they were packed off to Rome. King Alaric,[17] having no grace, bundled them down to Milan; where they remained, till it pleased God to inspire an ancient Archbishop with the fervent wish of depositing them at Cologne. There, these skeletons were taken into the most especial consideration, crowned with jewels, and filagreed with gold. Never were skulls more elegantly mounted; and I doubt, whether Odin's buffet could exhibit so fine an assortment. The chapel containing these beautiful bones, is placed in a dark extremity of the cathedral. Several golden lamps gleam along the polished marbles with which it is adorned, and afford just light enough to read the following monkish inscription:

CORPORA SANCTORUM RECUBANT HIC TERNA MAGORUM: EX HIS SUBLATUM NIHIL EST ALIBIVE LOCATUM.

After I had amply satisfied my curiosity, with respect to the peregrinations of the consecrated skeletons, I examined their shrine; and was rather surprized to find it, not only enriched with barbaric gold and pearl, but covered with cameos and intaglios of the best antique sculpture. Many an impious emperor and gross Silenus, many a wanton nymph and frantic bacchanal, figure in the fame range with the statutes of saints and evangelists. How St. Helena could tolerate such a mixed assembly (for the shrine was formed under her auspices) surpasses my comprehension. Perhaps you will say, it is no great matter; and give me a hint to move out of the chapel, lest the three kings and their star should lead me quite out of my way. Very well; I think I had better stop in time, to tell you, without further excursion, that we set off after dinner for Bonn. Our road-side was lined with beggarly children, high convent-walls, and scarecrow crucifixes; lubberly monks, dejected peasants, and all the delights of Catholicism. Such scenery not engaging a great share of my attention, I kept gazing at the azure,

---

15. Flavia Julia Helena Augusta (248–328), wife of Constantius Chlorus and mother of Constantine the Great. Legend had also credited Empress Helena with the discovery of the true Cross, which she was supposed to have made during her celebrated visit to the Holy Land.

16. Duchess of Portland, Lady Dorothy Cavendish, wife of the third Duke of Portland (William Henry Cavendish Bentinck).

17. Alaric I (c. 370–410), Visigoth King, conqueror of Rome.

irregular mountains, which bounded our view; and, in thought, was already transported to their summits. Various are the prospects I surveyed from this imaginary exaltation, and innumerable the chimeras which trotted in my brain. Mounted on these fantastic quadrupeds, I shot swiftly from rock to rock, and built castles, in the style of Piranesi,[18] upon most of their pinnacles. The magnificence and variety of my aerial towers, hindered my thinking the way long. I was still walking, with a crowd of phantoms, upon their terraces, when the carriage made a halt. Immediately descending the innumerable flights of steps, which divide such lofty edifices from the lower world, I entered the inn at Bonn; and was shewn into an apartment, which commands the chief front of the Elector's palace. You may guess how contemptible it appeared, to one just returned from the courts of fancy. In other respects, I saw it in a very favourable moment; for the twilight, shading the whole façade, concealed its plaistered walls and painted pillars; their pediments and capitals being tolerably well proportioned, and the range of windows beneath considerable, I gave the architect more credit than he deserved, and paced to and fro beneath the arcade, as pompously as if arrived at the Vatican; but the circumstance which rendered my walk in reality agreeable, was the prevalence of a delicious perfume. It was so dusky, that I was a minute or two seeking in vain the entrance of an orangery, from whence this reviving scent proceeded. At length I discovered it; and, passing under an arch, found myself in the midst of lemon and orange trees, now in the fullest blow, which form a continued grove before the palace, and extend, on each side of its grand portal, out of sight. A few steps separate this extensive terrace from a lawn, bordered by stately rows of beeches. Beyond, in the centre of this striking theatre, rises a romantic assemblage of distant mountains, crowned with the ruins of castles, whose turrets, but faintly seen, were just such as you have created to compleat a prospect. I was the only human being in the misty extent of the gardens, and was happier in my solitude than I can describe. No noise disturbed its silence, except the flutter of moths and trickling of fountains. These undecided sounds, corresponding with the dimness and haze of the scenery, threw me into a pensive state of mind, neither gay nor dismal. I recapitulated the wayward adventures of my childhood, and traced back each moment of a period, which has seen me happy. Then, turning my thoughts towards

18. Giambattista Piranesi (1720–1778), Italian draftsman and etcher who achieved fame through his depiction of fantasy architecture.

future days, my heart beat at the idea of that awful veil which covers the time to come. One moment, 'twas the brightest hope that glittered behind it; the next, a series of melancholy images clouded the perspective. Thus, alternately swayed by fears and exultation, I passed an interesting hour in the twilight, ranging amongst the orange-trees, or reclined by the fountain. I could not boast of being perfectly satisfied, since those were absent, without whom, not even the fields of Enna could be charming. However, I was far from displeased with the clear streams that bubbled around, and could willingly have dropt asleep by their margin. Had I reposed in so romantic a situation, the murmurs of trees and waters, would doubtless have invited "some strange mysterious dream" to hover over me; and, perhaps, futurity might have been unveiled.

Letter VIII.

Let those who delight in picturesque country, repair to the borders of the Rhine, and follow the road which we took, from Bonn to Coblentz. In some places it is suspended, like a cornice, above the waters; in others, it winds behind lofty steeps and broken acclivities, shaded by woods, and cloathed with an endless variety of plants and flowers. Several green paths lead amongst this vegetation to the summits of the rocks, which often serve as the foundation of abbeys and castles, whose lofty roofs and spires, rising above the cliffs, impress passengers with ideas of their grandeur, that might probably vanish upon a nearer approach. Not chusing to lose any prejudice in their favour, I kept a respectful distance whenever I left my carriage, and walked on the banks of the river. Just before we came to Andernach, an antiquated town with strange morisco-looking towers, I spied a raft, at least three hundred feet in length, on which ten or twelve cottages were erected, and a great many people employed in sawing wood. The women sat spinning at their doors, whilst their children played among the water-lilies, that bloomed in abundance on the edge of the stream. A smoke, rising from one of these aquatic habitations, partially obscured the mountains beyond, and added not a little to their effect. Altogether, the scene was so novel and amusing, that I sat half an hour contemplating it, from an eminence under the shade of some leafy walnuts; and should like extremely to build a moveable village, people it with my friends, and so go floating about from island to island, and from one woody coast of the Rhine to another. Would you dislike such a party? I am much deceived, or you would be the first to explore the shades and promontories, beneath which we should be wafted along; but I don't think you would find Coblentz, where we were obliged to take up our night's lodging, much to your taste. 'Tis a mean, dirty assemblage of plaistered houses, striped with paint and set off with wooden galleries, in the beautiful taste of St. Giles's. Above, on a rock, stands the palace of the Elector, which seems to be remarkable for nothing but situation. I did not bestow many looks on this structure whilst ascending the mountain, across which our road to Mayence conducted us.

(July 12.) Having attained the summit, we discovered a vast, irregular range of country, and advancing, found ourselves amongst downs, bounded by forests, and purpled with thyme. This sort of prospect extending for several leagues, I walked on the turf, and inhaled with avidity the fresh gales that blew over its herbage, till I came to a steep slope, overgrown with privet and a variety of luxuriant shrubs in blossom: there, reposing beneath the shade, I gathered flowers, listened to the bees, observed their industry, and idled away a few minutes with great satisfaction. A cloudless sky and bright sun-shine made me rather loth to move on, but the charms of the landscapes, increasing every instant, drew me forwards. I had not gone far, before a winding valley discovered itself, shut in by rocks and mountains, cloathed to their very summits with the thickest wood. A broad river, flowing at the base of the cliffs, reflected the impending vegetation, and looked so calm and grassy, that I was determined to be better acquainted with it. For this purpose, we descended by a zigzag path into the vale, and making the best of our way on the banks of the Lune (for so is the river called) came suddenly upon the town of Emms, famous in mineral story; where, finding very good lodgings, we took up our abode, and led an Indian life amongst the wilds and mountains. After supper, I walked on a smooth lawn by the river, to observe the moon journeying through a world of silver clouds, that lay dispersed over the face of the heavens. It was a mild, genial evening: every mountain cast its broad shadow on the surface of the stream: lights twinkled afar off on the hills: they burnt in silence. All were asleep, except a female figure in white, with glow-worms shining in her hair. She kept moving disconsolately about: sometimes I heard her sigh, and, if apparitions sigh, this must have been an apparition. Upon my return, I asked a thousand questions, but could never obtain any information of the figure and its luminaries.

July 13th. The pure air of the morning invited me early to the hills. Hiring a skiff, I rowed about a mile down the stream, and landed on a sloping meadow, level with the waters, and newly mown. Heaps of hay still lay dispersed under the copses, which hemmed in on every side this little sequestered paradise. What a spot for a tent! I could encamp here for months, and never be tired. Not a day would pass by without discovering some new promontory, some untrodden pasture, some unsuspected vale, where I might remain among woods and precipices, lost and forgotten. I would give you, and two or three more, the clew of my labyrinth: nobody else should be conscious of its entrance. Full of such agreeable dreams, I rambled about the meads, scarce knowing which way I was going: sometimes a spangled fly led me astray, and, oftener, my own strange fancies. Between both, I was perfectly bewildered; and should never have found my boat again, had not an old German Naturalist, who was collecting fossils on the cliffs, directed me to it.

When I got home it was growing late, and I now began to perceive, that I had taken no refreshment, except the perfume of the hay and a few wood strawberries: airy diet, you will observe, for one not yet received into the realms of Ginnistan.[19]

July 14th. I have just made a discovery, that this place is as full of idlers and water-drinkers, as their Highnesses of Orange and Hesse Darmstadt can desire; for to them accrue all the profits of its salubrious fountains. I protest, I knew nothing of all this yesterday, so entirely was I taken up with the rocks and meadows; no chance of meeting either card or billiard players in their solitudes. Both abound at Emms, where they hop and fidget from ball to ball, unconscious of the bold scenery in their neighbourhood, and totally insensible to its charms. They had no notion, not they, of admiring barren crags and precipices, where even the Lord would lose his way, as a coarse lubber, decorated with stars and orders, very ingeniously observed to me; nor could they form the least conception of any pleasure there was in climbing, like a goat, amongst the cliffs, and then diving into woods and recesses, where the sun had never penetrated; where there were neither card tables frequented, nor side-boards garnished; no *jambon de Mayence* in waiting; no supply of pipes, nor any of the commonest delights, to be met with in the commonest taverns.

To all this I acquiesced with most perfect submission; but, immediately, left the orator to entertain a circle of antiquated dames,

---

19. The Peries, inhabitants of Ginnistan, live upon perfumes, &c. &c. See Richardson's *Dissertations [on Languages, Literature, and Manners of Eastern Nations]* [Beckford's note.]

and weather-beaten officers, who were gathering around him. Scarcely had I turned my back upon this polite assembly, when *Monsieur l'Administrateur des bains,* a fine pompous fellow, who had been *maitre d'hotel* in a great German family, came forwards, purposely to acquaint me, I suppose, that their baths had the honour of possessing Prince Orloff,[20] *"avec sa grande Maitresse; son Chamberlain; et quelques Dames d'Honneur:"* moreover, that his Highness came hither to refresh himself, after his laborious employments at the court of Petersburg, and expected (*grace aux eaux!*) to return to the domains his august sovereign had lately bestowed upon him, in perfect health; and to become the father of his people. Wishing Monsieur d'Orloff all possible success, I should have left the company at a great distance, had not a violent shower stopped my career, and obliged me to return to my apartment. The rain, growing heavier, intercepted the prospect of the mountains, and spread such a gloom over the vale, as sunk my spirits fifty degrees; to which, a close foggy atmosphere not a little contributed. Towards night, the clouds assumed a darker and more formidable aspect. Thunder rolled awfully along the distant cliffs, and several rapid torrents began to run down the steeps. Unable to stay within, I walked into an open portico, listening to the murmur of the river, mingled with the roar of the falling waters. At intervals a blue flash of lightning discovered their agitated surface, and two or three scared women, rushing through the storm and calling all the saints in paradise to their assistance. Things were in this state, when the orator, who had harangued so brilliantly on the nothingness of ascending mountains, took shelter under the porch; and, entering immediately into conversation, regaled my ears with a woeful narration of murders which had happened the other day, on the precise road I was to follow next morning: "Sir," said he, "your route is to be sure very perilous; on the left, you have a chasm, down which, should your horses take the smallest alarm, you are infallibly precipitated: to the right, hangs an impervious wood, and there, Sir, I can assure you, are wolves enough to devour a regiment: a little farther on, you cross a desolate tract of forest-land: the roads so deep and broken, that, if you go ten paces in as many minutes, you may think yourself fortunate. There lurk the most

---

20. Grigori Grigorievich Orloff (1734–1783), Russian nobleman who gained prominence in St. Petersburg as the lover of Catherine II. With the aid of his brother Aleksei, he organized the *coup d'état* of 1762, which dethroned Catherine's husband Peter III.

savage banditti in Europe, lately irritated by the Prince of Orange's proscription; and so desperate, that if they once attack, you can expect no mercy. Should you venture through this hazardous district to-morrow, you will, in all probability, meet a company of people, who have just left the town to search for the mangled bodies of their relations; but, for Heaven's sake! Sir, if you value your life, don't suffer an idle curiosity to lead you over such dangerous regions, however picturesque their appearance." I own, I felt rather intimidated by so formidable a prospect, and was very near abandoning my plan of crossing the mountains, and so go back again and round about, the Lord knows where; but, considering this step would be quite unheroical, I resolved to attribute my fears to the gloom of the moment, and the dejection it occasioned. It was almost nine o'clock, before my kind adviser ceased inspiring me with terrors: then, finding myself at liberty, I retired to bed, not under the most agreeable impressions; and, after tossing and tumbling in the agitation of tumultuous slumbers, I started up at seven in the morning of July 15th, ordered the horses, and set forward, without further dilemmas. Though it had thundered almost the whole night, the air was still clogged with vapours, the mountains bathed in humid clouds, and the scene I had so warmly admired, no longer discernible. Proceeding along the edge of the precipices I had been forewarned of, for about an hour, and escaping that peril at least, we traversed the slopes of a rude, heathy hill, in instantaneous expectation of foes and murderers. A misty rain prevented our seeing above ten yards before us, and every uncouth oak, or rocky fragment, we approached, seemed lurking spies, or gigantic enemies. One time, the murmur of the winds amongst invisible woods of beech, sounded like the wail of distress; and, at another, the noise of a torrent we could not discover, counterfeited the report of musquetry. In this suspicious manner we journeyed through the forest, which had so recently been the scene of assaults and depredations. At length, after winding several restless hours amongst its dreary avenues, we emerged into open day-light. The sky cleared, a cultivated vale lay before us, and the evening sun, gleaming bright through the vapours, cast a chearful look upon some corn-fields, and seemed to promise better times. A few minutes more brought us safe to the village of Viesbaden, where we slept in peace and tranquillity.

July 16th. Our apprehensions entirely dispersed, we rose light and refreshed from our slumbers, and, passing through Mayence,

Oppenheim, and Worms, travelled gaily over the plain in which Manheim is situated. The sun set before we arrived there, and it was by the mild gleams of the rising moon, that I first beheld the vast electoral palace, and those long straight streets and neat white houses, which distinguish this elegant capital from almost every other.

Numbers of well-dressed people were amusing themselves with music and fire-works, in the squares and open spaces: other groups appeared conversing in circles before their doors, and enjoying the serenity of the evening. Almost every window bloomed with carnations; and we could hardly cross a street, without hearing the German flute. A scene of such happiness and retirement, contrasted, in the most agreeable manner, with the dismal prospects we had left behind. No storms, no frightful chasms, were here to alarm us; no ruffians, or lawless plunderers; all around was peace, security, and contentment, in their most engaging attire.

July 17th. Though all impatience to reach that delightful classic region which already possesses, as I have often said, the better half of my spirit, I could not think of leaving Manheim unexplored; and therefore resolved to give up this day to the halls and galleries of the electoral palace. Those, which contain the cabinet of paintings, and sculptures in ivory, form a regular suite of nine immense apartments, about three hundred and seventy-two feet in length, well-proportioned, and uniformly floored with inlaid wood. Each room has ample folding doors, richly gilt and varnished. When seen in perspective, these entrances have the most magnificent effect imaginable. Nothing can give nobler ideas of space than such an enfilade of saloons unincumbered by heavy furniture, where the eyes range without interruption: I wandered alone, from one to the other, and was never wearied with contemplating the variety of pictures which enliven the scene, and convey the highest idea of their collector's taste. When my curiosity was a little satisfied, I left this amusing series of apartments with regret, visited the library, which the prefect Elector Palatine has formed, upon the same great scale that characterizes his other collections; and, after viewing the rest of the palace, saw the opera-house, which may boast of having contained one of the first bands in Europe: from thence I returned home in a very musical humour. An excellent harpsichord seconded this disposition, which lasted me till late in the evening; when, growing drowsy, I yielded to the influence of sleep, and was in an instant transported to a far more delightful palace than that of the elector; where I expatiated in perfumed apartments with yellow light, and conversed with none but Albano and Claude Lorrain, till the beams of the morning sun entered my chamber, and forced my visiting companions to fly, murmuring to the shades. I cannot say but I was sorry to leave Manheim, though my acquaintance with it was entirely confined to inanimate objects. The chearful air and free range of the galleries would be sufficient, for several days, for my amusement; as you know I could people them with phantoms. Not many leagues out of town, lie the famous gardens of Schweidsing. The weather being extremely warm, we were glad to avail ourselves of their shades. There are a great many fountains inclosed by thickets of shrubs and cool alleys, which lead to arbours of trellis-work, festooned with nasturtiums and convolvuluses. Several catalpas and sumachs in full flower, gave considerable richness to the scenery; and whilst we walked amongst them, a fresh breeze gently waved their summits. The tall poplars and acacias, quivering with the air, cast innumerable shadows on the intervening plats of greensward, and, as they moved their branches, discovered other walks beyond, and distant jets of water rising above their foliage, and spangling in the sun. After passing a multitude of shady avenues, terminated by temples, or groups of statues, we followed our guide, through a kind of arched bower, to a little opening in the wood, neatly paved with different-coloured pebbles. On one side, appeared niches and alcoves, ornamented with spars and polished marbles; on the other, an aviary; in front, a superb pavilion, with baths, porticos, and cabinets, fitted up in the most elegant and luxurious style. The song of exotic birds; the freshness of the surrounding verdure heightened by falling streams; and that dubious poetic light admitted through thick foliage, so agreeable after the glare of a sultry day, detained me for some time in an alcove, reading Spenser, and imagining myself but a few paces removed from the Idle Lake. I would fain have loitered an hour more, in this enchanted bower, had not the gardener, whose patience was quite exhausted, and who had never heard of the red-cross knight and his achievements, dragged me away to a sun burnt, contemptible hillock, commanding the view of a serpentine ditch, and decorated with the title of *Jardin Anglois*. Some object like decayed lime-kilns and mouldering ovens, is disposed, in an amphitheatrical form, on the declivity of this tremendous eminence: and there is to be ivy, and a cascade, and what not, as my conductor observed. A glance was all I bestowed on this caricature upon English gardens; I then went off

in a huff, at being chased from my bower, and grumbled all the
road to Entsweigen; where, to our misfortune, we lay, amidst hogs
and vermin, who amply revenged my quarrels with their country.

July 20. After travelling a post or two, we came in sight of a
green moor, with many insulated woods and villages; the Danube
sweeping majestically along, and the city of Ulm rising upon its
banks. The fields in its neighbourhood were overspread with
cloths, bleaching in the sun, and waiting for barks, which convey
them down the great river, in ten days, to Vienna, and from
thence, through Hungary, into the midst of the Turkish empire.
I almost envied the merchants their voyage, and, descending to
the edge of the stream, preferred my orisons to Father Danube,
beseeching him to remember me to the regions through which he
flows. I promised him an altar and solemn rites, should he grant
my request, and was very idolatrous, till the shadows lengthening
over the unlimited plains on his margin, reminded me, that the
sun would be shortly sunk, and that I had still above fifteen miles
to go. Gathering a purple iris that grew from the bank, I wore
it to his honour; and have reason to fancy my piety was rewarded,
as not a fly, or an insect, dared to buzz about me the whole evening.
You never saw a brighter sky, nor more glowing clouds than
gilded our horizon. The air was impregnated with the perfume
of clover, and, for ten miles, we beheld no other objects than
smooth levels, enamelled with flowers, and interspersed with
thickets of oaks, beyond which appeared a long series of mountains, that distance and the evening tinged with an interesting
azure. Such were the very spots for youthful games and exercises,
open spaces for tilts, and spreading shades to screen the spectators.
Father Lafiteau tells us,[21] there are many such vast and flowery
meads in the interior of America, to which the roving tribes of
Indians repair once or twice in a century, to settle the rights of the
chase, and lead their solemn dances: and so deep an impression do
these assemblies leave on the minds of the savages, that the highest
ideas they entertain of future felicity, consist in the perpetual enjoyment of songs and dances upon the green, boundless lawns of
their elysium. In the midst of these visionary plains rises the
adobe of Aneantsic, encircled by choirs of departed chieftans,
leaping in cadence to the mournful sound of spears, as they ring
on the shell of the tortoise. Their favourite attendants, long separated from them whilst on earth, are restored again in this

---

21. Joseph François, Lafitau (1681–1746), author of *Moeurs des sauvages amer-
iquains, comparées aux moeurs des premiers temps* (1724).

etherial region, and skim freely over the vast level space; now, hailing one group of beloved friends; and, now, another. Mortals, newly ushered by death into this world of pure blue sky and boundless meads, see the long-lost objects of their affection, advancing across the lawn to meet them. Flights of familiar birds, the purveyors of many an earthly chace, once more attend their progress; whilst the shades of their faithful dogs seem coursing each other below. Low murmurs, and tinkling sounds, fill the whole region, and, as its new denizens proceed, encrease in melody, till, unable to resist the thrilling music, they spring forward in extacies to join the eternal round. A share of this celestial transport seemed communicated to me, whilst my eyes wandered over the plain, which appeared to widen and extend, in proportion as the twilight prevailed. The dusky hour, favourable to conjurations, allowed me to believe the spirits of departed friends not far removed from the clouds, which, to all appearance, reposed at the extremity of the prospect, and tinted the surface of the horizon with ruddy colours. This glow still lingered upon the verge of the landscape, after the sun disappeared; and 'twas in those peaceful moments, when no sound but the browsing of cattle reached me, that I imagined benign looks were cast upon me from the golden vapours, and I seemed to catch glimpses of faint forms moving amongst them, which were once so dear; and even thought my ears affected by well-known voices, long silent upon earth. When the warm hues of the sky were gradually fading, and the distant thickets began to assume a deeper and more melancholy blue, I fancied a shape, like Thisbe,[22] shot swiftly along; and, sometimes halting afar off, cast an affectionate look upon her old master, that seemed to say, When you draw near the last inevitable hour, and the pale countries of Aneantsic are stretched out before you, I will precede your footsteps, and guide them safe through the wild labyrinths which separate this world from yours. I was so possessed with the ideas, and so full of the remembrance of that poor, affectionate creature, whose miserable end you were the witness of, that I did not, for several minutes, perceive our arrival at Guntsberg. Hurrying to bed, I seemed in my slumbers to pass that interdicted boundary which divides our earth from the region of Indian happiness. Thisbe ran nimbly before me; her white form glimmered amongst dusky forests; she led me into an infinitely spacious plain, where I heard vast multitudes discoursing upon events to come. What further passed must never be revealed. I awoke in

---

22. Thisbe, a favourite greyhound, torn to pieces by a mad dog. [Beckford's note.]

tears, and could hardly find spirits enough to look around me, till we were driving through the midst of Augsburg.

July 21st. We dined, and rambled about this renowned city in the cool of the evening. The colossal paintings on the walls of almost every considerable building, gave it a strange air, which pleases upon the score of novelty. Having passed a number of streets decorated in this exotic manner, we found ourselves suddenly before the public hall, by a noble statue of Augustus, under whose auspices the colony was formed. Which way soever we turned, our eyes met some remarkable edifice, or marble bason, into which several groups of sculptured river gods pour a profusion of waters. These stately fountains and bronze statues, the extraordinary size and loftiness of the buildings, the towers rising in perspective, and the Doric portal of the town-house, answered in some measure the idea Montfaucon[23] gives us of the scene of an antient tragedy. Whenever a pompous Flemish painter attempts a representation of Troy, and displays in his back-ground those streets of palaces described in the Iliad, Augsburg, or some such city, may easily be traced. Sometimes a corner of Antwerp discovers itself; and, generally, above a Corinthian portico, rises a gothic spire. Just such a jumble may be viewed from the statue of Augustus, under which I remained till the Concierge came, who was to open the gates of the town-house, and shew me its magnificent hall. I wished for you exceedingly when, ascending a flight of a hundred steps, I entered it through a portal, supported by tall pillars and crowned with a majestic pediment. Upon advancing, I discovered five more entrances equally grand, with golden figures of guardian genii leaning over the entablature; and saw, through a range of windows, each above thirty feet high, and nearly level with the marble pavement, the whole city, with all its roofs and spires, beneath my feet. The pillars, cornices, and pannels of this striking apartment, are uniformly tinged with brown and gold; and the ceiling, enriched with emblematical paintings and innumerable canopies of carved work, casts a very magisterial shade. Upon the whole, I should not be surprised at a Burgomaster assuming a formidable dignity in such a room. I must confess it had a similar effect upon me, and I descended the flight of steps with as much pomposity, as if a triumphal car waited at their feet; or, as if on the point of giving audience to the Queen of Sheba. It

23. Bernard de Montfaucon (1655–1741), author of *Palaeographia Graeca* (1708) and *L'Antiquité expliquée et représentée en figures* (1719–24).

happened to be a saint's day, and half the inhabitants of Augsburg were gathered together in the opening before their hall; the greatest numbers, especially the women, still exhibiting the very identical dresses which Hollar engraved.[24] My lofty gait imposed upon this primitive assembly, which receded to give me passage, with as much silent respect, as if I had really been the wise sovereign of Israel. When I got home, an execrable supper was served up to my majesty: I scolded in an unroyal style, and soon convinced myself I was no longer Solomon.

July 22d. Joy to the Electors of Bavaria! for planting such extensive woods of fir in their dominions, as shade over the chief part of the road from Augsburg to Munich. Near the last-mentioned city, I cannot boast of the scenery changing to advantage. Instead of flourishing woods and verdure, we beheld a parched, dreary flat, diversified by fields of withering barley, and stunted avenues drawn formally across them; now and then a stagnant pool, and sometimes a dunghill, by way of regale. However, the wild rocks of the Tirol terminate the view, and to them imagination may fly, and walk amidst springs and lilies of her own creation. I speak from authority, having had the pleasure of anticipating an evening in this romantic style. Tuesday next is the grand fair, with horse-races and junkettings; a piece of news I was but too soon acquainted with; for the moment we entered the town, good-natured creatures from all quarters advised us to get out of it; since traders and harlequins had filled every corner of the place, and there was not a lodging to be procured. The inns, to be sure, were like hives of industrious animals, sorting their merchandise, and preparing their goods for sale. Yet, in spite of difficulties, we got possession of a quiet apartment.

July 23d. We were driven in the evening to Nymphenburg, the Elector's country palace, whose bosquets, jet d'eaux, and parterres, are the pride of the Bavarians. The principal platform is all of a glitter with gilded Cupids, and shining serpents, spouting at every pore. Beds of poppies, holyoaks, scarlet lychnis, and the most flaming flowers, border the edge of the walks, which extend till the perspective meets, and swarm with ladies and gentlemen in party-coloured raiment. The Queen of Golconda's gardens in a French opera, are scarcely more gaudy and artificial. Unluckily too, the evening was fine, and the sun so powerful, that we were half roasted before we could cross the great avenues and enter the

---

24. Wenceslaus Hollar (1607–1677), Bohemian artist and engraver.

thickets, which barely conceal a very splendid hermitage, where
we joined Mr. and Mrs. T,[25] and a party of fashionable Bavarians.
Amongst the ladies was Madame la Contesse, I forget who, a production of the venerable Haslang, with her daughter, Madame
de ———,[26] who has the honour of leading the Elector in her chains.
These goddesses, stepping into a car, vulgarly called a cariole, the
mortals followed, and explored alley after alley, and pavilion
after pavilion. Then, having viewed Pagotenburg, which is, as
they told me, all Chinese; and Marienburg, which is most as-
suredly all tinsel; we paraded by a variety of fountains in full
squirt, and though they certainly did their best (for many were
set agoing on purpose) I cannot say I greatly admired them. The
ladies were very gaily attired, and the gentlemen, as smart as
swords, bags, and pretty cloaks could make them, looked exactly
like the fine people one sees represented in a coloured print. Thus
we kept walking genteely about the orangery, till the carriages
drew up and conveyed us to Mr. T's. Immediately after supper,
we drove once more out of town, to a garden and tea-room, where
all degrees and ages dance jovially together till morning. Whilst
one party wheel briskly away in the valz, another amuse themselves
in a corner, with cold meat and rhenish. That dispatched, out they
whisk amongst the dancers, with an impetuosity and liveliness I
little expected to have found in Bavaria. After turning round and
round, with a rapidity that is quite inconceivable to an English
dancer, the music changes to a slower movement, and then follows
a succession of zigzag minuets, performed by old and young,
straight and crooked, noble and plebeian, all at once, from one
end of the room to the other. Tallow candles snuffing and stinking,
dishes changing, heads scratching, and all sorts of performances
going forwards at the same moment; the flutes, oboes, and bassoons
snorting and grunting with peculiar emphasis; now fast, now slow,
just as variety commands, who seems to rule the ceremonial of
this motley assembly, where every distinction of rank and privilege
is totally forgotten. Once a week, on sundays that is to say, the
rooms are open, and monday is generally somewhat advanced before they are deserted. If good-humour and coarse merriment are
all that people desire, here they are to be found in perfection;
though at the expense of toes and noses. Both these extremities of

25. John Trevor (1749–1824) and Harriot Burton Trevor (1751–1829). Trevor
was minister-plenipotentiary at Munich.
26. I.e. Madame de Baumgarten.

my person suffered most cruelly; and I was not sorry to retire, about one in the morning, to a purer atmosphere.

July 24th. Custom condemned us to visit the palace; which glares with looking-glass, gilding, and cut velvet. The chapel, though small, is richer than any thing Crœsus ever possessed, let them say what they will. Not a corner but shines with gold, diamonds, and scraps of martyrdom studded with jewels. I had the delight of treading amethysts and the richest gems under foot; which, if you recollect, Apuleius thinks such supreme felicity.[27] Alas! I was quite unworthy of the honour, and had much rather have trodden the turf of the mountains. Mammon would have never taken his eyes off the pavement: mine soon left the contemplation of it, and fixed on St. Peter's thumb, enshrined with a degree of elegance, and adorned by some malapert enthusiast, with several of the most delicate antique cameos I ever beheld: the subjects, Ledas and sleeping Venuses, are a little too pagan, one should think, for an apostle's finger. From this precious repository, we were conducted through the public garden, to a large hall, where part of the Sleitzom collection is piled up, till a gallery can be finished for its reception. 'Twas matter of great favour to view, in this state, the pieces that compose it, a very imperfect one too, since some of the best were under operation. But I would not upon any account have missed the sight of Reubens's massacre of the innocents. Such expressive horrors were never yet transferred to canvas, and Moloch himself might have gazed at them with pleasure. After dinner we were led round the churches, and if you are as much tired with reading my voluminous descriptions, as I was with the continual repetition of altars and reliquaries, the Lord have mercy upon you! However, your delivery draws near. The post is going out, and to-morrow we shall begin to mount the cliffs of the Tirol; but, don't be afraid of any long-winded epistles from their summits: I shall be too much fatigued in ascending them. Just now, as I have lain by a long while, I grow sleek, and scribble on in mere wantonness of spirit. What excesses such a correspondent is capable of, you will soon be able to judge.

---

27. Lucius Apuleius, Latin novelist and mystic of the second century A. D. Beckford is alluding to some early lines in Bk. V of Apuleius' *Metamorphoses* (*The Golden Ass*) : "The pavement was all of precious stone, divided and cut one from another, whereon was carved divers kinds of pictures, in such sort that blessed and thrice blessed were they which might go upon such a pavement of gems and ornaments,"

July 25th. The noise of the people, thronging to the fair, did not allow me to slumber very long in the morning. When I got up, every street was crouded with Jews and mountebanks, holding forth, and driving their bargains, in all the energetic vehemence of the German tongue. Vast quantities of rich merchandize glittered in the shops, as we passed along to the gates. Heaps of fruits and sweetmeats set half the grandams and infants in the place a cackling with felicity. Mighty glad was I to make my escape; and, in about an hour or two, we entered a wild tract of country, not unlike the skirts of a princely park. A little further on, stands a cluster of cottages, where we stopped to give our horses some bread, and were pestered with swarms of flies, most probably journeying to Munich fair, there to feast upon sugared tarts and bottlenoses. The next post brought us over hill and dale, grove and meadow, to a narrow plain, watered by rivulets and surrounded by cliffs, under which lies scattered the village of Wolfrathshausen, consisting of several cottages, built entirely of fir, with strange galleries hanging over the way. Nothing can be neater than the carpentry of these simple edifices, nor more solid than their construction: many of them looked as if they had braved the torrents, which fell from the mountains a century ago; and, if one may judge from the hoary appearance of the inhabitants, here are patriarchs who remember the Emperor, Lewis of Bavaria. Orchards of cherry-trees impend from the steeps above the village, which, to our certain knowledge, produce no contemptible fruit; for I can hardly think they eat better in the environs of Damascus. Having refreshed ourselves with their cooling juice, we struck into a grove of pines, the tallest and most flourishing, perhaps, we ever beheld. There seemed no end to these forests, save where little irregular spots of herbage, fed by cattle, intervened. Whenever we gained an eminence, it was only to discover more ranges of dark wood, variegated with meadows and glittering streams. White clover, and a profusion of sweet-scented flowers, cloath their banks: above, waves the mountain-ash, glowing with scarlet berries; and beyond, rise hills, and rocks, and mountains, piled upon one another, and fringed with fir to their topmost acclivities. Perhaps, the Norwegian forests alone, equal these, in grandeur and extent. Those which cover the Swiss highlands, rarely convey such vast ideas. There, the woods climb only half way up their ascents, and then are circumscribed by snows: here, no boundaries are set to their progress, and the mountains, from their bases to their summits, display rich, unbroken masses of vegetation. As we were surveying this prospect, a thick cloud, fraught with thunder, obscured the transparence of the horizon; whilst angry flashes startled our horses, whose snorts and stampings echoed through the woods. What from the shade of the firs and the impending tempests, we travelled several miles almost in total darkness. One moment, the clouds began to fleet, and a faint gleam promised serener hours; but the next, all was gloom and terror; presently, a deluge of rain poured down upon the valley, and, in a short time, the torrents beginning to swell, raged with such fury, as to be with difficulty forded. How we got over, the peasants best know; for, without their assistance, I think our heavy carriage must needs have been stranded. Twilight drew on, just as we had passed the most terrible; then ascending a steep hill, under a mountain, whose pines and birches rustled with the storm, we saw a little lake below. A deep azure haze veiled its eastern shore, and lowering vapours concealed the cliffs to the south; but over its western extremities a few transparent clouds, the remains of a struggling sun-set, were suspended, which streamed on the surface of the waters, and tinged with tender pink, the brow of a verdant promontory. I could not help fixing myself on the banks of the lake for several minutes, till this apparition was lost, and confounded with the shades of night. Looking round, I shuddered at a craggy mountain, cloathed in dark forests, and almost perpendicular, that was absolutely to be surmounted, before we could arrive at Wallersee. No house, not even a shed appearing, we were forced to ascend the peak, and penetrate these awful groves. Great praise is due to the directors of the roads across them; which, considering their situation, are wonderfully fine. Mounds of stones support the passage in some places; and, in others, it is hewn with incredible labour through the solid rock. Beeches and pines of an hundred feet high, darken the way with their gigantic branches, casting a chill around, and diffusing a woody odour. As we advanced, in the thick shade, amidst the spray of torrents, and heard their loud roar in the chasm beneath, I could scarcely help thinking myself transported to the Grand Chartreuse; and began to conceive hopes of once more beholding St. Bruno.[28] But, though that venerable father did not vouchsafe an apparition, or call to me again from the depths of the dells, he protected his votary from nightly perils, and brought us to the banks of Wallersee lake. We saw lights gleam upon its shores, which directed us to a cottage, where we reposed after our toils,

---

28. See the description of the Grand Chartreuse [Beckford's note.]

and were soon lulled to sleep by the fall of distant waters.

July 26th. The sun rose many hours before me; and, when I got up, was spangling the surface of the lake, which expands between steeps of wood, crowned by lofty crags and pinnacles. We had an opportunity of contemplating this bold assemblage as we travelled on the banks of the Meer, where it forms a bay sheltered by impending forests; the water, tinged by their reflection with a deep cerulean, calm and tranquil. Mountains of pine and beech, rising above, close every outlet; and, no village or spire peeping out of the foliage, impress an idea of more than European solitude. I could contentedly have passed a summer's moon in these retirements; hollowed myself a canoe; and fished for sustenance. From the shore of Wallersee, our road led us straight through arching groves, which the axe seems never to have violated, to the summit of a rock, covered with spurge-laurel, and worn, by the course of torrents, into innumerable craggy forms. Beneath, lay extended a chaos of shattered cliffs, with tall pines springing from their crevices, and rapid streams hurrying between their intermingled trunks and branches. As yet, no hut appeared, no mill, no bridge, no trace of human existence.

After a few hours journey through the wilderness, we began to discover a wreath of smoke; and, presently, the cottage from whence it arose, composed of planks, and reared on the very brink of a precipice. Piles of cloven spruce-fir were dispersed before the entrance, on a little spot of verdure browsed by goats: near them sat an aged man with hoary whiskers, his white locks tucked under a fur-cap. Two or three beautiful children, their hair neatly braided, played around him, and a young woman, dressed in a short robe and polish-looking bonnet, peeped out of a wicket-window. I was so much struck with the exotic appearance of this sequestered family, that, crossing a rivulet, I clambered up to their cottage, and begged some refreshment. Immediately there was a contention amongst the children, who should be the first to oblige me. A little black-eyed girl succeeded, and brought me an earthen jug full of milk, with crumbled bread, and a platter of strawberries, fresh picked from the bank. I reclined in the midst of my smiling hosts, and spread my repast on the turf: never could I be waited upon with more hospitable grace. The only thing I wanted, was language to express my gratitude; and it was this deficiency which made me quit them so soon. The old man seemed visibly concerned at my departure; and his children followed me a long way down the rocks, talking in a dialect which

passes all understanding, and waving their hands to bid me adieu.
I had hardly lost sight of them, and regained the carriage, before
we entered a forest of pines, to all appearance without bounds,
of every age and figure; some, feathered to the ground with flourishing branches; others, decayed into shapes like Lapland idols.
I can imagine few situations more dreadful than to be lost at
night amidst this confusion of trunks, hollow winds whistling
amongst the branches, and strewing their cones below. Even at
noon-day, I thought we should never have found our way out.
At last, having descended a long avenue, endless perspectives
opening on either side, we emerged into a valley bounded by
swelling hills, divided into agreeable shady inclosures, where
many herds were grazing. A rivulet flows along the pastures beneath; and, after winding through the village of Boidou, loses
itself in a narrow pass, amongst the cliffs and precipices which
rise above the cultivated slopes, and frame in this happy, pastoral
region. All the plain was in sun-shine, the sky blue, and the
heights illuminated, except one rugged peak with spires of rock,
shaped not unlike the views I have seen of Sinai, and wrapped,
like that sacred mount, in clouds and darkness. At the base of
this tremendous mass, lies a neat hamlet, called Mittenvald, surrounded by thickets and banks of verdure, and watered by frequent springs, whose sight and murmurs were so reviving in the
midst of a sultry day, that we could not think of leaving their
vicinity, but remained at Mittenvald, the whole evening. Our
inn had long, airy galleries, and a pleasant balcony fronting the
mountain. In one of these we dined upon trout, fresh from the
rills, and cherries, just culled from the orchards that cover the
slopes above. The clouds were dispersing, and the topmost peak
half visible, before we ended our repast. Every moment discovered some inaccessible cliff or summit, shining through the mists,
and tinted by the sun with pale golden colours. These appearances filled me with such delight, and with such a train of romantic associations, that I left the table, and ran to an open field
beyond the huts and gardens, to gaze in solitude, and catch the
vision before it dissolved away. You, if any human being is able,
may conceive true ideas of these glowing vapours, sailing over
the pointed rocks, and brightening them in their passage with
amber light. When all were faded and lost in the blue æther, I
had time to look around me and notice the mead in which I was
standing. Here, clover covered its surface; there, crops of grain;
further on, beds of herbs and the sweetest flowers. An amphi-

theatre of hills and rocks, broken into a variety of dales and precipices, guards the plain from intrusion, and opens a course for several clear rivulets, which, after gurgling amidst loose stones and fragments, fall down the steeps, and are concealed and quieted in the herbage of the vale. A cottage or two, peep out of the woods, that hang over the waterfalls; and on the brow of the hills above, appears a series of eleven little chapels, uniformly built. I followed the narrow path that leads to them, on the edge of the eminences, and met a troop of beautiful peasants, all of the name of Anna (for it was her saintship's day) going to pay their devotion, severally, at these neat white fanes. There were faces that Guercino[29] would not have disdained copying, with braids of hair, the softest and most luxuriant I ever beheld. Some had wreathed it simply with flowers; others with rolls of a thin linen (manufactured in the neighbourhood) ; and disposed it with a degree of elegance, one should not have expected on the cliffs of the Tirol. Being arrived, they knelt all together at the first chapel, on the steps, a minute or two; whispered a short prayer; and then dispersed each to her fane. Every little building had now its fair worshipper, and you may well conceive how much such figures, scattered about the landscape, increased its charms. Notwithstanding the fervour of their adorations (for at intervals they sighed, and beat their white bosoms with energy) several bewitching, profane glances were cast at me as I passed by. Don't be surprised then, if I became a convert to idolatry in so amiable a form, and worshipped Saint Anna on the score of her namesakes. When got beyond the last chapel, I began to hear the roar of a cascade, in a thick grove of beech and chesnuts, that cloaths the steeps of a wide fissure in the rock. My ear soon guided me to its entrance, which was marked by a shed encompassed with mossy fragments, and almost concealed by bushes of the caperplant in full red bloom. Amongst these I struggled, till reaching a goats-track, it conducted me, on the brink of the foaming waters, to the very depths of the cliff, whence issues a stream which dashes impetuously down, strikes against a ledge of grey rock, and sprinkles the impending thicket with dew. Big drops hung on every spray, and glittered on the leaves, partially gilt by the rays of the declining sun, whose mellow hues softened the summits of the cliffs, and diffused a repose, a divine calm over this deep retirement, which inclined me to imagine it the extremity of the earth, and the portal of some other region of

29. Name given to Giovanni Francesco Barbieri (1591–1666) , Italian religious painter.

existence; some happy world, behind the dark groves of pines, the caves and awful mountains, where the river takes its source. I hung eagerly on the gulph, impressed with this idea, and fancied myself listening to a voice that bubbled up with the waters; then looked into the abyss, and strained my eyes to penetrate its gloom: but all was dark, and unfathomable as futurity. Awaking from my reverie, I felt the damps of the water chill my forehead, and ran shivering out of the vale, to avoid them. A warmer atmosphere, that reigned in the meads I had wandered across before, tempted me to remain a good while longer, collecting the wild pinks with which they are strewed in profusion, and a species of thyme, scented like myrrh. Whilst I was thus employed, a confused murmur struck my ear, and, on turning towards a cliff, backed by the woods from whence the sound seemed to proceed, forth issued a herd of goats, hundreds after hundreds, skipping down the steeps: then followed two shepherd boys, gamboling together as they drove their creatures along: soon after, the dog made his appearance hunting a stray heifer, which brought up the rear. I followed them with my eyes, till lost in the windings of a valley, and heard the tinklings of their bells die gradually away. Now, the last blush of crimson left the summit of Sinai, inferior mountains being long since cast in deep blue shades. The village was already hushed when I regained it, and in a few moments I followed its example.

July 27th. We pursued our journey to Inspruck, through some of the wildest scenes of wood and mountain that were ever traversed; the rocks now beginning to assume a loftier and more majestic appearance, and to glisten with snows. I had proposed passing a day or two at Inspruck; visiting the castle of Ambras, and examining Count Eysenberg's cabinet, enriched with the rarest productions of the mineral kingdom, and a complete collection of the moths and flies peculiar to the Tirol; but, upon my arrival, the azure of the skies, and the brightness of the sunshine inspired me with an irresistible wish of hastening to Italy. I was now too near the object of my journey, to delay possession, any longer than absolutely necessary; so, casting a transient look on Maximilian's tomb, and the bronze statues of Tirolese Counts and Worthies, solemnly ranged in the church of the Franciscans, set immediately off. We crossed a broad, noble street, terminated by a triumphal arch, and were driven along the road, to the foot of a mountain waving with fields of corn, and variegated with wood and vineyards, incircling lawns of the finest verdure, scattered over with white houses, glistening in the sun. Upon ascending the mount, and beholding a vast range of prospects of a similar character, I almost repented my impatience, and looked down with regret upon the cupolas and steeples, we were leaving behind. But the rapid succession of lovely and romantic scenes, soon effaced the former from my memory. Our road, the smoothest in the world (though hewn in the bosom of rocks) by its sudden turns and windings, gave us, every instant, opportunities of discovering new villages, and forests rising beyond forests; green spots in the midst of wood, high above on the mountains; and cottages, perched on the edge of promontories. Down, far below, in the chasm, amidst a confusion of pines and fragments of stone, rages the torrent Inn, which fills the country far and wide with a perpetual murmur. Sometimes we descended to its brink, and crossed over high bridges; sometimes, mounted half way up the cliffs, till its roar and agitation became, through distance, inconsiderable. After a long ascent, the shades of evening reposing in the vallies, and the upland snows still tinged with a vivid red, we reached Schönberg, a village well worthy of its appellation; and then, twilight drawing over us, began to descend. We could now but faintly discover the opposite mountains veined with silver rills, when we came once more to the banks of the Inn. This turbulent stream accompanied us all the way to Steinach, and broke, by its continual roar, the stillness of the night, which had finished half its course, before we were settled to repose.

July 28th. I rose early, to scent the fragrance of the vegetation, bathed in a shower which had lately fallen; and, looking around me, saw nothing but crags hanging over crags, and the rocky shores of the stream, still dark with the shade of the mountains. The small opening in which Steinach is situated, terminates in a gloomy streight, scarce leaving room for the road and the torrent, which does not understand being thwarted, and will force its way, let the pines grow ever so thick, or the rocks be ever so considerable. Notwithstanding the forbidding air of this narrow dell, industry has contrived to enliven its steeps with habitations; to raise water by means of a wheel; and to cover the surface of the rocks with soil. By this means, large crops of oats and flax are produced, and most of the huts have gardens adjoining, which are filled with poppies, seeming to thrive in this parched situation:

Urit enim lini campum seges, urit avenæ,
Urunt Lethæo perfusa papavera somno.[30]

---

30. Virgil, *Georgics*, bk. I, ll. 77–78. "Exhausted are the fields that produce oats and flax or poppies filled with Lethean sleep."

The further we advanced in the dell, the larger were the planta-
tions which discoverd themselves. For what purpose these gaudy
flowers meet with such encouragement, I had neither time, nor
language to enquire; the mountaineers stuttering a gibberish,
unintelligible, even to Germans. Probably, opium is extracted
from them; or, perhaps, if you love a conjecture, Morpheus has
transferred his abode from the Cimmerians, and has perceived a
cavern somewhere or other, in the recesses of these endless mountains. Poppies, you know, in poetic travels, always denote the
skirts of his soporific reign, and I don't remember a region better
calculated for undisturbed repose, than the narrow clefts and
gullies which run up amongst the rocks, lost in vapours, impervious to the sun, and beaten by rills and showers, whose continual
tricklings inspire a drowsiness not easily to be resisted. Add to
these circumstances, the waving of the pines, with the hum of
bees seeking their food in the crevices, and you will have as sleepy
a region as that, in which Spenser and Ariosto have placed the
nodding deity. At present, I must confess I should not dislike
submitting to his empire for a few months or years, just as it
might happen, whilst Europe is distracted by dæmons of revenge
and war; whilst they are strangling at Venice, and tearing each
other to pieces in our unhappy London; whilst Ætna and Vesuvius give signs of uncommon wrath; America welters in her blood;
and almost every quarter of the globe is filled with carnage and
devastation. This is the moment to humble ourselves before the
God of sleep; to beseech him to open his dusky portals, and admit
us into the repose of his retired kingdom. If you are inclined to
become a suppliant, hasten to the Tirol, and we will search together about the mountains, traverse the poppy-meads, and look
into every chasm and fissure that excludes day-light, in hopes of
discovering the mansion of repose. Then, when we have found
this corner (or I think our search will be successful) Morpheus
will give us an approving nod, and beckon us in silence to a
couch, where, soon lulled by the murmurs of the place, we shall
sink into oblivion and tranquillity. But we may as well keep our
eyes open for the present, till we have made this important discovery, and look at the beautiful country round Brixen, whither
I arrived in the cool of the evening, and breathed the freshness
of a garden, immediately beneath my window. The thrushes,
warbling amongst its shades, saluted me, the moment I awoke
next morning.

July 29th. We proceeded over fertile mountains to Bolsano.

Here, first, I noticed the rocks cut into terraces, thick set with melons, and Indian corn; gardens of fig-trees and pomegranates hanging over walls, clustered with fruit; amidst them, a little pleasant cot, shaded by cypresses. In the evening, we perceived several further indications of approaching Italy; and, after sunset, the Adige, rolling its full tide between precipices, which looked awful in the dusk. Myriads of fire-flies sparkled amongst the shrubs on the bank. I traced the course of these exotic insects by their blue light, now rising to the summits of the trees, now sinking to the ground, and associating with vulgar glow-worms. We had opportunities enough to remark their progress, since we travelled all night; such being my impatience to reach the promised land! Morning dawned, just as we saw Trent dimly before us. I slept a few hours, then set out again, (July 30th) after the heats were in some degree abated; and, leaving Bergine, (where the peasants were feasting before their doors in their holiday dresses, with red pinks stuck in their ears in lieu of rings, and their necks surrounded with coral of the same colour) we came, through a woody valley, to the banks of a lake, filled with the purest and most transparent water, which loses itself in shady creeks, amongst hills, robed with verdure, from their base to their summits. The shores present one continual shrubbery, interspersed with knots of larches and slender almonds, starting from the underwood. A cornice of rock runs round the whole, except where the trees descend to the very brink, and dip their boughs in the water. It was five o'clock when I caught the sight of this unsuspected lake, and the evening shadows stretched nearly across it. Gaining a very rapid ascent, we looked down upon its placid bosom, and saw several airy peaks rising above the tufted foliage of the groves around. I quitted the contemplation of them with regret; and, in a few hours, arrived at Borgo di Valsugano, the scenes of the lake still present before the eye of my fancy.

July 31st. My heart beat quick, when I saw some hills, not very distant, which, I was told, lay in the Venetian state; and I thought an age, at least, had elapsed before we were passing their base. The road was never formed to delight an impatient traveller; loose pebbles and rolling stones render it, in the highest degree, tedious and jolting. I should not have spared my execrations, had it not traversed a picturesque valley, overgrown with juniper, and strewed with fragments of rock, precipitated, long since, from the surrounding eminences, blooming with cyclamens. I clambered up several of these crags, fra gli odoriferi ginepri,[31]

to gather the flowers I have just mentioned, and found them deliciously scented. Fratillarias, and the most gorgeous flies, many of which I here noticed for the first time, were fluttering about, and expanding their wings to the sun. There is no describing the numbers I beheld, nor their gayly varied colouring. I could not find in my heart to destroy their felicity; to scatter such bright plumage, and snatch them for ever, from the realms of light and flowers. Had I been less compassionate, I should have gained credit with that respectable corps, the torturers of butterflies; and might, perhaps, have enriched their cabinets with some unknown captives. However, I left them imbibing the dews of heaven, in free possession of their native rights; and, having changed horses at Tremolano, entered, at length, my long-desired Italy. The pass is rocky and tremendous, guarded by a fortress (Covalo) in possession of the Empress Queen, and only fit, one should think, to be inhabited by her eagles. There is no attaining this exalted hold, but by the means of a cord let down many fathoms by the soldiers, who live in dens and caverns, which serve also as arsenals, and magazines for powder; whose mysteries I declined prying into, their approach being a little too aerial for my earthly frame. A black vapour, tinging their entrance, compleated the terror of the prospect, which I shall never forget. For two or three leagues, it continued much in the same style; cliffs, nearly perpendicular, on both sides, and the Brenta foaming and thundering below. Beyond, the rocks began to be mantled with vines and gardens. Here and there a cottage, shaded with mulberries, made its appearance; and we often discovered, on the banks of the river, ranges of white buildings, with courts and awnings, beneath which vast numbers were employed in manufacturing silk. As we advanced, the stream gradually widened, and the rocks receded; woods were more frequent, and cottages thicker strewn. About five in the evening, we had left the country of crags and precipices, of mists and cataracts, and were entering the fertile territory of the Bassanese. It was now I beheld groves of olives, and vines clustering the summits of the tallest elms; pomegranates in every garden, and vases of citron and orange before almost every door. The softness and transparency of the air, soon told me I was arrived in happier climates; and I felt

---

31. Ludovico Ariosto, *Orlando Furioso*, can. VII, st. 32. "amidst the sweet odor of juniper."

sensations of joy and novelty run through my veins, upon beholding this smiling land of groves and verdure stretched out before
me. A few glooming vapours, I can hardly call them clouds, rested
upon the extremities of the landscape; and, through their medium, the sun cast an oblique and dewy ray. Peasants were
returning homeward from the cultivated hillocks and corn-fields,
singing as they went, and calling to each other over the hills;
whilst the women were milking goats before the wickets of the
cottages, and preparing their country fare. I left them enjoying
it, and soon beheld the ancient ramparts and cypresses of Bassano;
whose classic appearance recalled the memory of former times,
and answered exactly the ideas I had pictured to myself of Italian
edifices. Though encompassed by walls and turrets, neither soldiers nor customhouse officers start out from their concealments,
to question and molest a weary traveller; for such are the blessings of the Venetian state, at least of the Terra Firma provinces,
that it does not contain, I believe, above four regiments. Istria,
Dalmatia, and the maritime frontiers, are more formidably
guarded, as they touch, you know, the whiskers of the Turkish
empire. Passing under a Doric gateway, we crossed the chief part
of this town in the way to our locanda, pleasantly situated, and
commanding a level green, where people walk and eat ices by
moonlight. On the right, the Franciscan church and convent, half
hid in the religious gloom of pines and cypress; to the left, a perspective of walls and towers rising from the turf, and marking it,
when I arrived, with long shadows; in front where the lawn terminates, meadow, wood, and garden run quite to the base of the
mountains. Twilight coming on, this beautiful spot swarmed
with people, sitting in circles upon the grass, refreshing themselves with cooling liquors, or lounging upon the bank beneath
the towers. They looked so free and happy, that I longed to be
acquainted with them; and, by the interposition of a polite Venetian (who, though a perfect stranger, shewed me the most engaging marks of attention) was introduced to a group of the
principal inhabitants. Our conversation ended in a promise to
meet the next evening at a country house about a league from
Bassano, and then to return together, and sing to the praise of
Pachierotti,[32] their idol, as well as mine. You can have no idea
what pleasure we mutually found, in being of the same faith, and

---

32. Gasparo Pacchierotti (1740–1821), Italian male soprano, one of the foremost
artists of his day. Later in the year at Lucca, he performed in Bertoni's opera,
Quinto Fabio, which Beckford attended.

believing in one singer; nor can you imagine what effects that musical divinity produced at Padua, where he performed a few years ago, and threw his audience into such raptures, that it was some time before they recovered. One in particular, a lady of distinction, fainted away the instant she caught the pathetic accents of his voice, and was near dying a martyr to its melody. La Contessa Roberti, who sings in the truest taste, gave me the detail of the whole affair. *"Egli ha fatto veramente un fanatismo a Padua,"*[33] was her expression. I assured her we were not without idolatry in England upon his account; but that in this, as well as in other articles of belief, there were many abominable heretics.

August 1st. The whole morning, not a soul stirred who could avoid it. Those, who were so active and lively the night before, were now stretched languidly upon their couches. Being to the full as idly disposed, I sat down and wrote some of this dreaming epistle; then feasted upon figs and melons; then got under the shade of the cypress, and slumbered till evening, only waking to dine, and take some ice. The sun declining apace, I hastened to my engagement at Mosolente (for so is the villa called) placed on a verdant hill, encircled by others as lovely, and consisting of three light pavilions connected by porticos; just such as we admire in the fairy scenes of an opera. A vast flight of steps leads to the summit, where Signora Roberti and her friends received me, with a grace and politeness that can never want a place in my memory. We rambled over all the apartments of this agreeable edifice, characterized by airiness and simplicity. The pavement incrusted with a composition as cool and polished as marble; the windows, doors, and balconies adorned with silvered iron-work, commanding scenes of meads and woodland, that extend to the shores of the Adriatic; spires and cypresses rising above the levels; and the hazy mountains beyond Padua, diversifying the expanse, form altogether a landscape, which the elegant imagination of Horizonti[34] never exceeded. Behind the villa, a tumble of hillocks present themselves in variety of forms, with dips and hollows between, scattered over with leafy trees and vines dangling in continued garlands. I gazed on this rural view till it faded in the dusk; then, returning to Bassano, repaired to an illuminated hall, and had the felicity of hearing La Signora Roberti sing the very air

---

33. "He was truly made an object of fanatic devotion at Padua."

34. Jan Frans van Bloemen (1662–c.1748), Flemish painter. He was given the name Orizonte by the Society of Flemings in Rome because of his expert handling of distances in landscape paintings.

which had excited such transport at Padua. As soon as she had ended, and that I could hear no more those affecting sounds, which had held me silent and almost breathless for several moments, a band of various instruments, stationed in the open street, began a lively symphony, which would have delighted me at any other time; but, now, I wished them a thousand leagues away, so melancholy an impression did the air I had been listening to, leave on my mind. At midnight, I took leave of my obliging hosts, who were just setting out for Padua. They gave me a thousand kind invitations, and I hope some future day to accept them.

August 2d. Our route to Venice lay winding about the variegated plains I had surveyed from Mosolente; and, after dining at Treviso, we came, in two hours and a half, to Mestre, between grand villas, and gardens peopled with statues. Embarking our baggage at the last-mentioned place, we stepped into a gondola, whose even motion was very agreeable after the jolts of a chaise. Stretched beneath the awning, I enjoyed at my ease, the freshness of the gales, and the sight of the waters. We were soon out of the canal of Mestre, terminated by an isle, which contains a cell, dedicated to the holy virgin, peeping out of a thicket, from whence spire up two tall cypresses. Its bells tingled, as we passed along and dropped some paolis into a net tied at the head of a pole, stretched out to us for the purpose. As soon as we had doubled the cape of this diminutive island, an azure expanse of sea opened to our view, the domes and towers of Venice rising from its bosom. Now we began to distinguish Murano, St. Michele, St. Giorgio in Alga, and several other islands, detached from the grand cluster, which I hailed as old acquaintance; innumerable prints and drawings having long since made their shapes familiar. Still gliding forwards, the sun casting his last gleams across the waves, and reddening the distant towers, we every moment distinguished some new church, or palace in the city, suffused with the evening rays, and reflected with all their glow of colouring from the surface of the waters. The air was still; the sky cloudless; a faint wind, just breathing upon the deep, lightly bore its surface against the steps of a chapel in the island of Saint Secondo, and waved the veil before its portal, as we rowed by, and coasted the walls of its garden, overhung with fig-trees, and topped with Italian pines. The convent discovers itself through their branches, built in a style somewhat morisco, and level with the sea; except where the garden intervenes. Here, meditation may indulge her reveries in the midst of the surges, and walk in cloisters, alone vocal with the whispers of the pine. I passed this consecrated spot soon after sun-set, when day-light was expiring in the west, and when the distant woods of Fusina were lost in the haze of the horizon. We were now drawing very near the city; and a confused hum began to interrupt the evening stillness; gondolas were continually passing and repassing, and the entrance of the canal Reggio, with all its stir and bustle, lay before us. Our gondoliers turned, with much address, through a croud of boats and barges that blocked up the way, and rowed smoothly by the side of a broad pavement, covered with people in all dresses, and of all nations. Leaving the Palazzo Pesaro, a noble structure with two rows of arcades and a superb rustic, behind, we were soon landed before the Leon Bianco, which, being situated in one of the broadest parts of the grand canal, commands a most striking assemblage of buildings. I have no terms to describe the variety of pillars, of pediments, of mouldings, and cornices; some Grecian, others Saracenical, that adorn these edifices; of which the pencil of Canaletti[35] conveys so perfect an idea, as to render all verbal description superfluous. At one end of this grand perspective, appears the Rialto; the sweep of the canal conceals the other. The rooms of our hotel are as spacious and chearful, as I could desire: a lofty hall, or rather gallery, painted with grotesque, in a very good style, perfectly clean, floored with the stucco composition I have mentioned above, divides the house, and admits a refreshing current of air. Several windows near the ceiling, look into this vast apartment, which serves in lieu of a court, and is rendered perfectly luminous by a glazed arcade, thrown open to catch the breezes. Through it, I passed to a balcony, which impends over the canal, and is twined round with plants forming a grand festoon, and springing from two large vases of orange-trees placed at each end. Here I established myself, to enjoy the cool, and observe, as well as the dusk would permit, the variety of figures shooting by in their gondolas. As night approached, innumerable tapers glimmered through the awnings before the windows. Every boat had its lantern, and the gondolas, moving rapidly along, were followed by tracks of light, which gleamed and played on the waters. I was gazing at these dancing fires, when the sounds of music were wafted along the canals, and, as they grew louder and louder, an illuminated barge, filled with musicians, issued from the Rialto, and, stopping under

---

35. Antonio Canaletto (1697–1768), Venetian painter who found many of his subjects in the architecture of his native city. One of his most celebrated works, "View on the Grand Canal, Venice," is currently in the National Gallery, London.

one of the palaces, began a serenade, which was clamorous, and suspended all conversation in the galleries and porticos; till, rowing slowly away, it was heard no more. The gondoliers catching the air, imitated its cadences, and were answered by others at a distance, whose voices, echoed by the arch of the bridge, acquired a plaintive and interesting tone. I retired to rest, full of the sound, and, long after I was asleep, the melody seemed to vibrate in my ear.

August 3d. It was not five o'clock before I was roused, by a loud din of voices and splashing of water, under my balcony. Looking out, I beheld the grand canal so entirely covered with fruits and vegetables, on rafts and in barges, that I could scarcely distinguish a wave. Loads of grapes, peaches, and melons arrived, and disappeared in an instant; for every vessel was in motion, and the crowds of purchasers hurrying from boat to boat, formed one of the liveliest pictures imaginable. Amongst the multitudes, I remarked a good many, whose dress and carriage announced something above the common rank; and, upon enquiry, I found they were noble Venetians, just come from their casinos; and met to refresh themselves with fruit, before they retired to sleep, for the day. Whilst I was observing them, the sun began to colour the ballustrades of the palaces, and, the pure, exhilarating air of the morning drawing me abroad, I procured a gondola, laid in my provision of bread and grapes, and was rowed under the Rialto, down the grand canal, to the marble steps of S. Maria della Salute, erected by the senate in performance of a vow to the holy Virgin, who begged off a terrible pestilence in 1630. I gazed, delighted with its superb frontispiece and dome, relieved by a clear blue sky. To criticize columns, or pediments of the different façades, would be time lost; since one glance upon the worst view that has been taken of them, conveys a far better idea than the most elaborate description. The great bronze portal opened, whilst I was standing on the steps which lead to it, and discovered the interior of the dome, where I expatiated in solitude; no mortal appearing, except an old priest who trimmed the lamps, and muttered a prayer before the high altar, still wrapt in shadows. The sun-beams began to strike against the windows of the cupola, just as I left the church, and was wafted across the waves to the spacious platform in front of St. Giorgio Maggiore, by far the most perfect and beautiful edifice my eyes ever beheld. When my first transport was a little subsided, and I had examined the graceful design of each particular ornament, and united the just proportion and grand effect of the whole in my mind, I planted my umbrella on the margin of the sea, and reclining under its shade, my feet dangling over the waters, viewed the vast range of palaces, of porticos, of towers, opening on every side, and extending out of sight. The Doge's residence, and the tall columns at the entrance of the place of St. Mark, form, together with the arcades of the public library, the lofty Campanile, and the cupolas of the ducal church, one of the most striking groups of buildings that art can boast of. To behold at one glance these stately fabrics, so illustrious in the records of former ages; before which, in the flourishing times of the republic, so many valiant chiefs and princes have landed, loaded with the spoils of distant nations; was a spectacle I had long, and ardently desired. I thought of the days of Frederic Barbarossa, when looking up the piazza of St. Mark; along which he marched in solemn procession, to cast himself at the feet of Alexander the third, and pay a tardy homage to St. Peter's successor. Here were no longer those splendid fleets, that attended his progress: one solitary galeass was all I beheld, anchored opposite the palace of the Doge, and surrounded by crowds of gondolas, whose sable hues contrasted strongly with its vermilion oars and shining ornaments. A party-coloured multitude was continually shifting from one side of the piazza to the other; whilst senators and magistrates, in long black robes, were already arriving to fill their respective charges. I contemplated the busy scene from my peaceful platform, where nothing stirred but aged devotees, creeping to their devotions; and, whilst I remained thus calm and tranquil, heard the distant buzz and rumour of the town. Fortunately a length of waves rolled between me and its tumults; so that I eat my grapes, and read Metastasio,[36] undisturbed by officiousness, or curiosity. When the sun became too powerful, I entered the nef, and applauded the genius of Palladio. After I had admired the masterly structure of the roof, and the lightness of its arches, my eyes naturally directed themselves to the pavement of white and ruddy marble, polished, and reflecting, like a mirrour, the columns which rise from it. Over this I walked to a door that admitted me into the principal quadrangle of the convent, surrounded by a cloister supported on Ionic pillars, beautifully proportioned. A flight of stairs opens into the court, adorned with ballustrades and pedestals, sculptured with an elegance truly Grecian. This brought me to the refectory, where that *chef d'œuvre* of Paul Veronese,[37] rep-

36. Metastasio was the assumed name of Pietro Trapassi (1698–1782), Italian poet.

37. Paolo Veronese (1528–1588), otherwise known as Paolo Cagliari, was an Italian painter who worked in Venice. "The Marriage at Cana," a colossal painting containing about 120 figures, some of them larger than life, was completed in 1563.

resenting the marriage of Cana in Galilee, was the first object that presented itself. I never beheld so gorgeous a group of wedding-garments before: there is every variety of fold and plait, that can possibly be imagined. The attitudes and countenances are more uniform, and the guests appear a very genteel, decent sort of people; well used to the mode of their times, and accustomed to miracles. Having examined this fictitious repast, I cast a look on a long range of tables covered with very excellent realities, which the monks were coming to devour with energy, if one might judge from their appearance. These sons of penitence and mortification, possess one of the most spacious islands of the whole cluster; a princely habitation, with gardens and open porticos, that engross every breath of air; and, what adds not a little to the charms of their abode, is the liberty of making excursions from it, whenever they have a mind.

The republic, wisely jealous of ecclesiastical influence, connives at these amusing rambles; and, by encouraging the liberty of monks and churchmen, prevents their appearing too sacred and important in the eyes of the people, who have frequent proofs of their being mere flesh and blood, and that of the frailest composition. Had the rest of Italy been of the same opinion, and profited as much by Fra Paolo's maxims,[38] some of its fairest fields would not, at this moment, lie uncultivated; and its ancient spirit might have revived. However, I can scarcely think the moment far distant, when it will awake from its ignoble slumber, assert its natural prerogatives, and look back upon the tiara, with all its host of idle fears and scaring phantoms, as the offspring of a distempered dream. Scarce a sovereign supports any longer this vain illusion, except the old woman of Hungary; and, as soon as her dim eyes are closed, we shall probably witness great events.[39] Full of prophecies and bodings, I moved slowly out of the cloisters; and, gaining my gondola, arrived, I know not how, at the flights of steps which lead to the Redenptore, a structure so simple and elegant, that I thought myself entering an antique temple, and looked about for the statue of the God of Delphi, or some other graceful divinity. A huge crucifix of bronze soon brought me to times present: the charm being thus dissolved, I began to perceive

---

38. Paolo Sarpi (1552–1623), Venetian patriot, scholar, and church reformer advocated limiting the authority of the papacy and the subjection of the clergy to the state.

39. The conduct of the Emperor, since the death of his mother, seems to be accomplishing this prediction apace. [Beckford's note.]

the shapes of rueful martyrs, peeping out of the niches around, and the bushy beards of Capuchin friars, waggling before the altars. These good fathers had decorated their church, according to custom, with orange and citron trees, placed between the pilasters of the arcades; and on grand festivals, it seems, they turn the whole church into a bower, strew the pavement with leaves, and festoon the dome with flowers. I left them occupied with their plants and their devotions. It was mid-day, and I begged to be rowed to some woody island, where I might dine in shade and tranquillity. My gondoliers shot off in an instant; but, though they went at a very rapid rate, I wished to fly faster; and, getting into a bark with six oars, swept along the waters; soon left the Zecca and San Marco behind; and, launching into the plains of shining sea, saw turret after turret, and isle after isle, fleeting before me. A pale greenish light ran along the shores of the distant continent, whose mountains seemed to catch the motion of my boat, and to fly with equal celerity. I had not much time to contemplate the beautiful effects on the waters; the emerald and purple hues which gleamed along their surface. Our prow struck, foaming, against the walls of the Carthusian garden, before I recollected where I was; or could look attentively around me. Permission being obtained, I entered this cool retirement; and, putting aside with my hands the boughs of fig-trees and pomegranates, got under an ancient bay, near which several tall pines lift themselves up to the breezes. I listened to the conversation they held with a wind just flown from Greece, and charged, as well as I could understand this airy language, with many affectionate remembrances from their relations on mount Ida. I reposed amidst bay-leaves fanned by a constant air, till it pleased the fathers to send me some provisions, with a basket of fruit and wine. Two of them would wait upon me, and asked ten thousand questions about Lord George Gordon, and the American war. I, who was deeply engaged with the winds, and fancied myself hearing these rapid travellers relate their adventures, wished my interrogators in purgatory, and pleaded ignorance of the Italian language. This circumstance extricated me from my difficulties, and procured me a long interval of repose.

The rustling of the pines had the same effect, as the murmurs of other old story-tellers; and I slept undisturbed, till the people without, in the boat (who wondered not a little, I dare say, what the deuse was become of me within) began a sort of chorus in parts, full of such plaintive modulation, that I still thought myself under the influence of a dream; and, half in this world, and half in the other, believed, like the heroes in Fingal, that I had caught the music of the spirits of the hill. When I was thoroughly convinced of the reality of these sounds, I moved toward the shore, from whence they proceeded: a glassy sea lay full before me: no gale ruffled the expanse: every breath was subsided, and I beheld the sun go down in all its sacred calm. You have experienced the sensations this moment inspires: imagine what they must have been, in such a scene; and accompanied with a melody so simple and pathetic. I stepped into my boat, and, instead of encouraging the speed of the gondoliers, begged them to abate their ardour, and row me lazily home. They complied; and we were near an hour reaching the platform before the ducal palace, thronged as usual with a variety of nations. I mixed a moment with the crowd; then directed my steps to the great mosque, I ought to say the church, of St. Mark; but really its cupolas, slender pinnacles, and semicircular arches, have so oriental an appearance, as to excuse this appellation. I looked a moment at the four stately coursers of bronze and gold, that adorn the chief portal; and then, took in, at one glance, the whole extent of the square, with its towers and standards. So noble an assemblage never met my eyes; I envied the good fortune of Petrarch, who describes, in one of his letters, a tournament held in this princely opening. Many are the festivals which have been here celebrated. When Henry the Third left Poland to mount the throne of France, he passed through Venice, and found the republic waiting to receive him in their famous square; which, by means of an awning stretched from the ballustrades of opposite palaces, was metamorphosed into a vast saloon, sparkling with artificial stars, and spread with the richest carpets of the East. What a magnificent idea! The ancient Romans, in the zenith of power and luxury, never conceived a greater. It is to them the Venetians are indebted for the hint, since we read of the Coliseo and Pompey's theatre being sometimes covered with transparent canvass, to defend the spectators from the heat or sudden rain; and to tint the scene with soft, agreeable colours, like the hues of the declining sun. Having enjoyed the general perspective of the piazza, I began to enter into particulars, and examine the bronze pedestals of the three standards before the great church, designed by Sansovino[40] in the true spirit of the antique, and covered with relievos, at the same time bold and ele-

---

40. Jacopo Sansovino (1486–1570), Italian architect and sculptor.

gant. It is also to this celebrated architect we were indebted for the stately façade of the Proccuratie nuove, which form one side of the square, and present an uninterrupted series of arcades, and marble columns exquisitely wrought. Opposite this magnificent range, appears another line of palaces, whose architecture, though far removed from the Grecian purity of Sansovino, impresses veneration, and compleats the pomp of the view. There is something strange and singular in the tower, which rises distinct from the smooth pavement of the square, a little to the left, as you stand before the chief entrance of St. Mark's. The design is rather barbarous, and terminates in uncouth and heavy pyramids; yet, in spite of these defects, it struck me with awe. A beautiful building, called the Loggetta, and which serves as a guard-house, during the convocation of the grand council, decorates its base. Nothing can be more enriched, more finished, than this structure; which, though far from diminutive, is in a manner lost at the foot of the Campanile. This enormous mass seems to promise a very long duration, and will probably carry down the fame of Saint Mark and his lion, to the latest posterity. Both appear, in great state, towards its summit, and have nothing superior but an archangel perched on the topmost pinnacle, and pointing to the skies. The dusk prevented my remarking the various sculptures with which the loggetta is crouded. Crossing the ample space between this elegant edifice and the ducal palace, I passed through a labyrinth of pillars, and entered the principal court, of which nought but the great outline was visible, at so late an hour. Two reservoirs of bronze, rich with sculptured foliage, diversify the area. In front, a magnificent flight of stairs presents itself, by which the senators ascend through vast and solemn corridores, which lead to the interior of the edifice. The colossal statues of Mars and Neptune guard the entrance, and have given the appellation of *scala dei giganti* to the steps below; which I mounted, not without respect; and, leaning against the ballustrades, formed, like the rest of the building, of the rarest marbles, adored the tutelary divinities. My devotions were shortly interrupted by one of the *sbirri*, or officers of police, who take their stands, after sun-set, before the avenues of the palace; and who told me the gates were upon the point of being closed. So, hurrying down the stairs, I left half my vows unpaid, and a million of delicate sculptures unexplored; for every pilaster, every frieze, every entablature, is incrusted with porphyry, verde antique, or some other curious marble, carved into as many grotesque wreaths and mouldings, as we admire in the loggios of Raffaello. The various portals, the strange projections, the length of cloisters, in short, the noble irregularity of these imperial piles, delighted me beyond idea; and I was sorry to be forced to abandon them so soon; especially, as the twilight, which bats and owls love not better than I do, enlarged every portico, lengthened every colonnade, and encreased the dimensions of the whole, just as imagination dictated. This faculty would have had full scope, had I but remained an hour longer. The moon would then have gleamed upon the gigantic forms of Mars and Neptune, and discovered the statues of antient heroes, emerging from the gloom of their niches. Such an interesting assemblage of objects; such regal scenery, with the reflection, that half their ornaments once contributed to the decoration of Athens, transported me beyond mystelf. The *sbirri* thought me distracted. True enough, I was stalking proudly about, like an actor in an ancient Grecian tragedy, lifting up his hands to the consecrated fanes and images around, expecting the reply of his attendant Chorus, and declaiming the first verses of Oedipus Tyrannus. These fits of enthusiasm were hardly subsided, when I issued from the gates of the palace into the great square, which received a faint gleam from its casinos and palaces, just beginning to be lighted up, and become the resort of pleasure and dissipation. Numbers were walking, in parties, upon the pavement; some sought the shade of the porticos with their favourites; others were earnestly engaged in conversation, and filled the gay, illuminated apartments, where they resorted to drink coffee and sorbet, with laughter and merriment: a thoughtless, giddy transport prevailed; for, at this hour, any thing like restraint seems perfectly out of the question; and, however solemn a magistrate or senator may appear in the day, at night, he lays up wig, and robe, and gravity, to sleep together, runs intriguing about in his gondola, takes the reigning sultana under his arm, and so rambles half over the town, which grows gayer and gayer as the day declines. Many of the noble Venetians have a little suite of apartments in some out of the way corner, near the grand place, of which their families are totally ignorant. To these they sculk in the dusk, and revel undisturbed with the companions of their pleasures. Jealousy itself cannot discover the alleys, the winding passages, the unsuspected doors, by which these retreats are accessible. Many an unhappy lover, whose mistress disappears on a sudden with some fortunate rival, has searched for her haunts in vain. The gondoliers themselves, though often the prime managers of intrigues, are scarce ever acquainted with these interior cabinets. When a gallant has a mind to pursue his adventures with mystery, he rows to the piazza, orders his bark to wait, meets his goddess in the crowd, and vanishes from all beholders. Surely, Venice is the city in the universe best calculated for giving scope to the observations of a Devil upon two sticks. What a variety of lurking-places would one stroke of his crutch uncover! Whilst the higher ranks were solacing themselves in their casinos, the rabble were gathered in knots, round the strollers and mountebanks, singing and scaramouching in the middle of the square. I observed a great number of Orientals amongst the crowd, and heard Turkish and Arabic muttering in every corner. Here, the Sclavonian dialect predominated; there, some Grecian jargon, almost unintelligible. Had Saint Mark's church been the wonderous tower, and its piazza the chief square of the city of Babylon, there could scarcely have been a greater confusion of languages. The novelty of the scene afforded me no small share of amusement, and I wandered about from group to group, and from one strange exotic to another, asking, and being asked, innumerable ridiculous questions, and settling the politics of London and Constantinople, almost in the same breath. This instant, I found myself in a circle of grave Armenian priests and jewellers; the next, amongst Greeks and Dalmatians; who accosted me with the smoothest compliments, and gave proof, that their reputation for pliability and address, was not ill-founded. I was entering into a grand harum-scarum discourse with some Russian Counts; or Princes; or whatever you please; just landed, with dwarfs, and footmen, and governors; and staring, like me, about them, when Mad. de R.[41] arrived, to whom I had the happiness of being recommended. She very obligingly presented me to some of the most distinguished of the Venetian families, at their great casino which looks into the piazza, and consists of five or six rooms, fitted up in a gay, flimsy taste, neither rich nor elegant; where were a great many lights, and a great many ladies negligently dressed, their hair falling very freely about them, and innumerable adventures written in their eyes. The gentlemen were lolling upon the sophas, or lounging about the apartments. The whole assembly seemed upon the verge of gaping, till coffee was carried round. This magic beverage diffused a temporary animation; and, for a moment or two, conversation moved on with a degree of pleasing extravagance; but the

---

41. Giustiniana Wynne d'Orsini-Rosenberg (1727–1791), widow of Count d'Orsini-Rosenberg, former Austrian ambassador at Venice.

flash was soon dissipated, and nothing remained, save cards and stupidity. In the intervals of shuffling and dealing, some talked over the affairs of the grand council; with less reserve than I expected; and two or three of them asked some feeble questions about the late tumults in London; but mentioned not a syllable of their own commotions. As much, however, through indolence and forgetfulness, I should conjecture, as from any political motive; for I don't believe all those wise stories which some travellers have propagated, of Venetian subtlety and profound silence. They might have reigned during the dark periods of the republic; but, at this moment, the veil is rent in fifty places; and, without any wonderful penetration, the debates of the senate are discoverable. There doubtless was a time, when, society being greatly divided, and little communication subsisting amongst the nobles, secrets were inviolably kept; but since the establishment of casinos, which the ladies rule, where chit-chat and tittle-tattle are for ever going forwards, who can preserve a rigorous taciturnity, upon any subject in the universe? It was one o'clock before all the company were assembled, and I left them at three, still dreaming over their coffee and card-tables. Trieze is their favourite game: *uno, due, tre, quatro, cinque, fante, cavallo,* are eternally repeated, the apartments echoed no other sound. No lively people could endure such monotony; yet, I have been told the Venetians are remarkably spirited, and so eager in the pursuit of amusement, as hardly to allow themselves any sleep. Some, for instance, after declaiming in the senate, walking an hour in the square, and fidgeting about, from one casino to another, till morning dawns, will get into a gondola, row across the Lagunes, take the post at Mestre, or Fusina, and jumble over craggy pavements to Treviso, breakfast in haste, and rattle back again, as if the devil were charioteer. By eleven, the party is restored to Venice, resumes robe and periwig, and goes to council. This may be very true, and yet I will never cite the Venetians as examples of vivacity. Their nerves, unstrung by disease and the consequence of early debaucheries, impede all lively flow of spirits in its course, and permit, at best, but a few moments of a false and feverish activity. The approaches of rest, forced back by an immoderate use of coffee, renders them too weak and listless to like any active amusement; and the facility of being wafted from place to place in a gondola, adds not a little to their indolence. In short, I can scarcely regard their eastern neighbours in a more lazy light; and am apt to imagine, that instead of slumbering less than any other people, they pass their lives in one perpetual dose.

August 4th. The heats were so excessive in the night, that I thought myself several times on the point of suffocation, tossed about like a wounded fish, and dreamt of the devil and Senegal. Towards sun-rise, a faint breeze restored me to life and reason. I slumbered till late in the day; and, the moment I was fairly awake, ordered my gondolier to row out to the main ocean, that I might plunge into its waves, and hear and see nothing, but waters around me. We shot off, wound amongst a number of sheds, shops, churches, casinos, and palaces, growing immediately out of the canals, without any apparent foundation. No quay, no terrace, not even a slab is to be seen before the doors: one step brings you from the hall into the bark, and the vestibules of the stateliest structures lie open to the waters, and level with them. I observed several, as I glided along, supported by rows of well-proportioned pillars, adorned with terms and vases, beyond which the eye generally discovers a grand court, and sometimes, a garden. In about half an hour, we had left the thickest cluster of isles behind, and, coasting the place of St. Mark opposite to San Giorgio Maggiore, whose elegant frontispiece was painted on the calm waters, launched into the blue expanse of sea, from which rises the Chartreuse, and two or three other woody islands. I hailed the spot, where I had spent such a happy visionary evening, and nodded to my friends the pines. A few minutes more brought me to a dreary, sun-burnt shore, stalked over by a few Sclavonian soldiers, who inhabit a castle hard by, go regularly to an ugly unfinished church, and from thence, it is to be hoped, to paradise; as the air of their barracks is abominable, and kills them like blasted sheep. Forlorn as this island appeared to me, I was told it was the scene of the Doge's pageantry at the feast of the Ascension; and the very spot to which he sails in the Bucentaur, previous to wedding the sea. You have heard enough, and, if ever you looked into a show-box, seen full sufficient, of this gaudy spectacle, without my enlarging upon the topic. I shall only say, that I was obliged to pursue, partly, the same road as the nuptial procession, in order to reach the beach; and was broiled and dazzled accordingly. At last, after traversing some desart hillocks, all of a hop with toads and locusts (amongst which English heretics have the honour of being interred) I passed under an arch, and suddenly the boundless plains of ocean opened to my view. I ran to the smooth sands, extending on both sides out of sight, cast off my cloaths, and dashed into the waves; which were coursing one another with a gentle motion, and breaking lightly on the shores. The tide rolled over me as I lay floating about, buoyed up by the water, and carried me wheresoever it listed. It might have borne me far out into the main, and exposed me to a thousand perils, before I had been aware; so totally was I abandoned to the illusion of the moment. My ears were filled with murmuring, undecided sounds; my limbs, stretched languidly on the surge, rose, or sunk, just as it swelled, or subsided. In this passive, senseless state I remained, till the sun cast a less intolerable light, and the fishing vessels, lying out in the bay at a great distance, spread their sails and were coming home. Hastening back over the desart of locusts, I threw myself into the gondola; and, no wind nor wave opposing, was soon wafted across to those venerable columns, so conspicuous in the place of Saint Mark. Directing my course immediately to the ducal palace, I entered the grand court, ascended the Giant's stairs, and examined at my leisure its bas reliefs. Then, taking the first guide that presented himself, I was shewn along several cloisters and corridores, sustained by innumerable pillars, into the state apartments, which Tintoret and Paolo Veronese have covered with the triumphs of their country. A swarm of lawyers filled the Sala del Maggior Consiglio, and one of the first advocates in the republic, was pleading with all his might, before a solemn row of senators. The eyes and ears of the assembly seemed equally affected. Clouds of powder, and vollies of execrations issuing every instant from the disputants, I got out of their way; and was led, from hall to hall, and from picture to picture, with exemplary resignation. To be sure, I was heartily tired, but behaved with decency; having never once expressed, how much I wished the *chef d'œuvres* I had been contemplating less smoky and numerous. At last, I reached once more the colonades at the entrance, and caught the sea breeze in the open porticos which front San Giorgio Maggiore. The walls are covered in most places with grim visages, sculptured in marble, whose mouths gape for accusations, and swallow every lie that malice and revenge can dictate. I wished for a few ears of the same kind, dispersed about the Doge's residence, to which one might apply one's own, and catch some account of the mysteries within; some little dialogue between the Three Inquisitors, or debate in the Council of Ten. This is that tribunal, which holds the wealthy nobility in continual awe; before which they appear with trembling and terror; and whose summons they dare not disobey. Sometimes, by way of clemency, it condemns its victims to perpetual imprisonment, in close, stifling cells, between the leads and beams of the palace; or, unwilling to spill the blood of a fellow citizen, generously sinks them into dungeons, deep under the canals which wash its foundations; so that, above and below, its majesty is contaminated by the abodes of punishment. What sovereign could endure the idea of having his immediate residence polluted with tears? Or revel in his halls, conscious, that many of his species were consuming their hours in lamentations above his head, and that but a few beams separated him from the scene of their tortures? However gaily disposed, could one dance with pleasure on a pavement, beneath which lie damp and gloomy caverns, whose inhabitants waste away by painful degrees, and feel themselves whole years a dying? Impressed by these terrible ideas, I could not regard the palace without horror, and wished for the strength of a thousand antediluvians, to level it with the sea, lay open the secret recesses of punishment, and admit free gales and sunshine into every den. When I had thus vented my indignation, I repaired to the statue of Neptune, and invoked it to second my enterprize. Once upon a time, no deity had a freer hand at razing cities. His execution was renowned throughout all antiquity, and the proudest monarchs deprecated the wrath of ΚΡΕΙΩΝ ΕΝΟΣΙΧΘΩΝ. But, like the other mighty ones of antient days, his reign is past, and his trident disregarded. My supplications were fruitless, and I lamented being born three thousand years too late for propitious earthquakes, or heroic liberty. Formerly, any wild spirit found favour in the eyes of fortune, and was led along the career of glory to the deliverance of captives and the extirpation of monsters; but, in our degenerate days, this easy road to fame is no longer open, and the means of producing such signal events, perplexed and difficult. Abandoning therefore the sad tenants of the Piombi to their fate, I left the courts; and, stepping into my bark, was rowed down a canal, over which the lofty vaults of the palace cast a tremendous shade. Beneath these fatal waters, the dungeons I have been speaking of, are situated. There, the wretches lie marking the sound of the oars, and counting the free passage of every gondola. Above, a marble bridge, of bold, majestic architecture, joins the highest part of the prisons to the secret galleries of the palace; from whence criminals are conducted over the arch, to a cruel and mysterious death. I shuddered whilst passing below, and believe it is not without cause, this structure is named PONTE DEI SOSPIRI.[42] Horrors and dismal prospects haunted my fancy upon my return. I could not dine in peace, so strongly was my imagination affected; but, snatching my pencil, I drew chasms and subterraneous hollows, the domain of fear and torture, with chains, rocks, wheels, and dreadful engines, in the style of Piranesi. About sun-set, I went and refreshed myself with the cool air, and chearful scenery of the Fondamenti nuovi, a vast quay, or terrace of white marble, which commands the whole series of isles, from Saint Michele's to Torcello,

That rise and glitter o'er the ambient tide.

Nothing can be more picturesque than the groups of towers and cupolas which they present, mixed with flat roofs, and low buildings, and now and then a pine, or cypress. Afar off, a little woody isle, called Il Deserto, swells from the ocean, and diversifies its expanse. When I had spent a delightful half hour in viewing the distant islands, M. de B.[43] accompanied me to the Mendicanti, one of the four conservatorios, which give the best musical education conceivable, to near one hundred young women. You may guess how admirably those of the Mendicanti, in particular, are taught, since their establishment is under Bertoni's direction, who breathes around him the very soul of grace and harmony. The chapel, in which we sat to hear the oratorio, was dark and solemn; a screen of lofty pillars, formed of black marble, and highly polished, excluded the glow of the western sky, and reflected the lamps which burn perpetually before the altar. Every tribune was thronged with people, whose profound silence shewed them worthy auditors of Bertoni's compositions.[44] Here were no cackling old women, or groaning Methodists, such as infest our English churches, and scare one's ears with hoarse coughs, accompanied by the *naso obligato*. All were still and attentive, imbibing the plaintive notes of the voices with eager-

---

42. Bridge of Sighs
43. Count Bartolommeo Benincasa (1745–1825), Madame de Rosenberg's *cavaliere servente* and sometime diplomat at Modena, Italy.
44. Ferdinando Giuseppe Bertoni (1725–1813), Italian composer and choirmaster at the Ospedale San Lazzaro dei Mendicanti, Venice during the years 1757–1797. The opera *Quinto Fabio* was his greatest artistic success.

ness, and scarce a countenance but seemed deeply affected with David's sorrows, the subject of the performance. I sat retired in a solitary tribune, and felt them as my own. Night came on before the last chorus was sung, and I still seem to hear its sacred melody.

August 18th. It rains; the air is refreshed, and I have courage to resume my pen, which the sultry weather had forced to lie dormant so long. I like this odd town of Venice, and find every day some new amusement in rambling about its innumerable canals and alleys. Sometimes, I go and pry about the great church of Saint Mark, and examine the variety of marbles, and mazes of delicate sculpture, with which it is covered. The cupola, glittering with gold, mosaic, and paintings of half the wonders in the Apocalypse, never fails transporting me to the period of the eastern empire. I think myself in Constantinople, and expect Michael Paleologus[45] with all his train. One circumstance alone, prevents my observing half the treasures of the place, and holds down my fancy, just springing into the air: I mean, the vile stench, which exhales from every recess and corner of the edifice, and which all the altars cannot subdue. When oppressed by this noxious atmosphere, I run up the Campanile in the piazza; and, seating myself amongst the pillars of the gallery, breathe the fresh gales which blow from the Adriatic; survey at my leisure all Venice beneath me, with its azure sea, white sails, and long tracks of islands, shining in the sun. Having thus laid in a provision of wholesome breezes, I brave the vapours of the canals, and venture into the most curious, and musky quarters of the city, in search of Turks and Infidels, that I may ask as many questions as I please about Damascus and Suristan, those happy countries, which nature has covered with roses. Asiatics find Venice very much to their liking; and all those I conversed with, allowed its customs and style of living had a good deal of conformity to their own. The eternal lounging in coffee-houses, and sipping of sorbets, agrees perfectly well with the inhabitants of the Ottoman empire, who stalk about in their proper dresses, and smoke their own exotic pipes, without being stared and wondered at, as in most other European capitals. Some few of these Orientals are communicative and enlightened. But, generally speaking, they know nothing beyond the rule of three, and the commonest transactions of mercantile affairs. The Greeks are by far a more

---

45. Manuel Palaeologus (1350–1425), Byzantine emperor from 1391 to 1425.

lively generation, still retaining their propensity to works of
genius and imagination. Metastasio has been lately translated into
their modern jargon; and some obliging papa or other, has had
the patience to put the long-winded romance of Clelia[46] into
a Grecian dress. I saw two or three of these volumes exposed on a
stall, under the grand arcades of the public library, as I went one
day to admire the antiques in its vestibule. Whilst I was intent
upon my occupation, a little door, I should never have suspected,
flew open, and out popped Monsieur de V,[47] from a place where
nothing, I believe, but broomsticks and certain other utensils
were ever before deposited. This gentleman, the most active in-
vestigator of Homer since the days of the good bishop of Thessa-
lonica, bespatters you with more learning in a minute, than others
communicate in half a year; quotes Arabic, Greek, Hebrew,
Syriac, &c. with a formidable fluency, and drove me from one
end of the room to the other, with all the thunder of erudition. Syllables fell thicker than hail, and in an instant I found
myself so weighed down and covered, that I prayed, for mercy's
sake, to be introduced, by way of respite, to a Laplander, whom
he leads about as a curiosity; a poor harmless good sort of a
soul, calm and indifferent, who has acquired the words of several
oriental languages to perfection: ideas he has, in none. We
went together to view a collection of medals in one of the Grada-
nigo palaces, and two or three inestimable volumes, filled with
paintings that represent the dress of the antient Venetians; so
that I had an opportunity of observing to perfection all the
Lapland nothingness of my companion. What a perfect void!
Cold, and silent as the polar regions; not one passion ever
throbbed in his bosom; not one bright ray of fancy ever glittered
in his mind; without love or anger, pleasure or pain, his days
fleet smoothly along: all things considered, I must confess I envied
such comfortable apathy. After having passed a peaceful hour in
dreaming over the medals and rarities, M. de V was for conducting
me to the Armenian convent; but I begged to be excused, and
went to S. Giovanni e Paolo's, a church ever celebrated in the
annals of painting, since it contains that master-piece of Titian,
the martyrdom of St. Peter. It being a festival, the huge Gothic

---

46. I.e. *Clélia* by Madeleine de Scudéry (1607–1701).

47. Jean Baptiste Gaspard d'Ansse de Villoison (c. 1750–1805), French classical
scholar. He spent three years (1781–1783) in Venice at the expense of the French
government. During this period, he discovered the "Venetian Homer," a 10th
century MS. of the *Illiad*.

pillars were covered with red damask, and the shrines of saints and worthies glimmered with tapers. The dim chapels on each side the nave, received a feeble light, and discovered the tombs of ancient Doges, and the equestrian statues of many a doughty General. I admired them all, but liked nothing so much as a snug bas relief I found out in a corner, which represents St. Mark, and some other good soul, a prosing; whilst his lion and the old serpent squabble and scratch in the foreground of the sculpture, like cat and dog by the fire-side. After dinner, when the shadows of domes and palaces began lengthening across the waves, I rowed out

On the clear hyaline, the glassy sea,

to observe the last sun-beam fade on the tufted gardens of the Giudecca, and to contemplate the distant Euganean hills, once the happiest region of Italy; where wandering nations enjoyed the simplicity of a pastoral life, long before the arrival of Antenor.[48] In those antient times, deep forests and extensive pastures covered the shores[49] of the Adriatic; and innumerable flocks hung on the brow of the mountains. This golden period ended upon the incursion of the Trojans and Heneti; who, led by Antenor, drove away the unfortunate savages, and possessed themselves of their habitations.[50] The form of the hillocks is varied and picturesque; and the sun, sinking behind them, suffuses their summits with tints of the brightest orange. Scarce one evening have I failed to remark the changeful scenery of the clouds, and to fill my mind with recollections of primeval days, and happier ages. Night generally surprizes me in the midst of my reveries; I return, lulled in my gondola by the murmur of waters, pass about an hour with M—— de R——, whose imagination and sensibility almost equal your own; then, retire to sleep, and dream of the Euganeans.

---

48. History celebrates Antenor as one of the wisest Trojan counsellors. Beckford refers here to Livy's account of the founding of Patavium, when Antenor, as leader of the Eneti and the Trojans, drove the Euganei from their lands.

49. It is reasonably conjectured, that the sea formerly washed the walls of Padua. [Beckford's note.]

50. T[itus] Livius, [*History of Rome*], L. i. c. I. [Beckford's note].

Letter IX.

August 27th.

I am just returned from visiting the isles of Burano, Torcello, and Mazorbo; distant about five miles from Venice. To these amphibious spots the Romans, inhabitants of eastern Lombardy, fled from the rapine of Attila; and, if we may believe Cassiodorus,[51] there was a time when they presented a beautiful appearance. Beyond them, on the coast of the Lagunes, rose the once populous city of Altina, with its six stately gates, which Dandolo mentions.[52] Its neighbourhood was scattered with innumerable villas and temples, composing altogether a prospect, which Martial compares to Baiæ:

Æmula Baianis Altini littora villis.[53]

But this agreeable scene, like so many others, is past entirely away, and has left nothing, except heaps of stones and mis-shapen fragments, to vouch for its former magnificence. Two of the islands, Costanziaco and Amiano, that are imagined to have contained the bowers and gardens of the Altinatians, have sunk beneath the waters: those which remain, are scarcely worthy to rise above their surface. Though I was persuaded little was left to be seen above ground, I could not deny myself the imaginary pleasure of treading a corner of the earth, once so adorned and cultivated; and of walking over the roofs, perhaps, of concealed halls, and undiscovered palaces. M. de R, to whom I communicated my

---

51. Flavius Magnus Aurelius Cassiodorus (c. 490-c. 585), historian and statesman.

52. Lib. V. c. IV. p. 5. [Beckford's note.] Andrea Dandolo (c. 1307–1354) was an historian and doge of Venice from 1343 to 1354. His *Annals* to the year 1280 are considered to be a major source of Venetian history for the period covered.

53. Martial, *Epigrams,* bk. IV, st. XXV. "Altinum's shores that rival Baiae's villas."

ideas, entered at once into the scheme; hiring therefore a peiotte, we took some provisions and music (to us equally necessaries of life) and launched into the canal, between Saint Michael and Murano. The waves coursed each other with violence; and dark clouds hung over the grand sweep of northern mountains, whilst the west smiled with azure, and bright sunshine. Thunder rolled awfully at a distance, and those white and greyish birds, the harbingers of storms, flitted frequently before our bark. For some moments we were in doubt, whether to proceed; but, as we advanced by a little dome in the isle of Saint Michael, shaped like an antient temple, the sky cleared, and the ocean subsiding by degrees, soon presented a tranquil expanse, across which we were smoothly wafted. Our instruments played several delightful airs, that called forth the inhabitants of every island, and held them silent, and spell-bound, on the edge of their quays and terraces, till we were out of hearing. Leaving Murano far behind, Venice and its world of turrets, began to sink on the horizon, and the low, desert isles beyond Mazorbo, to lie stretched out before us.

Now, we beheld vast wastes of[54] purple flowers, and could distinguish the low hum of the insects which hover above them; such was the silence of the place. Coasting these solitary fields, we wound amongst several serpentine canals, bordered by gardens of figs and pomegranates, with neat, Indian looking inclosures of cane and reed: an aromatic plant clothes the margin of the waters, which the people justly dignify with the title of marine incense. It proved very serviceable in subduing a musky odour, which attacked us the moment we landed; and which proceeds from serpents that lurk in the hedges. These animals, say the gondoliers, defend immense treasures, which lie buried under the ruins. Woe to those who attempt invading them; or prying too curiously about. Not chusing to be devoured, we left many a mount of fragments unnoticed, and made the best of our way to a little green, free from weeds or adders; bounded on one side by a miserable shed, decorated with the name of the Podesta's residence; and, on the other, by a circular church. Some remains of tolerable antique sculpture are enchased in the walls; and the dome, supported by pillars of a smooth Grecian marble, though uncouth and ill-proportioned, impresses a sort of veneration, and transports the fancy to the twilight-glimmering period when it was raised. Having surveyed what little was visible, and given as

---

54. Called Roscani in Venetian, and reduced to ashes for the glass manufactory at Murano. [Beckford's note.]

much career to our imaginations as the scene inspired, we walked over a soil, composed of crumbling bricks and cement, to the cathedral; whose arches, turned on the antient Roman principle, convinced us that it dates as high as the sixth or seventh century. Nothing can be well more fantastic than the ornaments of this structure, formed from the ruins of the Pagan temples of Altina; and incrusted with a gold mosaic, like that which covers our Edward the Confessor's tomb. The pavement, composed of various precious marbles, is richer and more beautiful than one could have expected, in a place where every other object favours of the grossest barbarism. At the further end, beyond the altar, appears a semicircular niche, with seats like the gradines of a diminutive amphitheatre: above, rise the quaint forms of the apostles, in red, blue, green, and black mosaic; and in the midst of the goodly group, a sort of marble chair, cool and penitential enough, where Saint Lorenzo Giustiniani[55] sat to hold a provincial council, the Lord knows how long ago. The fount for holy water, stands by the principal entrance, fronting this curious recess; and seems to have belonged to some place of Gentile worship. The figures of horned imps cling around its sides; more devilish, more Egyptian, than any I ever beheld. The dragons on old china are not more whimsical: I longed to have filled it with bats' blood, and to have sent it by way of present to the sabbath. I can assure you, it would have done honour to their witcheries. The sculpture is not the most delicate; but I cannot say a great deal about it, as but little light reaches the spot where it is fixed. Indeed the whole church is far from luminous; its windows being narrow and near the roof, with shutters composed of blocks of marble, which nothing but the last whirlwind, one should think, could move from their hinges. By the time we had examined every nook and corner of this singular edifice, and caught perhaps some small portion of sanctity, by sitting in San Lorenzo's chair, dinner was prepared in a neighbouring convent; and the nuns, allured by the sound of our flutes and oboes, peeped out of their cells, and shewed themselves by dozens at the grate. Some few agreeable faces and interesting eyes enlivened the dark sisterhood: all seemed to catch a gleam of pleasure from the music: two or three of them, probably the last immured, let fall a tear, and suffered the recollection of the world and its prophane joys to interrupt, for a moment, their

---

55. Lorenzo Giustiniani (1380–1465), Bishop of Venice.

sacred tranquillity. We staid till the sun was low and the breezes blew cool from the ocean, on purpose that they might listen as long as possible to a harmony, which seemed to issue, as the old abbess expressed herself, from the gates of paradise a-jar. A thousand benedictions consecrated our departure: twilight came on, just as we entered the bark and rowed out upon the waves, agitated by a fresh gale; but fearing nothing, under the protection of Saint Margherita, whose good wishes our music had secured. In two hours, we were safely landed at the Fondamenti nuovi, and went immediately to the Mendicanti, where they were performing the oratorio of Sisera. The composer, a young man, had displayed great fire and originality in this performance, and a knowledge of character seldom found in the most celebrated masters. The supplication of the thirsty chieftain, and Jael's insinuating arts and pious treachery, are admirably expressed; but the agitation and boding slumbers which precede his death, are imagined in the highest strain of genius. The terror and agony of his dreams, made me start, more than once, from my seat; and all the horrors of his assassination seemed full before me: so fatal was the sound of the instruments, so just the conduct of the harmony! Too much applause cannot be given the Marchetti, who sung the part of Sisera, and seconded the composer's ideas by the most feeling and spirited execution. There are few things I shall regret more at Venice, than this conservativo. Whenever I am musically given, I fly to it, and hear the most striking finalis in Bertoni's and Anfosse's operas,[56] as long and often as I please. The sight of the orchestra still makes me smile. You know, I suppose, it is entirely of the female gender; and that nothing is more common, than to see a delicate white hand journeying across an enormous double bass; or a pair of roseate cheeks puffing with all their efforts, at a french-horn. Some that are grown old and Amazonian, who have abandoned their fiddles and their lovers, take vigorously to the kettle-drum; and one poor limping lady, who had been crossed in love, now makes an admirable figure on the bassoon. Good night! I am quite exhausted with composing a chorus for these same Amazons. The poetry I send you; which seems to be some of the most picturesque and nervous, an Italian ever produced. The music takes up too much room to travel at

---

56. Pasquale Anfossi (1727–1797), Italian composer. His most notable productions were *L'incognita perseguitata* (1773), *L'avaro* (1775), *La vera costanza* (1776), and *I viaggiatori felici* (1780).

present. One day or other, perhaps, we may hear it in some dark grove, when the moon is eclipsed, and nature in alarm. This is not the last letter you would receive from Venice, was I not hurrying to Lucca, where Pacchierotti sings next week, in the opera of *Quinto Fabio;* of all operas the most worthy to excuse such a musical fanaticism. Adieu!

Letter X.

I was sorry to leave Venice, and regretted my peaceful excursions upon the Adriatic, when the Euganean hills were lost in a golden haze, and the sun cast his departing gleams across the waters. No bright rays illuminated my departure; but the coolness and perfume of the air made some amends for their absence. About an hour's rowing from the isle of Saint Giorgio in Alga, brought us to the shores of Fusina, right opposite the opening, where the Brenta mixes with the sea. This river flows calmly between banks of verdure, crowned by poplars, with vines twining round every stalk, and depending from tree to tree, in beautiful festoons. Beds of mint and flowers, clothe the brink of the stream, except where a tall growth of reeds and oziers lift themselves to the breezes. I heard their whispers as we glided along; and, had I been alone, might have told you what they said to me; but such aerial oracles must be approached in solitude. The morning continued to lower as we advanced; scarce a wind ventured to breathe: all was still and placid as the surface of the Brenta. No sound struck my ears, except the bargemen hollowing to open the sluices, and deepen the water. As yet I had not perceived an habitation; no other objects than green meads and fields of Turkish corn, shaded with vines and poplars, met my eyes wherever I turned them. Our navigation, the tranquil streams and cultivated banks, in short the whole landscape, had a sort of Chinese cast, which led me into Quang-Si and Quang-Tong. The variety of canes, reeds, and blossoming rushes, shooting from the slopes, confirmed my fancies; and, when I beheld the yellow nenupha expanding its broad leaves to the current, I thought of the Tao-Sé, and venerated one of the chief ingredients in their beverage of immortality. Landing

133

where this magic vegetation appeared most luxuriant, I cropped the flowers; but searched in vain for the kernels, which, according to the doctrine of the Bonzes,[57] produce such wonderful effects. Though I was deceived in this pursuit, I gained, however, in another. The bank, upon which I had sprung, presented a continued walk of level turf, surrounded by vines, concealing the trees which supported them, and forming the most delightful bowers. Under these garlands I passed, and gathered the ripe clusters which dangled around; convinced that Noah had discovered a far superior beverage to that of the Tao-Sé. Whilst I was thus agreeably employed, it began to rain, and the earth to exhale a fresh reviving odour, highly grateful to one who had been so long confined to walls and waters. After breathing nothing but the essence of canals, and the flavours of the Rialto; after the jinglings of bells, and brawls of the gondoliers, imagine how agreeable it was, to scent the perfume of clover; to tread a springing herbage, and listen in silence to the flowers, pattering amongst the leaves. I staid so long amidst the vines, that it grew late before we rowed by the Mira, a village of palaces, whose courts and gardens, as magnificent as statues, terraces, and vases can make them, compose a grand, though far from a rural, prospect. Not being greatly delighted with such scenery, we staid no longer than our dinner required, and reached the Dolo, an hour before sun-set. Passing the great sluices, whose gates opened with a thundering noise, we continued our course along the peaceful Brenta, winding its broad, full stream through impenetrable copses, surmounted by tall waving poplars. Day was about to close when we reached Fiesso; and, it being a misty evening, I could scarcely distinguish the pompous façade of the Pisani palace. That, where we supped, looks upon a broad mass of foliage, which I contemplated with pleasure, as it sunk in the dusk. We walked a long while, under a pavilion stretched before the entrance, breathing the freshness of the wood after the shower, and hearing the drops trickle down the awning above our heads. The Galuzzi[58] sung some of her father Ferandini's compositions, with a fire, an energy, an expression, that, one moment, raised me to a pitch of heroism, and the next, dissolved me in tears. Her cheek was flushed with

---

57. Bonze derives from the Japanese term *bonzo* and in Europe referred to a member of the Buddhist religious orders of Japan and China.

58. Galuzzi Ferandini, daughter of Giovanni (1705–1793), Italian composer and vocal teacher. Among the operas he wrote were *Berenice* (1730), *Demofoonte* (1737), and *Diana Placata* (1758).

inspiration; her eyes glistened; the whole tone of her countenance was like that of a person rapt and inspired. I forgot both time and place, whilst she was breathing forth such celestial harmony. The night stole imperceptibly away, and morning dawned, before I awoke from my trance. I don't recollect ever to have passed an evening, which every circumstance conspired so much to improve. In general, my musical pleasures suffer terrible abatements from the phlegm and stupidity of my neighbourhood; but here, every one seemed to catch the flame, and to listen with reciprocal delight. The C—[59] threw quick around her the glancing fires of genius: and, what with the song of the Galuzzi, and those intellectual meteors, I scarcely knew to what element I was transported; and doubted, for several moments, whether I was not fallen into a celestial dream. I loathed the light of the morning star, which summoned me to depart; and, if I may express myself so poetically,

"cast many a longing, ling'ring look behind."

59. Beckford identified this person in the 1834 edition as "Marietta Cornaro," a member of the aristocratic Cornari family in Venice.

Letter XI.

The glow and splendor of the rising sun, for once in my life, drew little of my attention. I was too deeply plunged in my reveries, to notice the landscape which lay before me; and the walls of Padua presented themselves, some time, ere I was aware. At any other moment, how sensibly should I have been affected with their appearance! How many ideas of Antenor and his Trojans, would have thronged into my memory! but now, I regarded the scene with indifference; and passed many a palace, and many a woody garden, with my eyes rivetted to the ground. The first object that appeared upon lifting them up, was a confused pile of spires and cupolas, dedicated to blessed Saint Anthony,[60] who betook himself to the conversion of fish, after the heretics would lend no ear to his discourses. You are two well apprized of the veneration I have always entertained for this ingenious preacher, to doubt that I immediately repaired to his shrine, and offered up my little orizons before it. Mine was a disturbed spirit; and required all the balm of Saint Anthony's kindness, to appease it. Perhaps, you will say, I had better gone to bed, and applied myself to my sleepy friend, the pagan divinity. 'Tis probable that you are in the right; but I could not retire to rest, without venting some portion of effervescence, in sighs and supplications. The nave was filled with decrepit women and feeble children, kneeling by baskets of vegetables and other provisions; which, by good Anthony's interposition, they hoped to sell advantageously, in the course of the day. Beyond these, nearer the choir, and in a gloomier

---

60. St Anthony of Padua (1195–1231), Beckford's patron saint. He later built his own shrine for St. Anthony in Fonthill Abbey.

part of the edifice, knelt a row of rueful penitents, smiting their breasts, and lifting their eyes to heaven. Further on, in front of the dark recess, where the sacred relics are deposited, a few desperate, melancholy sinners lay prostrate. To these I joined myself, and fell down on the steps before the shrine. The sun-beams had not yet penetrated into this religious quarter; and the only light it received, proceeded from the golden lamps, which hung in clusters round the sanctuary. A lofty altar, decked with superstitious prodigality, conceals the holy pile from prophane glances. Those, who are profoundly touched with its sanctity, may approach, and, walking round, look through the crevices of the tomb, and rub their rosaries against the identical bones of St. Anthony; which, it is observed, exude a balsamic odour. But, supposing a traveller ever so heretical, I would advise him by no means to neglect this pilgrimage; since every part of the recess he visits, is decorated with the most exquisite sculptures. Sansovino and the best artists, have vied with each other in carving the alto-relievos of the arcade; which, for design and execution, would do honour to the sculptors of antiquity. Having observed these treasures, with much less exactness than they merited, and acted, perhaps, too capital a part amongst the devotees, I hastened to the inn, luckily, hard by, and one of the best I am acquainted with. Here I soon fell asleep, in defiance of sunshine. 'Tis true, my slumbers were not a little agitated. Saint Anthony had been deaf to my prayer, and I still found myself a frail, infatuated mortal. At five, I got up; we dined, and afterwards, scarcely knowing, nor much caring, what became of us, we strolled to the great hall of the town; an enormous edifice; as large as that of Westminster, but free from stalls, or shops, or nests of litigation. The roof, one spacious vault of brown timber, casts a solemn gloom, which was still encreased by the lateness of the hour, and not diminished by the wan light, admitted through the windows of pale blue glass. The size and shape of this colossal chamber, the coving of the roof, with beams, like perches for the feathered race, stretching across it; and, above all, the watery gleams that glanced through the casements, possessed my fancy with ideas of Noah's ark, and almost persuaded me I beheld that extraordinary vessel. The representation one sees of it in Scheutzer's *Physica Sacra*,[61] seems to be formed upon this very model; and, for several moments, I indulged the chimera, of imagining myself confined within its precincts. How

---

61. I.e. Johann Jacob Scheuchzer's *Jobi Physica Sacra* (1721).

willingly, could I but chuse my companions, would I encounter
a deluge, and float whole years, instead of months, upon the waves!
We remained walking to and fro in the ark, till the twilight faded
into total darkness. It was then full time to retire, as the guardian
of the place was by no means formed to divine our diluvian ideas.

Letter XII.

At Padua, I was too near the last, and one of the most celebrated abodes of Petrarch, to make the omission of a visit excuseable; had I not been in a disposition to render such a pilgrimage peculiarly pleasing. I set forwards from Padua after dinner, so as to arrive some time before sun-set. Nothing could be finer than the day; and I had every reason to promise myself a serene and delicious hour, before the sun might go down. I put the poems of Petrarch into my pocket; and, as my road lay chiefly through lanes, planted on either side with mulberries and poplars, from which vines hung dangling in careless festoons, I found many a bowering shade, where I sat, at intervals, to indulge my pensive humour, over some ejaculatory sonnet; as the pilgrim, on his journey to Loretto, reposes here and there, to offer his prayers and meditations to the Virgin. In little more than an hour and half, I found myself in the midst of the Euganean hills, and, after winding almost another hour amongst them, I got, before I was well aware, into the village of Arqua. Nothing can be more sequestered or obscure, than its situation. It had rather a deserted appearance; several of its houses being destitute of inhabitants, and crumbling into ruins. Two or three of them, however, exhibited antient towers, richly mantled with ivy, and surrounded with cypress, that retained the air of having once belonged to persons of consideration. Their present abandoned state, nourished the melancholy idea with which I entered the village. Could one approach the last retreat of genius, and not look for some glow of its departed splendor?

> "Dear to the pensive eye of fond regret,
> Is light still beaming from a sun that's set."

139

The residence of Petrarch at Arqua, is said to have drawn thither from Padua, the society of its more enlightened citizens. This city, whilst Petrarch lived in its neighbourhood, was engaged in rebellion against the Venetians; and Francis de Carrara,[62] the head of it, went often to Arqua, to consult Petrarch; when he found himself obliged to sue to Venice, for peace. The Poet was indeed deputed, upon this occasion, his ambassador to the state; as being a person, whose character and credit were most likely to appease its wrath. His success in this embassy, might, perhaps, have been some recompence for an employment he accepted with much regret, as it forced him from his beloved retirement. In a letter to one of his friends, written about this period of his life, he says: "I pass the greatest part of the year in the country, which I have always preferred to cities: I read; I write; I think: thus, my life, and my pleasures are like those of youth. I take pains to hide myself; but I cannot escape visits: it is an honour which displeases and wearies me. In my little house on the Euganean hills, I hope to pass my few remaining days in tranquillity, and to have always before my eyes my dead, or my absent, friends."—I was musing on these circumstances as I walked along the village, till a venerable old woman, seated at her door with her distaff in her hand, observing me, soon guessed the cause of my excursion; and offered to guide me to Petrarch's house. The remainder of my way was short, and well amused by my guide's enthusiastic expressions of veneration for the poet's memory; which, she assured me, she felt but in common with the other inhabitants of the village. When we came to the door of the house, we met the peasant, its present possessor. The old woman, recommending the stranger and his curiosity, to her neighbour's good offices, departed. I entered immediately, and ran over every room, which the peasant assured me, in confirmation of what I before learnt from better authority, were preserved, as nearly as they could be, in the state Petrarch had left them. The house and premises, having fortunately been transmitted from one enthusiast of his name to another, no tenants have been admitted, but under the strictest prohibition of making any change in the form of the apartments, or in the memorial relics belonging to the place: and, to say the truth, every thing I saw in it, save a few articles of the peasant's furniture in the kitchen, has an authentic appearance. Three of the rooms below stairs are particularly shewn, and they have nothing in them but what once belonged to the Poet. In one, which I think they call

---

62. Francesco da Carrara (d. 1393).

his parlour, is a very antique cupboard; where, it is supposed, he deposited some precious part of his literary treasure. The ceiling is painted in a grotesque manner. A niche in the wall contains the skeleton of his favourite cat, with a Latin epigram beneath, of Petrarch's composition. It is good enough to deserve being copied; but the lateness of the hour did not allow me time. A little room, beyond this, is said to have been his study: the walls of it, from top to bottom, are scribbled over with sonnets, and poetical eulogies on Petrarch, antient and modern: many of which are subscribed by persons of distinguished rank, and talents, Italians, as well as Strangers. Here, too, is the bard's old chair, and on it is displayed a great deal of heavy, ornamental carpentry; which required no stretch of faith to be believed the manufacture of the fourteenth century. You may be sure, I placed myself in it, with much veneration, and the most resigned assent to Mrs. Dobson's relation;[63] that Petrarch, sitting in this same chair, was found dead in his library, with one arm leaning on a book. Who could sit in Petrarch's chair, void of some effect? I rose not from it without a train of pensive sentiments and soft impressions; which I ever love to indulge. I was now led into a larger room, behind that I first saw; where, it is likely enough, the poet, according to the peasant's information, received the visits of his friends. Its walls were adorned with landscapes and pastoral scenes, in such painting as Petrarch himself might, and is supposed to have executed. Void of taste and elegance, either in the design or colouring, they bear some characteristic marks of the age to which they are, with no improbability, assigned; and, separate from the merit of exhibiting repeatedly the portraits of Petrarch and Laura, are a valuable sketch of the rude infancy of the art, where it rose with such hasty vigour to perfection. Having seen all that was left unchanged, in this consecrated mansion, I passed through a room, said to have been the Bard's bed-room, and stepped into the garden, situated on a green slope, descending directly from the house. It is now rather an orchard, than a garden; a spot of small extent, and without much else to recommend it, but that it once was the property of Petrarch. It is not pretended to have retained the form in which he left it. An agreeably wild and melancholy kind of view, which it commands over the Euganean hills, and which I beheld, under the calm glow of approaching sun-set, must often, at the same moment, have soothed the Poet's anxious feelings, and hushed his

---

63. Susannah Dobson (d. 1795), translator and author of *The Life of Petrarch* (1775).

active imagination, as it did my own, into a delicious repose. Having lingered here till the sun was sunk beneath the horizon, I was led a little way farther in the village, to see Petrarch's fountain. Hippocrene itself could not have been more esteemed by the Poet, than this, his gift, by all the inhabitants of Arqua. The spring is copious, clear, and of excellent water; I need not say with what relish I drank of it. The last religious act in my little pilgrimage, was a visit to the church-yard; where I strewed a few flowers, the fairest of the season, on the Poet's tomb; and departed for Padua by the light of the moon.

Letter XIII.

Immediately after breakfast, we went to Saint Justina's, a noble temple, designed by Palladio, and worthy of his reputation. The dimensions are vast, and the equal distribution of light and ornament, truly admirable. Upon my first entrance, the long perspective of domes above, and chequered marble below, struck me with surprize and pleasure. I roved about the spacious ailes for several minutes; then sat down under the grand cupola, and admired the beautiful symmetry of the building. Both extremities of the cross ailes are terminated by altars, and tombs of very remote antiquity, adorned with uncouth sculptures of the Evangelists, supported by wreathed columns of alabaster; round which, to my no small astonishment, four or five gawky, coarse fellows were waddling on their knees; persuaded, it seems, that this strange devotion would cure the rheumatism, or any other aches with which they were afflicted. You can have no conception of the ridiculous attitudes into which they threw themselves; nor the difficulty with which they squeezed along, between the middle column of the tomb, and those which surrounded it. No criminal in the pillory ever exhibited a more rueful appearance; no swine ever scrubbed itself more fervently than these infatuated lubbers. I left them hard at work; taking more exercise than had been their lot for many a day; and, mounting into the organ-gallery, listened to Turini's[64] music with infinite satisfaction. The loud harmonious tones of the instrument, filled the whole edifice; and, being repeated by the echoes of its lofty domes and arches, produced a wonderful effect. Turini, aware of this circumstance, adapts his compositions, with great intelligence, to the place; and makes his

64. A nephew of Bertoni, and worthy of his uncle. [Beckford's note.]

143

slave, the organ, send forth the most affecting long-protracted sounds, which languish in the air, and are some time a dying. Nothing can be more original than his style! deprived of sight by an unhappy accident, in the flower of his days, he gave up his entire soul to music, and scarcely exists but through its medium. When we came out of Saint Justina's, the azure of the sky and the softness of the air inclined us to think of some excursion. Where could I wish to go, but to the place in which I had been so delighted? Besides, it was proper to make the C. another visit; and proper to see the Pisani palace, which happily I had before neglected. All these proprieties considered, M. de R. accompanied me to Fiesso. The sun was just sunk when we arrived. The whole æther in a glow, and the fragrance of the citron alleys delightful. Beneath them I walked in the cool, till the Galuzzi began once more, her enchanting melody. She sung till the moon tempted the fascinating G—a,[65] and myself to stray on the banks of the Brenta. A profound calm reigned upon the woods and the waters, and moon-light added serenity, to a scene naturally peaceful. We listened to the faint murmurs of the leaves and the distant rural noises, observed the gleams that quivered on the river, and discovered a mutual delight in contemplating the same objects. We supped late: before the Galuzzi had repeated the airs which had most affected me, morning began to dawn.

September 8th. It was evening, and I was still asleep; not in a tranquil slumber, but at the mercy of fantastic visions. The want of sound repose, had thrown me into a feverish, impatient mood, that was alone to be subdued by harmony. Scarcely had I snatched some slight refreshment, before I flew to the great organ at St. Justina's, but tried, this time, to compose myself in vain. M. de R, finding my endeavours unsuccessful, proposed, by way of diverting my attention, that we should set out immediately for one of the Euganean hills about six or seven miles from Padua, at the foot of which some antique baths had been very lately discovered. I consented without hesitation, little concerned whither I went, or what happened to me, provided the scene was often shifted. The lanes and inclosures we passed in our road to the hills, appeared in all the gaiety that verdure, flowers, and sunshine could give them. But my pleasures were overcast, and I beheld every object, however chearful, through a dusky medium. Deeply engaged in conversation, distance made no impression; and we beheld the meadow, over which the ruins are scattered, lie before

---

65. I.e. Giustiniana, or Madame de Rosenberg.

us, when we still imagined ourselves several miles away. Had I
but enjoyed my former serenity, how agreeably would such a landscape have affected my imagination! How lightly should I not
have run over the herbage, and viewed the irregular shrubby hills,
diversified with clumps of cypress, verdant spots, and pastoral
cottages; such as Zuccarelli[66] loved to paint! No scene could be
more smiling than this which here presented itself, or answer, in
a fuller degree, the ideas I had formed of Italy. Leaving our carriage at the entrance of the mead, we traversed its flowery surface,
and shortly perceived among the grass, an oblong bason, encrusted
with pure white marble. Most of the slabs are large and perfect;
apparently brought from Greece, and still retaining their polished
smoothness. The pipes to convey the waters, are still discernible;
in short, the whole ground plan may be easily traced. Nothing
more remains: the pillars and arcades are fallen; and one or two
pedestals alone, vouch for their former existence. Near the principal bath, we remarked the platforms of several circular apartments, paved with mosaic, in a neat, simple taste, far from inelegant. Weeds have not yet sprung up amongst the crevices; and
the universal freshness of the ruin shews, that it has not been
long exposed. Theodoric is the prince to whom these structures
are attributed; and Cassiodorus, the prime chronicler of the
country, is quoted to maintain the supposition. My spirit was too
much engaged to make any learned parade, or to dispute upon a
subject, which I abandon, with all its glories, to calmer, and less
impatient minds. Having taken a cursory view of the ruins in the
mead, we ascended the hill which borders upon it, and surveyed
a prospect of the same nature, though in a more lovely and expanded style, than that which I beheld from Mosolente. Padua
crowns the landscape, with its towers and cupolas rising from a
continual grove; and, from the drawing I have seen, I should
conjecture that Damascus presents somewhat of a similar appearance. Taking our eyes off this extensive horizon, we turned
them to the fragments beneath our feet. These seem to announce
solidity and magnificence. The walls appear plainly composed of
the *opus reticulatum,* so universal in the environs of Naples. A
sort of terrace, with the bases of columns circling the mount, leads
me to imagine, here were formerly arcades and porticos, for enjoying the view; for, on the summit, I could trace no vestiges of
any considerable structure; and am therefore inclined to conclude,
that nothing more than a colonade surrounded the hill, leading

---

66. Francesco Zuccarelli (1702–1788), Italian painter.

perhaps to some slight fane, or pavilion, for the recreation of the bathers below. A profusion of aromatic flowers covered the slopes, and exhaled additional perfumes, as the sun declined, and the still hour approached, which was wont to spread over my mind a divine composure, and to restore the tranquillity, I might have lost in the day. But now, it diffused in vain its reviving coolness; and I remained, if possible, more sad and restless than before. To produce such a revolution, divine, how I must have been fascinated! and be not surprised at my repeating all the way, that pathetic sonnet of Petrarch:

> O giorno, o ora, o ultimo momento,
> O stelle congiurate a 'mpoverirme!
> O fido sguardo, or che volei tu dirme,
> Partend' io, per non esser mai contento?[67]

September 9th. You may imagine how I felt, when the hour of leaving Padua drew near. It happened to be a high festival, and mass celebrated at the grand church of Saint Anthony, with more than ordinary splendor. The music drawing us thither, we found every chapel twinkling with lights, and the choir fllled with a vapour of incense. Through its medium several cloth of gold figures discovered themselves, ministring before the altar, and acting their parts with a sacred pomposity, wonderfully imposing. I attended very little to their functions; but the plaintive tones of the voices and instruments, so consonant with my own feelings, melted me into tears, and gave me, no doubt, the exterior of exalted piety. Guadazni[68] sung amongst the other musicians, but seemed to be sinking apace into devotion and obscurity. The ceremony ended, I took leave of M. de R. with sincere regret, and was driven away to Vicenza. Of my journey I scarce know any more, than that the evening was cold and rainy, that I shivered and was miserable.

September 10th. The morning being overcast, I went, full of the spirit of Æschylus, to the Olympic theatre, and vented my evil temper in reciting some of the most tremendous verses of his furies. The august front of the scene and its three grand streets of fanes and palaces, inspired me with the lofty sentiments of the

---

67. *Rime e Trionfi*, No. CCCXXIX. "Oh day! Oh hour! Oh final moment! Oh stars conspiring to impoverish me! Oh faithful look! Now what did you want to tell me on my departure? I cannot be content any longer until I know."

68. Gaetano Guadagni (1725–1792), Italian male contralto singer. He had returned to Padua in 1777, but by this time he had changed his voice to a soprano and many complained of its shallow quality.

Grecian drama; but the dubious light, admitted through windows, scarce visible between the rows of statues which crown the entablature, sunk me into fits of gloom and sadness. I mused a long while in the darkest and most retired recess of the edifice; fancying I had penetrated into a real and perfect monument of antiquity, which till this moment had remained undiscovered. It is impossible to conceive a structure more truly classical, or to point out a single ornament which has not the best antique authority. I am not in the least surprised, that the citizens of Vicenza enthusiastically gave into Palladio's plan, and sacrificed large sums to erect so beautiful a model. When finished, they procured, at a vast expense, the representation of a Grecian tragedy, with its chorus and majestic decorations. You can enter into the rapture of an artist, who sees his fondest vision realized; and can easily conceive how it was, that Palladio esteemed this compliment, the most flattering reward. After I had given scope to the fancies which the scene suggested, we set out for Verona. The situation is striking and picturesque. A long line of battlement-walls, flanked by venerable towers, mounts the hills in a grand, irregular sweep, and incloses many a woody garden, and grove of slender cypresses. Beyond, rises an awful assembly of mountains; opposite to which, a fertile plain presents itself, decked with all the variety of meads and thickets, olive-grounds and vineyards. Amongst these our road kept winding, till we entered the city gate, and passed (the post knows how many streets and alleys in the way) to our inn, a lofty, handsome-looking building; but so full, that we were obliged to take up with an apartment on its very summit, open to all the winds, like the magic chamber Apuleius mentions; and commanding the roofs of half Verona. Here and there, a pine shot up amongst them, and the shady hills, terminating the perspective with their walls and turrets, formed a romantic scene. Placing our table in a balcony, to enjoy the prospect with greater freedom, we feasted upon fish from the Lago di Garda, and the delicious fruits of the country; grapes worthy of Canaan, and peaches, such as Eden itself might have gloried in producing. Thus did I remain, solacing myself; breathing the cool air, and remarking the evening tints of the mountains. Neither the paintings of Count this, nor the antiques of the Marquis t'other, could tempt me from my aerial situation: I refused hunting out the famous Paolos, scattered over the town, and sat like the owl in the *Georgics,*

Solis et occasum servans de culmine summo.[69]

69. Bk. I, 1. 402. "From some high point watching the setting of the sun."

Twilight drawing on, I left my haunt, and, stealing down stairs, enquired for a guide to conduct me to the amphitheatre; perhaps, the most entire monument of Roman days. The people of the house, instead of bringing me a quiet peasant, officiously delivered me up to an antiquary; one of those diligent, plausible young men, to whom, God help me! I have so capital an aversion. This sweet spark displayed all his little erudition, and flourished away upon cloacas and vomitoriums, with eternal fluency. He was very profound in the doctrine of conduits; and knew to admiration, how the filthiness of all the amphitheatre was disposed of: but perceiving my inattention, and having just grace enough to remark, that I chose one side of the street, when he preferred the other; and sometimes trotted, through despair, in the kennel, he made me a pretty bow, I tipped him half a crown; and, seeing the ruins before me, traversed a gloomy arcade, and emerged alone into the arena. A smooth turf carpets its surface, from which the spacious row of gradines rises to a majestic elevation. Four arches, with their simple doric ornament, alone remain of the grand circle, which once lifted itself above the highest seats of the amphitheatre; and, had it not been for gothic violence, this part of the structure would have equally resisted the ravages of time. Nothing can be more exact than the preservation of the gradines; not a block has sunk from its place; and whatever trifling injuries they may have received, have been carefully repaired. The two chief entrances are rebuilt with solidity, and closed by portals; no passage being permitted through the theatre, except at public shews and representations; sometimes, still given in the arena. When I paced slowly across it, silence reigned undisturbed amongst the awful ruins; and nothing moved, save the weeds and grasses which skirt the walls, and tremble with the faintest breeze. I liked the idea of being thus shut in one every side by endless gradines, abandoned to a stillness and solitude I was so peculiarly disposed to taste. Throwing myself upon the grass in the middle of the arena, I enjoyed the freedom of my situation; and pursued the last tracks of light, as they faded behind the solitary arches, which rise above the rest. Red and fatal were the tints of the western sky; the wind blew chill and hollow, and something more than common seemed to issue from the withering herbage on the walls. I started up; fled through a dark arcade, where water falls drop by drop; and arrived, panting, in the great square before the ruins. Directing my steps across it, I reached an antient castle; once inhabited by the Scaligeri, sovereigns of Verona. Hard by, appeared the ruins of a triumphal arch, which most antiquaries ascribe to Vitruvius, enriched with delicate scroles, and flowery ornaments. I could have passed half an hour very agreeably in copying these elegant sculptures; but night covering them with her shades, I returned home through the Corso; where the out-lines of several palaces, designed by Michael San Michele attracted my attention. But it was too dusky to examine their details.

September 11th. Traversing once more the grand piazza, and casting a last glance upon the amphitheatre, we passed under a lofty arch which terminates the perspective, and left Verona by a wide, airy street, commanding, whenever you look back, a striking scene of towers, cypress, and mountains. The country, between this beautiful town and Mantua, presents one continued grove of dwarfish mulberries, among which start up innumerable barren hills. Now and then a knot of poplars diversify their craggy summits; and, sometimes, a miserable shed. Mantua itself rises out of a morass formed by the Mincio; whose course, in most places, is so choaked up with reeds, as to be scarcely discernible. It requires a creative imagination, to discover any charms in such a prospect; and a strong prepossession, not to be disgusted with the scene where Virgil was born. For my own part, I approached this neighbourhood with proper deference, and began to feel the God; but finding no tufted tree on which I could suspend my lyre, or verdant bank which invited to repose, I abandoned poetry, and entered the city in despair. The beating of drums, and the sight of German whiskers, finished, what croaking frogs and stagnant ditches had begun. Every classic idea being scared by such sounds, and such objects, I dined in dudgeon; and refused stirring out, till late in the evening. A few paces from the town, stand the remains of the palace, where the Gonzagas[70] formerly resided. This, I could not resist looking at; and was amply rewarded. Several of the apartments, adorned by the bold pencil of Julio Romano,[71] merit the most exact attention; and the grotesque with which the stucco ceilings are covered, equal the celebrated loggios of the Vatican. I don't recollect ever having seen these elegant designs engraven; and believe, it would be perfectly worth the pains of some capital artist to copy them. Being in fresco, upon damp, neglected walls, each year diminishes their number; and every winter moulders some beautiful figure away. The subjects, mostly

70. An Italian noble family named after the town of Gonzaga.
71. Giulio Romano (1499–1546), Italian painter and architect who became head of the Roman school of painting after Raphael.

from antique fables, are treated with all the purity and gracefulness of Raffaelle. Amongst others, the story of Polypheme is very
conspicuous. Acis appears, reclined with his beloved Galatea, on
the shore of the ocean; whilst their gigantic enemy, seated above,
on the brow of Ætna, seems, by the paleness and horrors of his
countenance, to meditate some terrible revenge. When it was too
late to examine the paintings any longer, I walked into a sort of
court, or rather garden, which had been decorated with fountains
and antique statues. Their fragments still remain, amongst beds of
weeds and flowers; for every corner of the place is smothered
with vegetation. Here, nettles grow thick and rampant; there,
tuberoses and jessamines climb around mounds of ruins; which,
during the elegant reign of the Gonzagas, led to grottos and subterraneous apartments, concealed from vulgar eyes, and sacred to
the most refined enjoyments. I gathered a tuberose, that sprung
from a shell of white marble, once trickling with water, now, half
filled with mould; and carrying it home, shut myself up for the
rest of the night, inhaled its perfume, and fell a dreaming.

September 12th. A shower having fallen, the air was refreshed,
and the drops still glittered upon the vines, through which our
road conducted us. Three or four miles from Mantua, the scene
changed to extensive grounds of rice, and meads of the tenderest
verdure watered by springs, whose frequent meanders gave to the
whole prospect the appearance of a vast green carpet, shot with
silver. Further on, we crossed the Po; and, passing Guastalla, entered a woody country, full of inclosures and villages; herds feeding in the meadows, and poultry parading before every wicket.
The peasants were busied in winnowing their corn; or, mounted
upon the elms and poplars, gathering the rich clusters from the
vines, that hang streaming in braids from one branch to another.
I was surprized to find myself already in the midst of the vintage;
and to see every road crouded with carts and baskets, bringing
it along: you cannot imagine a pleasanter scene. Round Reggio
it grew still more lively; and, on the other side of that agreeable
little city, I remarked many a cottage, that Tityrus[72] might have
inhabited, with its garden, and willow hedge in flower, swarming
with bees. Our road, the smoothest conceivable, led us, perhaps
too rapidly, by so chearful a landscape. I caught glimpses of fields
and copses, as we fled along, that could have afforded me amusement for hours; and orchards on gentle acclivities, beneath which,
I could have walked till evening. The trees literally bent under

---

72. A fictitious monster said to be a cross between a sheep and a goat.

their loads of fruit, and innumerable ruddy apples lay scattered upon the ground:

Strata jacent passim sua quæque sub arbore poma.[73]

Beyond these rich masses of foliage, to which the sun lent additional splendor, at the utmost extremity of the pastures, rose the irregular ridge of the Appenines; whose deep blue presented a striking contrast to the glowing colours of the foreground. I fixed my eyes on the chain of distant mountains; and indulged, as usual, my conjectures, of what was going forwards on their summits; of those who tended goats on the edge of the precipice; traversed, at this moment, the dark thickets of pine; and passed their lives in yonder sheds, contented and unknown. Such were the dreams that filled my fancy, and kept it incessantly employed, till it was dusk, and the moon began to shew herself; the same moon which, but a few days ago, had seen me so happy at Fiesso. Her soft light reposed upon the meads, that had been newly mown; and the shadows of tall poplars were cast aslant them. I left my carriage; and, running into the dim haze, abandoned myself to the recollection it inspired. During an hour, I kept continually flying forwards; bounding from inclosure to inclosure, like a hunted antelope; and forgetting where I was; or whither I was going. One sole idea filled my mind, and led me on with such heedless rapidity, that I stumbled over stones and bushes, and entangled myself in every wreath of vines which opposed my progress. At length, having wandered where chance, or the wildness of my fancy led, till the lateness of the evening alarmed me, I regained the chaise as fast as I could, and arrived between ten and eleven at the place of my destination.

Sept. 13th. Having but a moment or two at liberty, I hurried early in the morning to the palace; and entered an elegant Ionic court, with arcades of the whitest stone, through which I caught peeps of a clear blue sky, and groves of cypresses. Some few good paintings still adorn the apartments, but the best part of the collection has been disposed of, for a hundred thousand sequins; amongst which was that inestimable picture, the Notte of Corregio. An excellent copy remains, and convinced me the original was not undeservedly celebrated. None but the pencil of Corregio ever designed such graceful angels; nor imagined such a pearly dawn to cast around them. Ten thousand times, I dare say, has the

---

73. Virgil, *Bucolics,* Ec. VII, 1. 54. "The apples lie scattered here and there under the tree."

subject of the nativity been treated, and as many painters have failed in rendering it so pleasing. The break of day, the first smiles of the celestial infant, and the truth, the simplicity, of every countenance, cannot be too warmly admired. In the other rooms, no picture gave me more pleasure than Jacob's vision, by Domenico Feti.[74] I gazed several minutes at the grand confusion of clouds and seraphim descending around the patriarch; and wished for a similar dream.

Having spent the little time I had remaining in contemplating this object, I hastened from the palace, and left Modena. We traversed a champain country in our way to Bologna, whose richness and fertility encreased, in proportion as we drew near that celebrated mart of lap-dogs and sausages. A chain of hills commands the city, variegated with green inclosures and villas innumerable, almost every one of which has its grove of chestnuts and cypresses. On the highest acclivity of this range, appears the magnificent convent of Madonna del Monte, embosomed in wood, and joined to the town by a corridor, a league in length. This vast portico ascending the steeps, and winding amongst the thickets, sometimes concealed and sometimes visible, produces an effect wonderfully grand and singular. I longed to have mounted the height by so extraordinary a passage; and hope, on some future day, to be better acquainted with Saint Maria del Monte. At present, I thought of little else, to say truth, but what I had seen at Fiesso; and, what I was to hear at Lucca. The anxiety inspired by the one, and impatience by the other, rendered me shamefully insensible to the merit of Bologna; where I passed near two hours, and of which I can add nothing, but that it is very much out of humour at this present moment; an earthquake and cardinal Buoncompagni[75] having disarranged both land and people. For half a year, the ground continued trembling; and, for these last months, the legate and senators have grumbled and scratched incessantly; so that, between natural and political commotions, the Bolognese must have passed an agreeable summer. Such a report of the situation of things, you may suppose, was not likely to retard my journey: I put off delivering my letters to another opportunity; ran up a tall, slender tower, as high as the Campanile di San Marco, by way of exercise; and proceeded, immediately

---

74. Feti (1589–1624) had achieved a considerable reputation in Italy as a painter of Biblical and mythological subjects.

75. Buoncompagni was the name of a famous Italian noble family to which Gregory XIII belonged. They had presided for years in Bologna.

after dinner, towards the mountains. We were soon in the midst of crags, and stony channels, that stream with ten thousand rills in the winter season; but, during the summer months, reflect every sun-beam, and harbour half the scorpions in the country. For many a toilsome league, our prospect consisted of nothing but dreary hillocks, and intervening wastes, more barren and mournful than those to which Mary Magdalene retired. Sometimes a crucifix, or chapel, peeped out of the parched fern and grasses, with which these desolated fields are cloathed; and now and then, we met a goggle-eyed pilgrim, trudging along, and staring about him, as if he waited only for night and opportunity to have additional reasons for hurrying to Jerusalem. During three or four hours that we continued ascending, the scene increased in sterility and desolation; but, at the end of our second post, the landscape began to alter for the better: little green valleys at the base of tremendous steeps, discovered themselves; scattered over with oaks, and freshened with running waters, which the nakedness of the impending rocks set off to advantage. The sides of the cliffs in general consist of rude mis-shapen masses; but their summits are smooth and verdant, and continually browsed by herds of white goats, which were gamboling on the edge of the precipices, as we passed beneath. I joined one of these frisking assemblies, whose shadows were stretched by the setting sun, along the level herbage. There I sat a few minutes, whilst they shook their beards at me, and tried to scare me with all their horns; but I was not to be frightened, and would offer up my adorations to departing day, in spite of their caperings. Being tired with skipping and butting at me in vain, the whole herd trotted away; and I after them. They led me a rare dance from crag to crag, and from thicket to thicket. It was growing dusky apace, and wreaths of smoke began to ascend from the mysterious depths of the valleys. I was ignorant what monster inhabited such retirements, so gave over my pursuit, lest some Polypheme or other might make me repent it. I looked around, the carriage was out of sight; but hearing the neighing of horses at a distance, I soon came up with them, and mounted another rapid ascent; from whence an extensive tract of cliff and forest-land was discernible. The rocks here formed a spacious terrace; along which I continued surveying the distant groves, and marking the solemn approach of night. The sky was hung with storms, and a pale moon seemed to advance with difficulty amongst broken and tempestuous clouds. It was an hour to reap plants with brazen sickles, and to meditate upon revenge. A chill wind blew from the highest peak of the Appenines, inspiring evil; and making a dismal rustle amongst the woods of chestnuts that hung on the mountains' side, through which we were forced to pass. I never heard such fatal murmurs; nor felt myself so gloomily disposed. I walked out of the sound of the carriage, where the glimmering moon-light prevailed, and began interpreting the language of the leaves, not greatly to my own advantage, or that of any being in the universe. I was no prophet of good, but full of melancholy bodings, and something that bordered upon despair. Had I but commanded an oracle, as antient visionaries were wont, I should have thrown whole nations into dismay. How long I continued in this strange temper, I cannot pretend to say, but believe it was midnight before we emerged from the oracular forest, and saw faintly before us the huts of Lognone, where we were to sleep. This blessed hamlet is suspended on the brow of a bleak mountain, and every gust that stirs, shakes the whole village to its foundations. At our approach, two hags stalked forth with lanterns, and invited us with a grin, which I shall always remember, to a dish of mustard and crows gizzards; a dish I was more than half afraid of tasting, lest it should change me to some bird of darkness, condemned to mope eternally on the black rafters of the cottage. After repeated supplications, we procured a few eggs, and some faggots to make a fire. Its blaze gave me courage to hear the hallow blasts, that whistled in the crevices; and, pitching my bed in a warm corner, I soon fell asleep; and forgot all my cares and inquietudes.

Sept. 14th. The sun had not been long above the horizon, before we set forwards upon a craggy pavement, hewn out of the rough bosom of cliffs and precipices. Scarce a tree was visible; and the few that presented themselves, began already to shed their leaves. The raw nipping air of the deserts, with difficulty spares a blade of vegetation; and in the whole range of these extensive eminences, I could not discover a single corn-field, or pasture. Inhabitants, you may guess, there were none: I would defy even a Scotch highlander to find means of subsistence in so rude a soil. Towards mid-day, we had surmounted the dreariest part of our journey, and began to perceive a milder landscape. The climate improved, as well as the prospect; and, after a continual descent of several hours, we saw groves and villages in the dips of the hills; and met a string of mules and horses laden with fruit. I purchased some figs and peaches from this little caravan, and, spreading my repast upon a bank, basked in the sunshine, and gathered large spikes

of lavender in full bloom. Continuing our route, we bid adieu
to the realms of poverty and barrenness, and entered a cultivated
vale, shaded by woody acclivities. Amongst these we wound along
—the peasants singing upon the hills, and driving their cattle to
springs by the road's side; near one of which we dined, in a
patriarchal manner; and, afterwards, pursued our course, through
a grove of taper cypresses, waving with the cool gales of the evening. The heights were suffused with a ruddy glow, proceeding
from the light pink clouds which floated on the horizon. No others
were to be seen. All nature seemed in a happy, tranquil state; the
herds penned in their folds, and every rustic going to repose. I
shared the general calm, for the first time this many a tedious
hour; and traversed the dales in peace, abandoned to flattering
hopes and gay illusions. The full moon shone propitiously upon
me, as I ascended a hill, and discovered Florence at a distance,
surrounded with gardens and terraces, rising one above another.
The serene moon-light on the pale grey tints of the olive, gave an
elysian, visionary appearance to the landscape. I never beheld so
mild a sky, nor such soft gleams: the mountains were veiled in
azure mists, which concealed their rugged summits; and the plains
in vapours, that smoothed their irregularities, and diffused a faint
aerial hue, to which no description can render justice. I could
have contemplated such scenery for hours, and was sorry when I
found myself shut up from it, by the gates of Florence. We passed
several lofty palaces of the true Tuscan order, with rustic arcades
and stout columns, whose solidity and magnificence were not
diminished by the shades of midnight. Whilst these grand masses
lay dark and solemn, the smooth flag-stone, with which every
street is paved, received a chequered gleam, and the Arno, the
brightest radiance. Though tired with my jumble over the Appen-
nines, I could not resist the pleasure of walking upon the banks
of so celebrated a river, and crossing its bridges; which still echoed
with music and conversation. Having gratified the first impulse
of curiosity, I returned to Vaninis, and slept as well as my impatience would allow, till it was time next morning (September
15th) to visit the gallery, and worship the Venus de Medicis. I
felt, upon entering this world of taste and elegance, as though I
could have taken up my abode in it for ever; but, confused with
the multitude of objects, I knew not where to turn myself, and
ran childishly by the ample ranks of sculptures; like a butterfly
in a parterre, that skims, before it fixes, over ten thousand flowers.
Having taken my course down one side of the gallery, I turned

the angle, and discovered another long perspective, equally stored
with prodigies of bronze and marble; paintings on the walls, on
the ceilings, in short, every where. A minute brought me, vast
as it was, to the extremity of this range; then, flying down a third,
adorned in the same delightful manner, I paused under the bust
of Jupiter Olympius; and began to reflect a little more maturely,
upon the company in which I found myself. Opposite, appeared
the majestic features of Minerva, breathing divinity; and Cybele,
the mother of the gods. I bowed low to the awful powers; but
seeing a black figure just by, whose colour and attitude seemed
to announce the deity of sleep, I made immediately up to it. You
know my fondness for this drowsy personage; and that it is not
the first time I have quitted the most splendid society for him.
I found him at present, of touchstone, with the countenance of
a towardly brat, sleeping ill, through indigestion. The artist had
not conceived such high ideas of the god as live in my bosom;
or else he never would have represented him with so little grace,
or dignity. Displeased at finding my favourite subject prophaned,
the lively transports of enthusiasm began in some degree to be
dissipated, and I felt myself calm enough to follow the herd of
guides and spectators, from chamber to chamber, and cabinet to
cabinet, without falling into errors of rapture and inspiration.
We were led slowly and moderately through the large rooms, containing the portraits of painters, good, bad, and indifferent, from
Raffaelle to Liotard; then into a museum of bronzes, which would
afford both amusement and instruction for years. To one who can
never behold an antient lamp or tripod, without the associations
of those who sacrificed on the one, and meditated by the other;
imagine what pleasure such a repository must have communicated.
When I had alarmed, not satisfied, my curiosity, by rapidly running over this multitude of candelabrums, urns, and sacred utensils; we entered a small, luminous apartment, surrounded with
cases, richly decorated, and filled with the most exquisite models
of workmanship, in bronze and various metals, classed in exact
order. Here are crowds of diminutive deities and tutelary lars,
to whom the superstition of former days attributed those midnight
murmurs, which were believed to presage the misfortunes of a
family. Amongst these now neglected images, are preserved a vast
number of talismans, cabalistic amulets, and other grotesque relics
of antient credulity. In the center of the room, I remarked a table,
beautifully formed of polished gems; and, hard by it, the statue
of a genius with his familiar serpent, and all his attributes; the

guardian of the treasured antiquities. From this chamber we were conducted into another, which opens to that part of the gallery, where the busts of Adrian and Antinous are placed. Two pilasters, delicately carved in trophies and clusters of antient armour, stand on each side the entrance; within, are several perfumed cabinets of miniatures, and a single column of oriental alabaster about ten feet in heighth,

> lucido, e terfo, e bianco, più che latte.[76]

I put my guide's patience to the proof, by remaining much longer than any one else ever did, in admiring the pillar, and rummaging the drawers of the cabinets. At last the musk, with which they are impregnated, obliged me to desist; and I moved on to a suite of saloons, with low arched roofs, glittering with arabesque, in azure and gold. Several medallions appear amongst the wreaths of foliage, tolerably well painted, with representations of splendid feasts and tournaments; for which Florence was once so famous. A vast collection of small pictures, most of them Flemish, covers the walls of these apartments. But nothing struck me more than a Medusa's head by that surprizing genius Leonardo da Vinci. It appears just severed from the body, and cast on the damp pavement of a cavern: a deadly paleness covers the countenance, and the mouth exhales a pestilential vapour; the snakes, which fill almost the whole picture, beginning to untwist their folds; one or two seemed already crept away, and crawling up the rock in company with toads and other venomous reptiles. The colouring of these disgustful objects is faithful to a great degree; the effect of light, prodigious; the whole so masterly, that I could not help entering into this description, though I fear to little purpose; as words, at best, convey but a weak idea of objects addressed to the sight alone. Here are a great many Polemburgs; one, in particular, the strangest I ever beheld. Instead of those soft scenes of woods and waterfalls, he is in general so fond of representing, he has chosen for his subject, Virgil ushering Dante into the regions of eternal punishment, amidst the ruins of flaming edifices, that glare across the infernal waves. These mournful towers harbour innumerable shapes, all busy in preying upon the damned. One capital devil, in the form of an enormous lobster, seems very strenuously employed in mumbling a miserable mortal; who sprawls, though in vain, to escape from his claws. This perfor-

---

76. "Polished and clear, and whiter than milk itself."

mance, whimsical as it is, retains all that softness of tint, and delicacy of pencil, for which Polemburg is renowned. Had not the subject so palpably contradicted the execution, as to become remarkable, I should have passed it over, like a thousand more, and brought you immediately to the Tribune. I dare engage our sensations were similar upon entering this apartment, and beholding such a circle of celestials. Need I say I was enchanted, the moment I set my feet within it, and saw full before me the Venus de Medicis? The warm ivory hue of the original marble, is a beauty no copy has ever imitated; and the softness of the limbs exceeded the liveliest idea I had formed to myself of their perfection. Their symmetry every artist is acquainted with; but do you recollect a faint ruddy cast in the hair; which admirably relieves the whiteness of the forehead? This circumstance, though perhaps accidental, struck me as peculiarly charming: it increased the illusion, and helped me to imagine I beheld a breathing divinity. When I had taken my eyes reluctantly from this beautiful object, I cast them upon a Morpheus of white marble, who lies slumbering at the feet of the goddess, in the form of a graceful child. A dormant lion serves him for a pillow: two ample wings, carved with the utmost delicacy, are gathered under him; two others, budding from his temples, half concealed by a flow of lovely ringlets. His languid hands scarce hold a bunch of poppies; near him creeps a lizard, the companion of his cave. Nothing can be more just than the expression of sleep, in the countenance of the little divinity. His lion too, seems perfectly lulled, and rests his muzzle upon his fore paws, as quiet as a domestic mastiff. I contemplated the God with infinite satisfaction, till I felt an agreeable sleepiness steal over my senses, and should have liked very well to doze away a few hours by his side. My ill-humour, at seeing this deity so grossly sculptured in the gallery, was dissipated by the gracefulness of his appearance in the Tribune. I was now contented; for the artist (to whom the Lord give a fair seat in paradise!) had realized my ideas; and, if I may venture my opinion, sculpture never arrived to higher perfection; or, at the same time, kept more justly within its province. Sleeping figures, with me, always produce the finest illusion. I easily persuade myself, that I behold the very personage cast into the lethargic state, which is meant to be represented; and I can gaze whole hours upon them, with complacency. But when I see an archer, in the very act of discharging his arrow; a dancer, with one foot in the air; or a gladiator, extending his fist to all eternity; I grow tired, and ask, when will they perform what they are about? When will the bow twang? the foot come to the ground? or the fist meet its adversary? Such wearisome attitudes I can view with admiration; but never, with pleasure. The wrestlers, for example, in the same apartment, filled me with disgust: I cried out, For heaven's sake! give the throw, and have done. In taking my turn round the enchanted circle, I discovered still another Morpheus; stretched carelessly on a mantle, with poppies in his hands; but no wings grow from his temples, nor lion supports his head. A moth just issuing from his chrysolite, is the only being which seems to have felt his soporific influence; whereas the other god I have mentioned, may vaunt the glory of subduing the most formidable of animals. The morning was gone, before I could snatch myself from the Tribune. In my way home, I looked into the cathedral; an enormous fabric, inlaid with the richest marbles, and covered with stars and chequered work, like an old-fashioned cabinet. The architect seems to have turned his building inside out; nothing in art being more ornamented than the exterior, and few churches so simple within. The nave is vast and solemn, the dome amazingly spacious, with the high altar in its center, inclosed by a circular arcade near two hundred feet in diameter. There is something imposing in this decoration, as it suggests the idea of a sanctuary, into which none but the holy ought to penetrate. However prophane I might feel myself, I took the liberty of entering, and sat myself down in a niche. Not a ray of light reaches this sacred inclosure, but through the medium of narrow windows, high in the dome, and richly painted. A sort of yellow tint predominates, which gives additional solemnity to the altar, and paleness to the votary before it. I was sensible of the effect, and obtained at least the colour of sanctity. Having remained some time in this pious hue, I returned home, and feasted upon grapes and ortolans with great edification; then walked to one of the bridges across the Arno, and surveyed the hills at a distance, purpled by the declining sun. Its mild gleams tempted me to the garden of Boboli, which lies behind the Palazzo Pitti, stretched out on the side of a mountain. I ascended terrace after terrace, robed by a thick underwood of bay and myrtle, above which rise several nodding towers, and a long sweep of venerable wall, almost entirely concealed by ivy. You would have been enraptured with the broad masses of shade and dusky alleys, that opened as I advanced, with white statues of fawns and sylvans glimmering amongst them; some of which pour water into sarcophagi of the purest marble, covered

with antique relievos. The capitals of columns and antient friezes,
are scattered about, as seats. On these I reposed myself, and looked
up to the cypress-groves spiring above the thickets; then, plunging into their retirements, I followed a winding path, which led
me by a series of steep ascents, to a green platform, overlooking
the whole extent of wood, with Florence deep beneath, and the
tops of the hills which encircle it, jagged with pines; here and
there, a convent, or villa, whitening in the sun. This scene extends
as far as the eye can reach. Still ascending, I attained the brow of
the mountain, and had nothing but the fortress of Belvedere, and
two or three open porticos above me. On this elevated situation,
I found several walks of trellis-work, cloathed with luxuriant
vines, that produce, to my certain knowledge, the most delicious
clusters. A colossal statue of Ceres, her hands extended in the act
of scattering fertility over the prospect, crowns the summit; where
I lingered, to mark the landscape fade, and the bright skirts of the
western clouds die gradually away. Then descending, alley after
alley, and bank after bank, I came to the orangery in front of the
palace, disposed in a grand amphitheatre, with marble niches relieved by dark foliage, out of which spring tall aerial cypress. This
spot brought the scenery of an antique, Roman garden full into
my mind. I expected every instant to be called to the table of
Lucullus[77] hard by, in one of the porticos, and to stretch myself
on his purple triclinias; but waiting in vain for a summons, till
the approach of night, I returned delighted with a ramble, that
had led me so far into antiquity.

Friday, September 16th. My impatience to hear Pacchierotti,
called me up with the sun. I blessed a day which was to give me
the greatest of musical pleasures, and travelled gayly towards
Lucca, along a fertile plain, bounded by rocky hills, and scattered
over with towns and villages. We passed Pistoia in haste, and,
about three in the afternoon, entered the Lucchese territory, by
a clean paved road, which runs through some of the pleasantest
copses imaginable, bordered with variety of heaths and broom,
in blossom. Sometimes it conducted us down slopes, overgrown
with shrubby chesnuts and arbor vitae; sometimes, between
groves of cypress and pines laden with cones: a red soil peeping
forth from the vegetation, adds to the richness of the landscape,
which swells, all the way, into gentle acclivities; and, round the
town, spreads into mountains, green to their very summits, and

---

77. Lucius Licinius Lucullus (c. 110–56 B.C.), Roman general.

diversified with gardens and palaces. A more pleasing scenery can with difficulty be imagined. I was quite charmed with beholding it, as I knew very well the opera would keep me a long while, chained down in its neighbourhood. Happy for me, that the environs of Lucca were so beautiful; since I defy almost any city to contain more ugliness within its walls. Narrow streets and dismal alleys; wide gutters and cracked pavements; every body in black, like mourners for the gloom of their habitations, which however are large and lofty enough of conscience; but, having all grated windows, they convey none but dark, and dungeon-like ideas. My spirits fell many degrees upon entering this sable capital; and when I found Friday was meagre day, in every sense of the word, with its inhabitants, and no opera to be performed, I grew terribly out of humour, and shut myself up in a chamber of the inn; which, to compleat my misfortune, was crowded with human lumber. Instead of a delightful symphony, I heard nothing for some time but the clatter of plates and the swearing of waiters. Amongst the number of my tormentors was a whole Genoese family of distinction; very fat and sleek, and terribly addicted to the violin. Hearing of my fondness for music, they speedily got together a few scrapers, and began such an academia, as drove me to one end of the room, whilst they possessed the other. The hopes and heir of the family, a coarse chubby dolt of about eighteen, played out of all time, and, during the intervals of repose he gave his elbow, burst out into a torrent of common-place, which compleated, you may imagine, my felicity. Pacchierotti, whom they all worshipped in their heavy way, sat silent the while in a corner; the second Soprano warbled, not absolutely ill, at the harpsichord; whilst the old lady, young lady, and attendant females, kept ogling him with great perseverance. Those who could not get in, squinted through the crevices of the door. Abbés and greyhounds were fidgetting continually about. In short, I was so worried, that, pleading head-aches and lassitudes, I escaped about ten o'clock, and shook myself, when I got safe into my apartment, like a spaniel just fresh from a dripping copse.

Letter XIV.

You ask how I pass my time. Generally upon the hills, in wild spots where the arbutus flourishes; from whence I may catch a glimpse of the distant sea; my horse tied to a cypress, and myself cast upon the grass, like Palmarin of Oliva,[78] with a tablet and pencil in my hand, a basket of grapes by my side, and a crooked stick to shake down the chesnuts. I have bidden adieu, several days ago, to the dinners and glories of the town, to visits and conversationes, and only come thither in an evening, just time enough for the grand march which precedes Pacchierotti in *Quinto Fabio.* Sometimes he accompanies me in my excursions, to the utter discontent of the Lucchese, who swear I shall ruin their opera, by leading him such confounded rambles amongst the mountains, and exposing him to the inclemency of winds and showers. One day, they made a vehement remonstrance, but in vain; for the next, away we trotted over hill and dale, and stayed so late in the evening, that cold and hoarseness were the consequence. The whole republic was thrown into a commotion, and some of its prime ministers deputed to harangue Pacchierotti, upon the rides he had committed. Billingsgate never produced such furious orators. Had the safety of their mighty state depended upon this imprudent excursion, they could not have vociferated with greater violence. You know I am rather energetic, and, to say truth, I had very near got into a scrape of importance, and drawn down the execrations of the Gonfalonier and all his council upon my head, in defending him, and in openly declaring our intention of taking, next morning, another ride over the rocks, and absolutely losing ourselves in the clouds, which veil their acclivities. These threats

---

78. The hero of *Palmerin de Oliva* (1511), a Renaissance romance of chivalry.

162

were put into execution, and, yesterday, we made a tour of about
thirty miles upon the high lands, and visited a variety of castles
and palaces. The Conte Nobili conducted us, a noble Lucchese,
but born in Flanders, and educated at Paris. He possesses the
greatest elegance of imagination, and a degree of sensibility, rarely
met with upon our gross planet. The way did not appear tedious
in such company. The sun was tempered by light clouds, and a
soft autumnal haze rested upon the hills, covered with shrubs and
olives. The distant plains and forests appeared tinted with deep
blue; and I am now convinced the azure so prevalent in Velvet
Breughel's landscapes, is not exaggerated. After riding for six or
seven miles along the cultivated levels, we began to ascend a
rough slope, overgrown with chesnuts; here and there, some vines
streaming in garlands displayed their clusters. A great many loose
fragments and stumps of antient pomegranates perplexed our
route; which continued, turning and winding through this sort
of wilderness, till it opened on a sudden to the side of a lofty
mountain covered with tufted groves; amongst which hangs the
princely castle of the Garzonis, on the very side of a precipice.
Alcina[79] could not have chosen a more romantic situation. The
garden lies extended beneath, gay with flowers, and glittering
with compartments of spar; which, though in no great purity of
taste, has an enchanted effect, for the first time. Two large marble
basons, with *jet d'eaux* seventy feet in height, divide the parterres; from the extremity of which rises a rude cliff, shaded with
firs and ilex, and cut into terraces. Leaving our horses at the
great gate of this magic inclosure, we passed through the spray
of the fountains, and, mounting an almost endless flight of steps,
entered an alley of oranges, and gathered ripe fruit from the trees.
Whilst we were thus employed, the sun broke from the clouds,
and lighted up the vivid greens of the vegetation; at the same
time spangling the waters, which pour copiously down a succession of rocky terraces, and sprinkle the impending citron-trees
with perpetual dew. These streams issue from a chasm in the cliff,
surrounded by cypresses, which conceal, by their thick branches,
some pavilions with baths. Above arises a colossal statue of Fame,
boldly carved, and in the very act of starting from the precipices.
A narrow path leads up to the feet of the goddess, on which I
reclined; whilst a vast column of water arched over my head, and
fell, without even wetting me with its spray, into the depths below.

---

79. The witch in *Orlando Furioso*. Beckford had in mind can. VI, st. XXXV,
which refers to Alcina's "mansion seated by the sea."

I could with difficulty prevail upon myself to abandon this cool recess, which the fragrance of bay and orange, extracted by constant showers, rendered uncommonly luxurious. At last, I consented to move on, through a dark walk of ilex, which, to the credit of Signior Garzoni be it spoken, is suffered to grow as wild, and as forest-like, as it pleases. This grove is suspended on the mountain side, whose summit is cloathed with a boundless wood of olives, and forms, by its azure colour, a striking contrast with the deep verdure of its base. After resting a few moments in the shade, we proceeded to a long avenue (bordered by aloes in bloom, forming majestic pyramids of flowers thirty feet high) which led us to the palace. This was soon run over. Then, mounting our horses, we wound amongst sunny vales, and inclosures with myrtle hedges, till we came to a rapid steep. We felt the heat most powerfully in ascending it, and were glad to take refuge under a bower of vines, which continues for miles along its summit, almost without interruption. These arbours afforded us both shade and refreshment: I fell upon the clusters, which formed our ceiling, like a native of the north, unused to such luxuriance; like one of those Goths, which Gray so poetically describes, who

> Scent the new fragrance of the breathing rose,
> And quaff the pendant vintage as it grows.[80]

I wish you had journeyed with us under this fruitful canopy, and observed the partial sunshine through its transparent leaves, and the glimpses of blue sky, it every now and then admitted. I say only, every now and then; for, in most places, a sort of verdant gloom prevailed, exquisitely agreeable in so hot a day. But such luxury did not last, you may suppose, for ever. We were soon forced from our covert, and obliged to traverse a mountain, exposed to the sun, which had dispersed every cloud, and shone with intolerable brightness. On the other side of this extensive eminence, lies an agreeable hillock, surrounded by others, woody and irregular. Wide vineyards and fences of Indian corn lay between, across which the Conte Nobili conducted us to his house, where we found a very comfortable dinner prepared. We drank the growth of the spot, and defied Constantia and the Cape to exceed it. Afterwards, retiring into a wood of the Marchese Mansi, with neat pebble walks and trickling rivulets, we sipped coffee, and loitered till sun-set. It was then time to return: the dews began to

---

80. ll. 56–57 of Gray's fragment "The Alliance of Education and Government."

fall, and the mists to rise from the valleys. The profound calm and silence of evening, threw us all three into our reveries. We went pacing along heedlessly, just as our horses pleased, without hearing any sound but their steps. Between nine and ten we entered the gates of Lucca. Pacchierotti coughed, and half its inhabitants wished us at the devil. I think now I have detained you long enough with my excursions; you must require a little repose; for my own part, I am heartily tired. I intended to say some things about certain owls, amongst other grievances, I am pestered with in this republic; but shall cut them all short, and wish you good night; for the opera is already begun, and I would not miss the first, glorious recitative for the empire of Trebizond.[81]

---

81. A city in Turkey located near the southeastern angle of the Black Sea.

Letter XV.

No sooner were we beyond the gates, than we found ourselves in narrow roads, shut in by vines and grassy banks of canes and oziers, rising high above our carriage, and waving their leaves in the air. Through the openings, which sometimes intervene, we discovered a variety of hillocks, cloathed with shrubberies and verdure; ruined towers looking out of the bushes: not one without a romantic tale attending it. This sort of scenery lasted till, passing the baths, we beheld Pisa, rising from an extensive plain, the most open we had as yet seen in Italy, crossed by an aqueduct. We were set down immediately before the Duomo, which stands insulated in a verdant opening, and is by far the most curious and highly-finished edifice my eyes ever viewed. Don't ask of what shape, or architecture; it is almost impossible to tell, so great is the confusion of ornaments. The capitals of the columns and carving of the architraves, as well as the form of the arches, are evidently of Grecian design, but Gothic proportions. The dome gives the mass an oriental appearance, which helped to bewilder me; in short, I have dreamt of such buildings, but little thought they existed. On one side you survey the famous tower, as perfectly awry as I expected; on the other, the baptistery, a circular edifice, distinct from the church, and right opposite its principal entrance; crouded with sculptures, and topped by the strangest of cupolas. Having indulged my curiosity with this singular prospect for some moments, we entered the cathedral, and admired the stately columns of porphyry, and the rarest marbles, supporting a roof, which, like the rest of the building, shines with gold. A pavement of the brightest mosaic compleats its magnificence: all around are sculptures by M. Ang. Buonaroti, and paintings by the most dis-

166

tinguished artists. We examined them all, and then walked down the nave, and remarked the striking effect of the baptistery, seen in perspective, through the bronze portals, which you know, I suppose, are covered with relievos of the finest workmanship. These noble valves were thrown wide open, and we passed between to examine the alabaster fount in the baptistery, constructed after the primitive ritual, and exquisitely wrought. Many palm-trees appear amongst the carved work, which seem to indicate the former connexions of the Pisanese with Palestine. Our next object was the Campo Santo, which forms one side of the opening in which the cathedral is situated. The walls, and gothic tabernacle above the entrance, rising from a level turf, appear as fresh, as if built within the century, and, preserving a neat straw-colour, have the cleanliest effect imaginable. Our guide unlocking the gates, we entered a spacious cloister, forming an oblong quadrangle, inclosing the sacred earth of Jerusalem, conveyed thither about the period of the crusades, in the days of Pisanese prosperity. The holy mould produces a rampant crop of weeds; but none are permitted to spring from the pavement, which is entirely composed of tombs with slabs and monumental inscriptions, smoothly laid. Ranges of slender pillars, formed of the whitest marble and glistening in the sun, support the arcades, which are carved with innumerable stars and roses, partly gothic, and partly saracenial. Strange paintings of hell and the devil, mostly taken from Dante's rhapsodies, cover the walls of these fantastic galleries, attributed to the venerable Giotto,[82] and Bufalmacco,[83] whom Boccace mentions in his *Decamerone*. Beneath, along the base of the columns, rows of Pagan sarcophagi are placed, to my no small surprise; as I could not have supposed the Pisanese sufficiently tolerant to admit prophane sculptures within such consecrated precincts. However, there they are, as well as fifty other contradictory ornaments. I was quite seized by the strangeness of the place, and paced fifty times round and round the cloisters, discovering at every time, some odd novelty. When tired, I seated myself on a fair slab of *giallo antico,* that looked a little cleaner than its neighbours, (which I only mention to identify the precise point of view) and looking through the fillagreed covering of the arches, observed the domes of the cathedral,

---

82. Giotto di Bondone (c. 1267–1337), the Italian painter.

83. Cristofani Buonamico (1262–1340), Italian painter, nicknamed Buffalmacco by Boccaccio. In the *Decameron* he is mentioned in the third, sixth, and ninth tales of the eighth day and the third and fifth tales of the ninth day.

cupola of the baptistery, and roof of the leaning tower, rising
above the leads, and forming the strangest assemblage of pinnacles,
perhaps, in Europe. The place is neither sad, nor solemn; the
arches are airy; the pillars light; and there is so much caprice,
such an exotic look in the whole scene, that, without any violent
effort of imagination, one might imagine one's self in fairy land.
Every object is new; every ornament original: the mixture of
antique sarcophagi, with gothic sepulchres, compleats the vagaries
of the prospect, to which, one day or other, I think of returning,
to act a visionary part, hear visionary music, and commune with
sprites; for I shall never find in the whole universe besides, so
whimsical a theatre. It was between ten and eleven when we
entered the Campo Santo, and one o'clock struck, before I could
be persuaded to leave it; and 'twas the sun which then drove me
away; whose heat was so powerful, that all the inhabitants of Pisa
shewed their wisdom, by keeping within doors. Not an animal
appeared in the streets, except five camels laden with water, stalking along a range of garden walls, and pompous mansions, with
an awning before every door. We were obliged to follow their
steps, at least, a quarter of a mile, before we reached our inn. Ice
was the first thing I sought after, and when I had swallowed an
unreasonable portion, I began not to think quite so much of the
deserts of Africa, as the heat and the camels had induced me, a
moment ago. Early in the afternoon, we proceeded to Livourno,
through a wild tract of forest, somewhat in the style of our English
parks. The trees, in some places, formed such shady arbours, that
we could not resist the desire of walking beneath them, and were
well rewarded; for after struggling through a rough thicket, we
entered a lawn, hemmed in by oaks and chesnuts, which extends
several leagues along the coast, and conceals the prospect of the
ocean; but we heard its murmur. Nothing could be smoother or
more verdant, than the herbage, which was sprinkled with daisies
and purple crocuses, as in the month of May. I felt all the genial
sensations of spring steal into my bosom, and was greatly delighted upon discovering vast bushes of myrtle, in bloom. The
softness of the air, the sound of the distant surges, the evening
gleams, and repose of the landscape, quieted the tumult of my
spirits; and I experienced the calm of my instant hours. I lay
down in the open turf-walks between the shrubberies; listlessly
surveyed the cattle browsing at a distance, and the blue hills, that
rose above the foliage and bounded the view. During a few moments I had forgotten every care; but when I began to enquire

into my happiness, I found it vanish. I felt myself without those I love most, in situations they would have warmly admired; and, without them, these pleasant meads and woodlands were of little avail. On the contrary, they reminded me so strongly of their absence, that my joy was changed into tears. I looked earnestly at the distant hills, and sighed: I scattered the blossoms I had gathered, and cried out incessantly, Let us drive away. We had not left this woody region far behind, when the Fanalè[84] began to lift itself above the horizon; the Fanalè you have so often mentioned: the sky and ocean glowing with amber light, and the ships out at sea, appearing in a golden haze, of which we have no conception in our northern climates. Such a prospect, together with the fresh gales from the Mediterranean, charmed me: I hurried immediately to the port, and sat on a reef of rocks, listening to the waves, that broke amongst them.

---

84. A tower.

Letter XVI.

October 3d.

I went, as you would have done, to walk on the mole as soon as the sun began to shine upon it. Its construction you are no stranger to; therefore I think I may spare myself the trouble of saying more about it, except that the port which it embraces is no longer crouded. Instead of ten ranks of vessels, there are only three; and those consist chiefly of Corsican galleys, that look as poor and tattered as their masters. Not much attention did I bestow upon such objects; but, taking my seat at the extremity of the quay, surveyed the smooth plains of ocean, the coast scattered over with watch-towers, and the rocky isle of Gorgona, emerging from the morning mists, which still lingered upon the horizon. Whilst I was musing upon the scene, and calling up all that train of ideas before my imagination, which possessed your own upon beholding it, an antient figure, with a beard that would have suited a sea-god, stepped out of a boat, and, tottering up the steps of the quay, presented himself before me, with a basket in his hand. He staid dripping a few moments before he pronounced a syllable, and when he began his discourse, I was in doubt, whether I should not have moved off in a hurry; there was something so wan and singular in his countenance. Except this being, no other was visible, for a quarter of a mile at least. I knew not what strange adventure I might be upon the point of commencing; or what message I was to expect from the submarine divinities. However, after all my conjectures, the figure turned out to be no other than an old fisherman, who, having picked up a few large branches of red coral, offered them to sale. I eagerly made the purchase, and thought myself a favourite of Neptune; since he allowed me to acquire, for next to nothing, some of his most beautiful ornaments.

170

My bargain thus expeditiously finished, I ran along the quay with my basket of coral, and, jumping into a boat, was rowed back to the gate of the port. The carriage waited there: I filled it with jasmine, shut myself up in the shade of the green blinds, and was driven away at a rate that favoured my impatience. We bowled smoothly over the lawns, I attempted describing in my last letter, amongst myrtles in flower, that would have done honour to Juan Fernandes. Arrived at Pisa, I scarcely allowed myself a moment to revisit the Campo Santo; but, after taking my usual portion of ice and pomegranate-seeds, hurried on to Lucca as fast as the horses could carry me, threw the whole idle town into a stare by my speedy return, and gave myself up to *Q. Fabio.*

Next day (October 4th) was passed in running over my old haunts upon the hills, and bidding farewell to several venerable chesnuts, for which I had contracted a sort of friendship, by often experiencing their protection. I could not help feeling some melancholy sensations, when I turned round, the last time, to bid them adieu. Who knows but some dryad, inclosed within them, was conscious of my gratitude, and noted it down on the bark of her tree? It was late before I finished my excursion, and soon after I had walked as usual upon the ramparts, the opera began.

Letter XVII.

Florence, October 5th.

It was not without regret, that I forced myself from Lucca. We had all the same road to go over again that brought us to this important republic, but we broke down by way of variety. The wind was chill, the atmosphere damp, and clogged with unwholsome vapours, through which we were forced to walk for a league, whilst our chaise lagged after us. Taking shelter in a miserable cottage, we remained shivering and shaking, till the carriage was in some sort of order, and then proceeded so slowly, that we did not arrive at Florence till late in the evening. We found an apartment over the Arno prepared for our reception. The river, swollen with rains, roared like a mountain torrent. Throwing open my windows, I viewed its agitated course by the light of the moon, half concealed in stormy clouds, which hung above the fortress of Belvedere, and cast a lowering gleam over the hills, which rise above the town, and wave with cypress. I sat contemplating the effect of the shadows on the bridge, on the heights of Boboli, and the mountain covered with pale olive-groves, amongst which a convent is situated, till the moon sunk into the blackest quarter of the sky, and a bell began to toll. Its sullen sound filled me with sadness: I closed the casements, called for lights, ran to a harpsichord Vannini had prepared for me, and played somewhat in the strain of Jomelli's[85] *Miserere*.

October 6th. Every cloud was dispersed when I arose; the sunbeams glittered on the stream, and the purity and transparence of the æther, added new charms to the woody eminences around. Such was the clearness of the air, that even objects on the distant mountains were distinguishable. I felt quite revived by this ex-

---

85. Niccolò Jommelli (1714–1774), Neapolitan composer.

hilarating prospect, and walked in the splendor of sunshine to the porticos beneath the famous gallery, then to an antient castle, raised in the days of the republic, which fronts the grand piazza. Colossal statues and venerable terms are placed before it. On one side a fountain clung round with antic figures of bronze, by John of Bologna,[86] so admirably wrought as to hold me several minutes in astonishment. On the other, three lofty gothic arches, and, under one of them, the Perseus of Benvenuto Cellini raised on a pedestal, incomparably designed and executed; which I could not behold uninterested, since its author has ever occupied a distinguished place in my kalendar of genius. Having examined some groups of sculptures, by Baccio Bandinelli[87] and other mighty artists, I entered the court of the castle, dark and deep, as if hewn out of a rock; surrounded by a vaulted arcade, covered with arabesque ornaments, and supported by pillars, as uncouthly carved as those of Persepolis. In the midst appears a marble fount with an image of bronze, that looks quite strange and cabalistic. I leaned against it, to look up to the summits of the walls, which rise to a vast height; from whence springs a slender tower. Above, in the apartments of the castle, were preserved numbers of curious cabinets; tables of inlaid gems, and a thousand rarities, collected by the house of Medici, but exposed by the present sovereign of Tuscany to public sale. It was not without indignation, that I learnt this new mark of contempt, which the Austrians bestow on the memory of those illustrious patrons of the arts; whom, being unwilling to imitate, they affect to despise, as a race of merchants, whose example it would be abasing their dignity to follow. I could have staid much longer to enjoy the novelty and strangeness of the place; but it was right to pay some compliments of form. That duty over, I dined in peace and solitude, read over your letters, and repaired, as evening drew on, to the thickets of Boboli. What a serene sky! What mellowness in the tints of the mountains! A purple haze concealed the bases, whilst their summits were invested with saffron light, discovering every white cot, and every copse, that cloathed their declivities. The prospect widened as I ascended the terraces of the garden. After traversing many long alleys, brown with impending foliage, I emerged into a green opening on the brow of the hill, and seated myself under the statue of Ceres. From this high point I surveyed the mosaic cupolas

---

86. Giovanni Bologna, or Giambologna (1529–1608), a major figure in Italian sculpture.
87. Also known as Bartolommeo Bandinelli (1493–1560).

of the Duomo, its quaint turret, and one still more grotesque in its neighbourhood, built not improbably in the style of antient Etruria. Beyond this singular group of buildings, a plain stretches itself far and wide, scattered over with villas, gardens, and groves of pine and olive, quite to the feet of the mountains. After I had marked the sun's going down, I went, through a plat of vines hanging on the steeps, to a little eminence, round which the wood grows wilder and more luxuriant, and the cypresses shoot up to a surprising elevation. The pruners have spared this sylvan corner, and suffered the bays to put forth their branches, and the ilex to dangle over the walks, many of whose entrances are nearly overgrown. I enjoyed the gloom of these shady arbours, in the midst of which rises a lofty pavilion with galleries running round it, not unlike the idea one forms of Turkish chiosks. Beneath, lies a garden of vines and rose-trees, which I visited, and found a spring under a rustic arch of grotto-work fringed round with ivy. Millions of fish inhabit here, of that beautiful, glittering species which comes from China. This golden nation were leaping after insects, as I stood gazing upon the deep clear water, and listening to the drops that trickle from the cove. Opposite to which, at the end of an alley of vines, you discover an oval bason, and, in the midst of it, a statue of Ganymede, sitting reclined upon the eagle, full of that graceful languor so peculiarly Grecian. Whilst I was musing on the margin of the spring (for I returned to it after casting a look upon the sculpture) the moon rose above the tufted foliage of the terraces. Her silver brightness was strongly contrasted by the deep green of the holm-oak and bay, amongst which I descended by several flights of stairs, with neat marble ballustrades crowned by vases of aloes. It was about seven o'clock, and every body was jumbling to my Lord T—'s,[88] who lives in a fine house, all over blue and silver, with stuffed birds, alabaster Cupids, and a thousand prettinesses more; but, after all, neither he nor his abode are worth mentioning. I found a deal of slopping and sipping of tea going forwards, and many dawdlers assembled. As I can say little good of the party, I had better shut the door, and conduct you to the opera, which is really a striking spectacle. However, it being addressed to the sight alone, I was soon tired, and gave myself up to conversation. Bedini, first Soprano, put my patience to severe proof, during the few minutes I attended. You

---

88. John (Tylney, formerly Child), Earl Tylney of Castlemaine (1712–1784) a notorious homosexual, who died in exile without an heir after he had "left his country for his country's good."

never beheld such a porpoise. If these animals were to sing, I should conjecture it would be in his style. You may suppose how often I invoked Pacchierotti, and regretted the lofty melody of *Quinto Fabio*. Every body seemed as well contented as if there were no such thing as good music in the world, except a Neapolitan Duchess, who delighted me by her vivacity. We took our fill of maledictions, and went home equally pleased with each other, for having mutually execrated both singers and audience. This, you will say, is not infinitely to our advantage. That I allow; but, tell you truth I must, whether I will or not. Some dæmon, envious of your having too favourable an opinion of me, forces me every now and then to confessions, which ought to go great lengths to destroy it. Least, therefore, I should transgress all bounds during this communicative moment, and disclose adventures, sacred as the mysteries of Eleusis,[89] I had better fold up my letter, and assure you abruptly of my remaining ever, your affectionate, &c. &c.

---

89. Religious ceremonies celebrated in honor of Demeter and Persephone at Eleusis near Athens.

Letter XVIII.

October 22d.

They say the air is worse this year at Rome than ever, and that it would be madness to go thither during its malign influence. This was very bad news indeed, to one heartily tired of Florence; at least of its society. Merciful Powers! what a set harbour within its walls! ****. You may imagine, I do not take vast, or vehement delight in this company, though very ingenious, praise-worthy, &c. The woods of the Cascini shelter me every morning; and there grows an old crooked ilex at their entrance, twisting round a pine, upon whose branches I sit for hours; hear, without feeling, the showers trickling above my head, and see the cattle browsing peacefully in their pastures, which hazle copses, Italian pines, and groves of cypress inclose. In the afternoon, I never fail hiding myself in the thickets of Boboli, and marking the golden glimmer of sun-set between their leaves. The other evening I varied my walks, and ascended one of those pleasant[90] hills which rise in the vicinity of the city, and commands a variegated scene of spires, towns, villas, cots, and gardens. On the right, as you stand upon the brow, appears Fesule, with its turrets and white houses, covering a rocky mount; to the left, the vast Val d' Arno, lost in immensity. A Franciscan convent stands on the summit of the eminence, wrapped up in antient cypresses, which hinder its holy inhabitants from seeing too much of so gay a view. The paved ascent, leading up to their abode, receives also a shade from the cypresses which border it. Beneath which venerable avenue, crosses with inscriptions, are placed at stated distances, to mark the various moments of Christ's passion; as when, fainting under his burthen, he halted to repose himself, or when he met his

---

90. Mentioned by Dante in his Purgatorio. [Beckford's note.]

176

afflicted mother. (*Giesu incontra la sua afflitta Madre.*) [91] Above, at the end of the perspective, rises a chapel, designed with infinite taste, and simple elegance, by M. A. Buonarotti. Further on, an antient church, in the corrupt Greek style of the primitive Christians, encrusted with white marble, porphyry, and verd antique. The interior presents a crouded assemblage of ornaments, elaborate mosaic pavements, and inlaid work without end. The high altar, placed in a semicircular recess, which reminded me of the church at Torcello, glitters with barbaric paintings on a gold ground, and receives the strongest glow of light imaginable, from five windows, filled up with transparent marble clouded like tortoise-shell. A smooth polished stair-case leads to this sacred place; another, brought me to a subterraneous chapel, supported by confused groups of variegated pillars, just visible by the glimmer of lamps. I thought of the Zancaroon at Cordova, and began reciting the first verses of the Koran. Passing on, not unawed, I followed some flights of steps, which terminate in the neat cloisters of the convent, in perfect preservation; but totally deserted. Ranges of citron and aloes fill up the quadrangle, whose walls are hung with superstitious pictures, most singularly fancied. The Jesuits were the last tenants of this retirement, and seem to have had great reason for their choice. Its peace and stillness delighted me. I staid till sun-set, and then, stretching myself out at length upon the level green which forms the summit of the hill, looked down upon the plains below, between the cypresses, and marked the awful waving of their boughs. Next day, a very opposite scene engaged me, though much against my will. Her R. H. the G. Duchess having produced a princess in the night, every body put on grand gala in the morning; and I was carried, along with the glittering tide of courtiers, ministers, and ladies, to see the christening. After hearing the Grand Duke talk politics for some time, the doors of a temporary chapel were thrown open. Trumpets flourished, processions marched, and the archbishop began his business, at an altar of massive gold, placed under a yellow silk pavilion, with pyramids of lights before it. Wax tapers, though it was noon-day, shone in every corner of the apartments. Two rows of pages, gorgeously accoutered, and holding enormous torches, stood on each side his Royal Highness, and made him the prettiest courtesies imaginable, to the sound of an execrable band of music, though led by Nardini. [92] The poor old archbishop, who

---

91. "Jesus encounters his afflicted mother."
92. Pietro Nardini (1722–1793), Italian violinist and composer.

looked very piteous and saint-like, struck up the Te Deum with a quavering voice, and the rest followed him full gallop. That ceremony being dispatched (for his R. H. was in a mighty fidget to shrink back into his beloved obscurity) the crowd dispersed, and I went, with a few others, to dine at my Lord Tilney's. Evening drawing on, I ran to throw myself into the woods of Boboli, and remained till it was night, in their profound recesses. Really, this garden is enough to bewilder an enthusiastic spirit; there is something so solemn in its shades, its avenues, and spires of cypresses. When I had mused for many a melancholy hour amongst them, I emerged into the orangery before the palace, which overlooks the largest district of the town, and beheld, as I slowly descended the road which leads up to it, certain bright lights glancing across the cupola of the Duomo and the points of the highest towers. At first, I thought them meteors, or those illusive fires which often dance before the eye of my imagination; but soon I was convinced of their reality; for in a few minutes the battlements of the old castle, which I remember mentioning in a former letter, shone with lamps; the lantern of the cathedral was lighted up on a sudden; whilst a stream of torches ran along its fantastic turrets. I enjoyed this prospect at a distance: when near, its pleasures were greatly diminished, for half the fish in the town were frying to rejoice the hearts of H. R. Highness's loyal subjects, and bonfires blazing in every street and alley. Hubbubs and stinks of every denomination, drove me quickly to the theatre; but that was all glitter and glare. No taste, no arrangement; paltry looking-glasses, and rat's-tail candles. I had half a mind to return to Boboli.

Letter XIX.

Do you recollect our evening rambles last year, upon the hill of pines; and the dark valley, where we used to muse in the twilight? I remember, we often fancied the scene like Valombrosa; and vowed, if ever an occasion offered, to visit that deep retirement. I had put off the execution of this pilgrimage from day to day, till the warm weather was gone; and the Florentines declared, I should be frozen if I attempted it. Every body stared, last night at the opera, when I told them, I was going to bury myself in fallen leaves, and hear no music but their rustlings. Mr. ——[93] was just as eager as myself to escape the chit-chat and nothingness of Florence: so we finally determined upon our expedition; and mounting our horses, set out this morning; happily without any company, but the spirit which led us along. We had need of inspiration, since nothing else, I think, would have tempted us over such dreary, uninteresting hillocks, as rise from the banks of the Arno. The hoary olive is their only vegetation; so that nature, in this country, seems in a withering decrepit state; and may not unaptly be compared to "an old woman cloathed in grey." However, we did not suffer the prospect to damp our enthusiasm, which was the better preserved for Valombrosa. About half way, our palfreys thought proper to look out for some oats; and I, to creep into a sort of granary in the midst of a barren waste, scattered over with white rocks, that reflected more heat than I cared for; although I had been told, snow and ice were to be my portion. Seating myself on the floor between heaps of corn, I reached down a few purple clusters of muscadine grapes, which hung to dry in the ceiling; and amused myself very pleasantly with them, till the

---

93. John Lettice, Beckford's private tutor and traveling companion.

horses had finished their meal, and it was lawful to set forwards. We met with nothing but rocky steeps, shattered into fragments, and such roads as half inclined us to repent our undertaking; but cold was not yet amongst the number of our evils. At last, after ascending a tedious while, we began to feel the wind blow sharp from the peaks of the mountains; and to hear the murmur of the forests of pine, which shade their acclivities. A paved path leads across them, quite darkened by boughs, which, meeting over our heads, cast a gloom and a chill below, that would have stopped the proceedings of reasonable mortals, and sent them back to bask in the plain; but, being not so easily discomfited, we threw ourselves boldly into the grove. It presented one of those confusions of tall straight stems I am so fond of; and exhaled a fresh aromatic odour, that revived my spirits. The cold to be sure was piercing; but, setting that at defiance, we galloped on, and issued shortly into a vast amphitheatre of lawns and meadows, surrounded by thick woods beautifully green. Flocks of sheep were dispersed on the slopes, whose smoothness and verdure equal our English pastures. Steep cliffs, and mountains, cloathed with beech to their very summits, guard this retired valley. The herbage, moistened by streams which fall from the eminences, has never been known to fade; and, whilst the chief part of Tuscany is parched by the heats of summer, these upland meadows retain the freshness of spring. I regretted not having visited them sooner, as autumn had, already, made great havock amongst the foliage. Showers of leaves blew full in our faces, as we rode towards the convent, placed at an extremity of the vale, and sheltered by remote firs and chesnuts, towering one above another. Alighting before the entrance, two fathers came out, and received us into the peace of their retirement. We found a blazing fire, and tables spread very comfortably before it, round which five or six over-grown friars were lounging, who seemed, by the sleekness and rosy hue of their countenances, not totally to have despised this mortal existence. My letters of recommendations soon brought the heads of the order about me, fair round figures, such as a Chinese would have placed in his pagoda. I could willingly have dispensed with their attention; yet, to avoid this, was scarcely within the circle of possibility. All dinner we endured the silliest questions imaginable; but, that dispatched, away flew your humble servant to the fields and forests. The fathers made a shift to waddle after, as fast and as complaisantly as they were able; but were soon distanced. Now, I found myself at liberty; and ran up a narrow path overhung by rock, with bushy chesnuts starting from the crevices. This led me into wild glens of beech-trees, mostly decayed, and covered with moss; several were fallen. It was amongst these, the holy hermit Gualbertus[94] had his cell. I rested a moment upon one of their huge branches, listening to the roar of a water-fall which the wood concealed: then, springing up, I clambered over crags and fragments, guided by the sound; and, presently, discovered a full stream, precipitating itself down a cliff of pines, amongst which I remained several minutes, watching the falling floods; till, tired with their endless succession, I plunged into the thickest of the grove. A beech received me, like a second Gualbertus, in its hollow trunk. The dry leaves chased each other down the steeps on the edge of the torrents, with hollow rustlings; whilst the solemn wave of the forests above, exactly answered the idea I had formed of Valombrosa,

> where th' Etrurian shades
> High overarch't imbowr.

The scene was beginning to take effect, and the Genius of Milton to move across his favourite valley, when the fathers arrived, puffing and blowing, by an easier ascent than I knew of. Pardon me, if I cursed their intrusion, and wished them as still as Gualbertus. "You have missed the way," cried the youngest; "the Hermitage, with the fine picture by Andrea del Sarto, which all the English admire, is on the opposite side of the wood: there! don't you see it, on the point of the cliff?" "Yes, yes," said I, a little peevishly; "I wonder the devil has not pushed it down long ago; it seems to invite his kick." "Satan," answered the old Pagod, very dryly, "is full of malice; but whoever drinks of a spring which the Lord causeth to flow, near the Hermitage, is freed from his illusions." "Are they so?" replied I, with a sanctified accent, "then prithee conduct me thither, for I have great need of such salutary waters; being troubled with strange fancies and imaginations, such as the evil-one himself ought to be ashamed of inspiring." The youngest father shook his head, as much as to say, this is nothing more than a heretic's whim: the senior, muddled, I conjecture, set forwards with greater piety, and began some legendary tales, of the kind which my soul loveth; rare stories of caves and dens of the earth, inhabited by antient men familiar with spirits, and not the least discomposed by a party of angels coming to dinner, or playing a

---

94. Giovanni Gualberto (c. 990–1073), founder and abbot of the Vallombrosian Order.

game at miracles to pass away the evening. He pointed to a chasm in the cliff, round which we were winding by a spiral path, where Gualbertus used to sleep, and, turning himself towards the west, see a long succession of saints and martyrs sweeping athwart the sky, and tinging the clouds with brighter splendors than the setting sun. Here, he slumbered till his last hour; when the bells of the convent beneath (which till that moment would have made dogs howl, had there been any within its precincts) struck out such harmonious jingling, that all the country round was ravished, and began lifting up their eyes with singular devotion; when, behold, cherubim appeared, light dawned, and birds chirped, although it was midnight. Alas! alas! what would I not give to witness such a spectacle, and read my prayer book by the effulgence of opening heaven! However, willing to see something at least, I crept into the consecrated cleft, and extended myself on its rugged surface—A very penitential couch! but commanding glorious prospects of the world below, which lay, this evening, in deep blue shade; the sun looking red and angry through misty vapours, which prevented our discovering the Tuscan sea. Finding the rock as damp as might be expected, I soon shifted my quarters, and followed the youngest father up to the Romitorio, a snug little hermitage, with a neat chapel, and altar-piece by Andrea del Sarto, which I should have more minutely examined in any other place, but where the wild scenery of hanging woods and meadows, steep hills and nodding precipices, possessed my whole attention. I just staid to taste the holy fountain; and then, escaping from my conductors, ran eagerly down the path, leaping over the springs that crossed it, and entered a lawn of the smoothest turf, grazed by sheep, and swelling into gentle acclivities skirted by groves of fir, whose solemn verdue formed a contrast with its tender green. Beyond this pleasant opening rises a second, hemmed in with copses; and, still higher, a third; from whence a forest of young pines spires up into a lofty theatre, terminated by peaks, universally concealed under a thick mantle of beech, tinged with ruddy brown. Pausing in the midst of the lawns, and looking upward to the sweeps of wood which surrounded me, I addressed my orisons to the Genius of the place, and prayed that I might once more return into its bosom, and be permitted to bring you along with me; for, surely, such meads, such groves, were formed for our enjoyment! This little rite performed, I walked on quite to the extremity of the pastures, traversed a thicket, and found myself on the edge of precipices, beneath whose base the whole Val d' Arno lies expanded. I listened to distant murmurings in the plain, saw smokes rise from the cottages, and viewed a vast tract of barren country, which evening rendered still more desolate, bounded by the high mountain of Radicofani. Then, turning round, I beheld the whole extent of rock and forest, the groves of beech, and wilds above the convent, glowing with firey red; for the sun, making a last effort to pierce the vapours, produced this effect; which was the more striking, as the sky was dark, and the rest of the prospect of a melancholy blue. Returning slowly homeward, I marked the warm glow deserting the eminences, and heard the bell toll sullenly to vespers. The young boys of the seminary were moving in a body to their dark inclosure, all dressed in black. Many of them looked pale and wan. I wished to ask them, whether the solitude of Valombrosa suited their age and vivacity; but a tall spectre of a priest drove them along, like a herd, and presently, the gates opening, I saw them no more. A sadness, I could scarcely account for, came over me: I shivered at the bare idea of being cooped up in such a place, and seeing no other living objects than scarecrow priests and friars; to hear every day the same dull service, and droning organ; view the same cloisters; be led the same walks; watched, cribbed, confined, and filled with superstitious terrors. The night was growing chill, the winds boisterous, and, in the intervals of the gusts, I had the addition of a lamentable screech-owl to raise my spirits. Upon the whole, I was not at all concerned to meet the fathers, who came out to show me to my room, and entertain me with various gossipings, both sacred and profane, till supper appeared.

Next morning, the Padre Decano gave us chocolate in his apartments; and, afterwards, led us round the convent, insisting most unmercifully upon our viewing every cell, and every dormitory. However, I was determined to make a full stop at the organ, which is perhaps the most harmonious I ever played upon; but placed in a dark, dingy recess, feebly lighted by lamps, not calculated to inspire triumphant voluntaries. The music partook of the sadness of the scene. The monks, who had all crowded round me, when I first began, in expectation of brisk jigs and lively overtures, soon took themselves away, upon hearing a strain ten times more sorrowful, than that, to which they were accustomed. I did not lament their departure; but played dismally on, till our horses came round to the gate. We mounted; spurred back, through the grove of pines which protect Valombrosa from intrusion; descended the steeps, and, gaining the plains, galloped in three hours to Florence.

Letter XX.

At last, fears were overcome, the epidemical fever at Rome allowed to be no longer dangerous, and myself permitted to quit Florence. The weather was neither gay nor dismal; the country neither fine nor ugly; and your friend full as indifferent as the scenes he looked at. Towards afternoon, a thunder-storm gave character to the landscape, and we entered a narrow vale inclosed by rocks, with streams running at their base. Poplars with faded yellow leaves, sprung from the margin of the rivulets, which seemed to lose themselves in the ruins of a castle, built in the gothic times. Our road led through its court, and passed the antient keep, still darkened by its turrets: a few mud cottages are scattered about the opening, where formerly the chieftain exercised his vassals, and trained them to war. The dungeon, once filled with miserable victims, serves only at present to confine a few goats, which were milking before its entrance. As we were driven along under a tottering gateway, and then through a plain, and up a hill, the breeze whispering amongst the fern which covers it, I felt the sober autumnal cast of the evening bring back the happy hours I passed last year, at this very time, calm and sequestered. Full of these recollections, my eyes closed of their own accord, and were not opened for many hours; in short, till we entered Sienna.

October 27th. Here my duty of course was to see the cathedral, and I got up much earlier than I wished, in order to perform it. I wonder our holy ancestors did not chuse a mountain at once, scrape it into shrines, and chissel it into scripture stories. It would have cost them almost as little trouble as the building in question, which may certainly be esteemed a master-piece of ridiculous taste, and elaborate absurdity. The front, encrusted with alabaster, is worked into a million of fretted arches and puzzling ornaments. There are statues without number, and relievos without end. The church within, is all of black and white marble alternately; the roof blue and gold, with a profusion of silken banners hanging from it; and a cornice running above the principal arcade, composed entirely of bustos, representing the whole series of sovereign pontiffs, from the first bishop of Rome to Adrian the Fourth. Pope Joan figured amongst them, between Leo the Fourth and Benedict the Third, till the year 1600, when she was turned out, at the instance of Clement the Eighth, to make room for Zacharias the First. I hardly knew which was the nave, or which the cross aile, of this singular edifice; so perfect is the confusion of its parts. The pavement demands attention, being inlaid so curiously as to represent variety of histories taken from holy writ, and designed in the true style of that hobgoblin tapestry, which used to bestare the halls of our ancestors. Near the high altar stands the strangest of pulpits, supported by polished pillars of granite, rising from lions backs, which serve as pedestals. In every corner of the place, some chapel or other offends and astonishes you. That, however, of the Chigi family,[95] it must be allowed, has infinite merit with respect to design and execution; but it is so lost in general disorder, as to want the best part of its effect.

From the church, one enters a vaulted chamber erected by the Picolominis,[96] filled with valuable missals most exquisitely illuminated. The paintings in fresco on the walls, are rather barbarous, though executed after the designs of the mighty Raffaelle; but then we must remember, he had but just escaped from Pietro Perugino.[97] Not staying long in the Duomo, we left Sienna in good time; and, after being shaken and tumbled in the worst roads that ever pretended to be made use of, found ourselves beneath the rough mountains round Radicofani, about seven o'clock, on a cold and dismal evening. Up we toiled a steep, craggy ascent, and reached, at length, the inn upon its summit. My heart sunk, when I entered a vast range of apartments with high black roofs, once intended for a hunting palace of the Grand Dukes, but now desolate and forlorn. The wind having risen, every door began to shake, and every board substituted for a window, to clatter; as

---

95. A Roman family of Sienese extraction. Fabio Chigi was Pope Alexander VII; his nephew, Agostino, was made prince of the Holy Roman Empire in 1659.
96. Prominent Italian noble family in Siena.
97. Perugino (c. 1450–1524) was Raphael's teacher for a time.

if the severe Power who dwells on the topmost peak of Radicofani, according to its village mythologists, was about to visit his abode. My only spell, to keep him at a distance, was kindling an enormous fire; whose charitable gleams cheared my spirits, and gave them a quicker flow. Yet, for some minutes, I never ceased looking, now to the right, now to the left, up at the dark beams, and down the long passages, where the pavement broken up in several places, and earth newly strewn about, seemed to indicate that something horrid was concealed below. A grim fraternity of cats kept whisking backwards and forwards in these dreary avenues, which I am apt to imagine is the very identical scene of the sabbath of witches, at certain periods. Not venturing to explore them, I fastened my door, pitched my bed opposite the hearth, which glowed with embers, and crept under the coverlids, hardly venturing to go to sleep, lest I should be roused from it by the sudden glare of torches, and be more initiated than I wished, into the mysteries of the place. Scarce was I settled, before two or three of the brotherhood just mentioned, stalked in at a little opening under the door. I insisted upon their moving off faster than they had entered, suspecting they would soon turn wizards; and was surprized, when midnight came, to hear nothing more than their mewings, doleful enough, and echoed by the hollow walls and arches.

Letter XXI.

Radicofani, Oct. 28th.

I begin to despair of magical adventures, since none happened at Radicofani; which nature seems wholly to have abandoned. Not a tree, not an acre of soil, has she bestowed upon its inhabitants, who would have more excuse for practicing the gloomy art, than the rest of mankind. I was very glad to leave their black hills and stony wilderness behind, and, entering the Papal territory, to see some shrubs and corn-fields at a distance, near Aquapadente, which is situated on a ledge of cliffs, mantled with chesnut-copses and tufted ilex. The country grew varied and picturesque. St. Lorenzo, the next post, built upon a hill, overlooks the lake of Bolsena, whose woody shores conceal many ruined buildings. We passed some of them in a retired vale, with arches from rock to rock, and grottos beneath, half lost in thickets; from which rise craggy pinnacles, crowned by mouldering towers; just such scenery as Polemburg and Peter de Laer[98] introduce in their paintings. Beyond these truly Italian prospects, which a mellow evening tint rendered still more interesting, a forest of oaks presents itself, upon the brows of hills, which extends almost the whole way to Monte Fiascone. It was late when we ascended it. The whole country seems full of inhabited caverns, that began, as night drew on, to shine with fires. We saw many dark shapes glancing before them; and perhaps a subterraneous people, like the Cimmerians, lurk in their recesses. The crackling of flames, and confused hum of voices, struck our ears, as we passed along. I wished to have mixed in these nocturnal assemblies; but prudently repressed my curiosity, lest I might have intruded upon some mysterious rites, and have suffered the punishment due to sacrilege. As we drew

98. Sometimes called Bamboccio (c. 1592–1642), a Dutch painter.

187

near Viterbo, the lights in the fields grew less and less frequent; and, when we entered the town, all was total darkness. Tomorrow I hope to pay my vows before the high altar of St. Peter, and tread the Vatican. My heart beats quick with the idea of approaching Rome. Why are you not here to usher me into that imperial city; to watch my first glance of the Coliseo; and lead me up the stairs of the Capitol? I shall rise before the sun, that I may see him set from Monte Cavallo.

Letter XXII.

Rome, Oct. 29th.

We set out in the dark. Morning dawned over the Lago di Vico: its waters, of a deep ultramarine blue, and its surrounding forests catching the rays of the rising sun. It was in vain I looked for the cupola of St. Peter's, upon descending the mountains beyond Viterbo. Nothing but a sea of vapours was visible. At length, they rolled away; and the spacious plains began to shew themselves, in which the most warlike of nations reared their seat of empire. On the left, afar off, rises the rugged chain of Appenines, and on the other side, a shining expanse of ocean terminates the view. It was upon this vast surface so many illustrious actions were performed, and I know not where a mighty people could have chosen a grander theatre. Here was space for the march of armies, and verge enough for encampments. Levels for martial games, and room for that variety of roads and causeways, that led from the Capital to Ostia. How many triumphant legions have trodden these pavements! how many captive kings! What throngs of cars and chariots once glittered on their surface! savage animals dragged from the interior of Africa; and the ambassadors of Indian princes followed by their exotic train, hastening to implore the favour of the senate. During many ages, this eminence commanded, almost every day, such illustrious scenes; but all are vanished; the splendid tumult is passed away; silence and desolation remain. Dreary flats thinly scattered over with ilex, and barren hillocks crowned by solitary towers, were the only objects we perceived for several miles. Now and then, we passed a flock of black, ill-favoured sheep feeding by the way's side, near a ruined sepulchre; just such animals as an antient would have sacrificed to the Manes. Sometimes we crossed a brook, whose riplings were the only sounds which broke the general stillness, and observed the shepherds huts on its banks, propped up with broken pedestals and marble friezes. I entered one of them, whose owner was abroad, tending his herds, and began writing upon the sand, and murmuring a melancholy song. Perhaps, the dead listened to me from their narrow cells. The living I can answer for; they were far enough removed. You will not be surprized at the dark tone of my musings in so sad a scene; especially, as the weather lowered; and you are well acquainted how greatly I depend upon skies and sunshine. To-day I had no blue firmament to revive my spirits; no genial gales, no aromatic plants to irritate my nerves, and give at least a momentary animation. Heath and furze were the sole vegetation which covers this endless wilderness. Every slope is strewed with the relics of a happier period; trunks of trees, shattered columns, cedar beams, helmets of bronze, skulls, and coins, are frequently dug up together. I cannot boast of having made any discoveries, nor of sending you any novel intelligence. You knew before how perfectly the environs of Rome were desolate, and how compleatly the papal government contrives to make its subjects miserable. But, who knows that they were not just as wretched, in those boasted times we are so fond of celebrating? All is doubt and conjecture in this frail existence; and I might as well attempt proving to whom belonged the mouldering bones which lay dispersed around me, as venture to affirm, that one age was more fortunate than another. Very likely, the poor cottager, under whose roof I reposed, is happier than the luxurious Roman, upon the remains of whose palace, perhaps his shed is raised; and yet, that Roman flourished in the purple days of the empire, when all was wealth and splendor, triumph and exultation. I could have spent the whole day by the rivulet, lost in dreams and meditations; but recollecting my vow, I ran back to the carriage, and drove on. The road, not having been mended, I believe, since the days of the Cæsars, would not allow our motions to be very precipitate. When you gain the summit of yonder hill, you will discover Rome, said one of the postillions: up we dragged; no city appeared. From the next, cried out a second; and so on, from height to height, did they amuse my expectations. I thought Rome fled before us, such was my impatience; till, at last, we perceived a cluster of hills, with green pastures on their summits, inclosed by thickets, and shaded by flourishing ilex. Here and there, a white house, built in the antient style, with open porticos, that received a faint gleam of the evening sun, just emerged from the clouds and tinting the meads below. Now, domes and towers began to discover themselves in the valley, and St. Peter's to rise above the magnificent roofs of the Vatican. Every step we advanced, the scene extended; till, winding suddenly round the hill, all Rome opened to our view. A spring flowed opportunely into a marble cistern close by the way; two cypresses and a pine waved over it. I leaped out, poured water upon my hands, and then, lifting them up to the sylvan Genii of the place, implored their protection. I wished to have run wild in the fresh fields and copses above the Vatican, there to have remained, till fauns might peep out of their concealments, and satyrs begin to touch their flutes in the twilight; for the place looks still so wonderous classical, that I can never persuade myself, either Constantine, Attila, or the Popes themselves, have chased them all away. I think I should have found some out, who would have fed me with milk and chesnuts, have sung me a Latian ditty, and mourned the woeful changes which have taken place, since their sacred groves were felled, and Faunus[99] ceased to be oracular. Who can tell but they would have given me some mystic skin to sleep on, that I might have looked into futurity? Shall I ever forget the sensations I experienced, upon slowly descending the hills, and crossing the bridge over the Tyber? when I entered an avenue between terraces and ornamented gates of villas, which leads to the Porto del Popolo? and beheld the square, the domes, the obelisk; the long perspective of streets and palaces opening beyond, all glowing with the vivid red of sun-set? You can imagine how I enjoyed my beloved tint, my favourite hour, surrounded by such objects. You can fancy me ascending Monte Cavallo, leaning against the pedestal which supports Bucephalus; then, spite of time and distance, hurrying to St. Peter's in performance of my vow. I met the Holy Father in all his pomp, returning from vespers. Trumpets flourishing, and a legion of guards drawn out upon Ponte St. Angelo. Casting a respectful glance upon the Moles Adriani, I moved on, till the full sweep of St. Peter's colonade opened upon me, and fixed me, as if spellbound, under the obelisk; lost in wonder. The edifice appears to have been raised within the year, such is its freshness and preservation. I could hardly take my eyes from off the beautiful symmetry of its front, contrasted with the magnificent, though irregular courts of the Vatican, towering over the colonade; till, the sun sinking

---

99. Faunus, son of Picus, was an oracular deity and a protector of agriculture and shepherds.

behind the dome, I ran up the steps, and entered the grand portal, which was on the very point of being closed. I knew not where I was, or to what scene transported. A sacred twilight concealing the extremities of the structures, I could not distinguish any particular ornament, but enjoyed the effect of the whole. No damp air, or fetid exhalation offended me. The perfume of incense was not yet entirely dissipated. No human being stirred. I heard a door close with the sound of thunder, and thought I distinguished some faint whisperings, but am ignorant from whence they came. Several hundred lamps twinkled round the high altar, quite lost in the immensity of the pile. No other light disturbed my reveries, but the dying glow, still visible through the western windows. Imagine how I felt upon finding myself alone in this vast temple, at so late an hour; and think, whether I had not revelations. It was almost eight o'clock before I issued forth, and, pausing a few minutes under the porticos, listened to the rush of the fountains. Then, traversing half the town, I believe, in my way to the Villa Medici, under which I am lodged, fell into a profound repose, which my zeal and exercise may be allowed, I think, to have merited.

October 30th. It was a clear morning; I mounted up to the roof of the house, and sat under a set of open pavilions, surveying the vast group of stately buildings below; then repaired, immediately after breakfast, to St. Peter's, which even exceeded the heighth of my expectations. I could hardly quit it. I wished his Holiness would allow me to erect a little tabernacle under the dome, I should desire no other prospect during the winter; no other sky, than the vast arches glowing with golden ornaments, so lofty as to lose all glitter, or gaudiness. But I cannot say, I should be perfectly contented, unless I could obtain another pavilion for you. Thus established, we would take our evening walks on the field of marble; for is not the pavement vast enough to excuse the extravagance of the appellation? Sometimes, instead of climbing a mountain, we should ascend the cupola, and look down on our little encampment below. At night I should wish for a constellation of lamps dispersed about in clusters, and so contrived as to diffuse a mild equal light for us to read, or draw by. Music should not be wanting; one day, to breathe in the subterraneous chapels, another, to mount high in the dome. The doors should be closed, and not a mortal admitted. No priests, no cardinals; God forbid! We should have all the space to ourselves, and to such creatures too as resemble us. The windows I should shade with transparent

William Beckford at 21. From an engraving of the Sir Joshua Reynolds portrait done by T. A. Dean in 1835.

The Gordon Riots. Burning of Newgate. From an engraving by H. Roberts after a drawing by O'Neil.

Pacchierotti in 1782. From an engraving published by Charles Bretherton.

Pacchierotti

B.M. 6092.

Venice. From an engraving by Edward Goodall after a drawing by
J. M. W. Turner.

St. Mark's Palace. From an engraving by D. Allen after a drawing
by Titian.

Ducal Palace at Venice. From an engraving by J. Tingle after a drawing by Samuel Prout.

The Rialto at Venice. From an engraving by J. Henshall after a drawing by Samuel Prout.

Bridge of Sighs. From an engraving by Robert Wallis after a drawing by Samuel Prout.

Petrarch's House at Arqua. From an engraving by Charles Heath after a drawing by Samuel Prout.

View of Verona. From an engraving by J. T. Willmore after a drawing by Samuel Prout.

St. Peter's Basilica. From an engraving by Robert Wallis after a drawing by J. M. W. Turner.

The Roman Forum. From an engraving by Edward Goodall after a drawing by J. M. W. Turner.

The Guilty Lovers. Letter XXIII. From an engraving by F. Bartolozzi after an original drawing by G. B. Cipriani. Appeared as frontispiece to the first edition.

St. Bruno. From an engraving by F. Bartolozzi after an original drawing by G. B. Cipriani. Appeared in the first edition.

curtains of yellow silk, to admit the glow of perpetual summer. Lanterns, as many as you please, of all forms and sizes; they would remind us of China, and, depending from the roofs of the palace, bring before us that of the Emperor Ki; which was twice as large as St. Peter's (if we may credit the grand annals) and lighted alone by tapers; for, his imperial majesty, being tired of the sun, would absolutely have a new firmament of his own creation, and an artificial day. Was it not a rare fantastic idea? For my part, I should like of all things to immure myself, after his example, with those I love; forget the divisions of time, have a moon at command, and a theatrical sun to rise and set, at pleasure. I was so absorbed in my imaginary palace, and exhausted with contriving plans for its embellishment, as to have no spirits left for the Pantheon; which I visited late in the evening, and entered with a reverence approaching to superstition. The whiteness of the dome offending me, I slunk into one of the recesses; closed my eyes; transported myself into antiquity; then, opened them again, tried to persuade myself, the Pagan gods were in their niches, and the saints out of the question; was vexed at coming to my senses, and finding them all there, St. Andrew with his cross and St. Agnes with her lamb, &c. &c. Then, I paced disconsolately into the portico, which shews the name of Agrippa on its pediment. I leaned a minute against a Corinthian column, and lamented, that no pontiff arrived with victims and aruspices, of whom I might enquire, what, in the name of birds and garbage, put me so terribly out of humour; for you must know I was very near being disappointed, and began to think Piranesi and Paolo Panini[100] had been a great deal too colossal, in their view of this venerable structure. But, though it is not so immense as I expected, yet a certain venerable air, an awful gloom, breathed inspiration, though of the sorrowful kind. I left the column, walked in the center of the temple, and, folding my arms, stood as fixed as a statue. Some architects have celebrated the effect of light from the opening above, and pretended it to be so equally distributed around, as to give those who walk beneath, the appearance of mystic substances beaming with radiance. Mighty fine, if that were the case! I appeared, to be sure, a luminous figure; and never stood I more in need of something to distinguish me, being forlorn and dismal in the supreme degree. I had expected a heap of Venetian letters, but could not discover one: I had received no

---

100. Giovanni Paolo (c. 1691–1764), painter of Roman scenes. One of his works was entitled "The Pantheon."

intelligence from England, this many a tedious day; and, for aught I can tell to the contrary, you may have been dead these three weeks. I think, I shall wander soon in the Catacombs, which I am half inclined to imagine communicate with the lower world; and perhaps I may find some letter there from you, lying upon a broken sarcophagus, dated from the realms of Night, and giving an account of your descent into her bosom. Yet, I pray continually, notwithstanding my curiosity to learn what passes in the dark regions beyond the tomb, that you will condescend to remain a few years longer on our planet; for what would become of me, should I lose sight of you? Stay, therefore, as long as you can, and let us have the delight of dozing a little more of this poor existence away together, and steeping ourselves in pleasant dreams.

October 31st. I absolutely will have no antiquary to go prating from fragment to fragment, and tell me, that were I to stay five years at Rome, I should not see half it contained. The thought alone, of so much to look at, is quite distracting, and makes me resolve to view nothing at all in a scientific way; but straggle and wander about, just as the spirit chuses. This evening, it led me to the Coliseo, and excited a vehement desire in me to break down and pulverize the whole circle of saints' nests and chapels, which disgrace the arena. You recollect, I dare say, the vile effect of this holy trumpery, and would join with all your heart in kicking it into the Tyber. A few lazy abbots were at their devotion before them; such as would have made a lion's mouth water; fatter, I dare say, than any saint in the whole martyrology, and ten times more tantalizing. I looked first, at the dens where wild beasts used to be kept, to divert the magnanimous people of Rome with devastation and murder; then, at the tame cattle before the altars. Heavens! thought I to myself, how times are changed! Could ever Vespasian[101] have imagined, his amphitheatre would have been thus inhabited? I passed on, making these reflections, to a dark arcade, overgrown with ilex. In the openings which time and violence have made, a distant grove of cypresses discover themselves; springing from heaps of mouldering ruins, relieved by a clear transparent sky, strewed with a few red clouds. This was the sort of prospect I desired, and I sat down on a shattered frieze, to enjoy it. Many stories of antient Rome thronged into my mind as I mused; triumphal scenes, but tempered by sadness, and the awful thoughts of their being all passed away. It would be

---

101. Roman emperor A.D. 70–79.

in vain to recapitulate the ideas which chased one another along. Think where I sat, and you may easily conjecture the series. When the procession was fleeted by, (for I not only thought, but seemed to see warriors moving amongst the cypresses, and consuls returning from Parthian expeditions, loaded with strange spoils, and received with the acclamations of millions upon entering the theatre) I arose, crossed the arena, paced several times round and round, looked up to arcade rising above arcade, and admired the stately height and masses of the structure, considered it in various points of view, and felt, as if I never should be satisfied with gazing, hour after hour, and day after day. Next, directing my steps to the arch of Constantine, I surveyed the groups of ruins which surrounded me. The cool breeze of the evening played in the beds of canes and oziers, which flourished under the walls of the Coliseo: a cloud of birds were upon the wing to regain their haunts in its crevices; and, except the sound of their flight, all was silent; for happily no carriages were rattling along. I observed the palace and obelisk of Saint John of Lateran, at a distance; but it was too late to take a nearer survey; so, returning leisurely home, I traversed the Campo Vaccino, and leaned a moment against one of the columns which supported the temple of Jupiter Stator. Some women were fetching water from the fountain hard by, whilst another group had kindled a fire under the shrubs and twisted fig-trees, which cover the Palatine hill. Innumerable vaults and arches peep out of the vegetation. It was upon these, in all probability, the splendid palace of the Cæsars was raised. Confused fragments of marble, and walls of lofty terraces, are the sole traces of its antient magnificence. A wretched rabble were roasting their chestnuts, on the very spot, perhaps, where Domitian[102] convened a senate, to harangue upon the delicacies of his entertainment. The light of the flame cast upon the figures around it, and the mixture of tottering wall with foliage impending above their heads, formed a striking picture, which I staid contemplating from my pillar, till the fire went out, the assembly dispersed, and none remained but a withered hag, raking the embers and muttering to herself. I thought also it was high time to retire, lest the unwholesome mists, which were steaming from the opening before the Coliseo, might make me repent my stay. Whether they had already taken effect, or no, I will not absolutely determine; but, something or

---

102. Emperor of Rome A.D. 81–96.

other had grievously discouraged me. A few centuries ago, I should have taxed the old hag with my head-ache, and have attributed the uncommon oppression I experienced, to her baleful power. Hastening to my hotel, I mounted into the open portico upon its summit, nearly upon a level with the Villa Medici, and sat, several hours, with my arms folded in one another, listening to the distant rumours of the town. It had been a fine moment to have bestrode one of the winds which piped around me, offering, no doubt, some compact from Lucifer.

November 1st. Though you find I am not yet snatched away from the earth, according to my last night's bodings, I was far too restless and dispirited to deliver my recommendatory letters. St. Carlos, a might day of gala at Naples, was an excellent excuse for leaving Rome, and indulging my roving disposition. After spending my morning at St. Peter's, we set off about four o'clock, and drove by the Coliseo, and a Capuchin convent, whose monks were all busied in preparing the skeletons of their order, to figure by torch-light, in the evening. St. John's of Lateran astonished me. I could not help walking several times round the obelisk, and admiring the noble open space in which the palace is erected, and the extensive scene of towers and aqueducts, discovered from the platform in front. We went out at the Porta Appia, and began to perceive the plains which surround the city, opening on every side. Long reaches of walls and arches, but seldom interrupted, stretch across them. Sometimes, indeed, a withered pine, lifting itself up to the mercy of every blast that sweeps the champain, breaks their uniformity. Between the aqueducts to the left, nothing but wastes of fern, and tracts of ploughed land, dark and desolate, are visible, the corn not being yet sprung up. On the right, several groups of ruined fanes and sepulchres diversify the levels; with, here and there, a garden or woody inclosure. Such objects are scattered over the landscape, that, towards the horizon, bulges into gentle ascents, and, rising by degrees, swells, at length, into a chain of mountains, which received the pale gleams of the sun, setting in watery clouds. By this uncertain light, we discovered the white buildings of Albano, sprinkled about the steeps. We had not many moments to contemplate them; for it was night when we passed the Torre di mezza via, and began breathing a close pestilential vapour. Half suffocated, and recollecting a variety of terrifying tales about the malaria, we advanced, not without fear, to Veletri, and hardly ventured to fall asleep, when arrived there.

November 2d. I arose at day-break, and, forgetting fevers and mortalities, ran into a level meadow without the town, whilst the horses were putting to the carriage. Why should I calumniate the air? it seemed purer and more transparent than any I had before inhaled. The mountains were covered with thin mists, and the morning star sparkled above their summits. Birds were twittering amongst some sheds and bushes, which border the sides of the road. A chestnut hung over it, against which I leaned till the chaise came up. Being perfectly alone, and not discovering any trace of the neighbouring city, I fancied myself existing in the antient days of Hesperia, and hoped to meet Picus in his woods, before the evening. But, instead of those shrill clamours which used to echo through the thickets, when Pan joined with mortals in the chace, I heard the rumbling of our carriage, and the curses of its postillions. Mounting an horse, I flew before them, and seemed to catch inspiration from the breezes. Now, I turned my eyes to the ridge of precipices, in whose grots and caverns Saturn and his people passed their life; then, to the distant ocean. Afar off, rose the cliff, so famous for Circe's incantations, and the whole line of coasts, which was once covered with her forests. Whilst I was advancing with full speed, the sun-beams began to shoot athwart the mountains, the plains to light up by degrees, and their shrubberies of myrtle to glisten with dew-drops. The sea brightened, and the Circean rock soon glowed with purple. I never felt my spirits so exhilarated, and they could not have flowed with more vivacity, even had I tasted the cup, which Helen gave Telemachus. You will think me gone wild, when I tell you, I was, in a manner, drunk with the dews of the morning, and so enraptured with the prospects which lay before me, as to address them in verse, and compose charms to dispel the enchantments of Circe. All day were we approaching her rock: towards evening, Terracina appeared before us, in a bold romantic scite; house above house, and turret looking over turret, on the steeps of a mountain, inclosed with mouldering walls, and crowned by the ruined terraces of a delightful palace: one of those, perhaps, which the luxurious Romans inhabited during the summer, when so free and lofty an exposition (the sea below, with its gales and murmurs) must have been exquisitely agreeable. Groves of oranges, and citrons hang on the declivity, rough with the Indian fig, whose bright red flowers, illumined by the sun, had a magic splendor. A palm-tree growing on the highest crag, adds not a little to its singular appearance. Being the largest I had ever seen, and clustered with fruit, I climbed up the rocks to take a close survey of it; and found a spring trickling near its trunk, bordered by fresh herbage. On this I stretched myself by the very edge of the precipice, and, looking down upon the beach, and glassy plains of ocean, exclaimed with Martial:

> O nemus! O fontes! solidumque madentis arenæ
> Littus, et æquoreis splendidus Anxur aquis![103]

Glancing my eyes athwart the sea, I fixed them on the Circean promontory, which lies right opposite to Terracina, joined to the continent by a very narrow strip of land, and appearing like an island. The roar of the waves lashing the base of the precipices, might still be thought the howl of savage monsters; but where are those woods which shaded the dome of the goddess? Scarce a tree appears. A few thickets, and but a few, are the sole remains of this once impenetrable vegetation; yet, even these, I longed to visit; such was my predilection for the spot. Who knows, but Circe might have led me to some other palace, in a more secret and retired vale, where she dwells, remote from modern mariners, and the present inhabitants of her environs; universally changed to swine for these many ages? Their metamorphosis being so thoroughly established as to leave no future pretence for her operations; I can imagine her given up to solitude, and the consciousness of her potent influence. Notwithstanding the risks of the adventure, I wished to have attempted it, and seen, whether she would have allowed me, as night came on, to warm myself by her cedar fire, and hear her captivating song. Perhaps, had the goddess been propitious, I might have culled some herbs of wonderous efficacy. You recollect, I dare say, how renowned the cliff was for them, and remember that Circe's attendants, deeply skilled like their mistress in pharmacy,[104] were continually gathering plants, in the woods and wilds which enriched her abode. It was thus, the companions of Ulysses found them employed, when, entering her palace, they unwarily drank the beverage she offered. Ovid has told this story in a masterly manner, and formed a lively picture of the magic dome, with the occupations of its inhabitants. We see them judiciously arranging their plants, whilst Circe

---

103. *Epigrams*, bk. X, st. LI. "O grove and founts! and shores of firm damp sand, and Anxur shining in the ocean waves."

104. Όρ☉ Κιρκαῖον πολυφάρμακον. Schol[ia] in Apoll[onius] Argon[autica] Lib. iv. v. 331. Theophrast[us] de Plant. [*Enquiry into Plants*] 1. viii. c. 15. [Beckford's note.]

directs, and points out, with the nicest discernment, the simple and compound virtues of every flower. Descending the cliff, and pursuing our route to Mola, along the shore, by a grand road, formed on the ruins of the Appian, we drove under an enormous perpendicular rock, standing detached, like a watch-tower, and cut into arsenals and magazines. Day closed, just as we got beyond it, and a new moon gleamed faintly on the waters. We saw fires afar off in the bay, some twinkling on the coast, others upon the waves, and heard the murmur of voices; for the night was still and solemn, like that of Cajetas's[105] funeral. I looked anxiously on a sea, where the heroes of the Odyssey and Æneid had failed, in search of fate and empire; then, closed my eyes, and dreamed of those illustrious wanderers. Nine struck when we arrived at Mola di Cajeta. The boats were just coming in (whose lights we had seen, out upon the main) and brought such fish, as Neptune, I dare say, would have grudged Æneas and Ulysses.

November 3d. The morning was soft, but hazy. I walked in a grove of oranges, white with blossoms, and at the same time glowing with fruit; some of which I obtained leave to gather. The spot sloped pleasantly toward the sea, and here, I amused myself with my agreeable occupation, till the horses were ready; then, set off on the Appian, between hedges of myrtle and aloes, catching fresh gales from the sea as I flew along, and breathing the perfume of an aromatic vegetation, which covers the fields on the shore. We observed variety of towns, with battlemented walls and antient turrets, crowning the pinnacles of rocky steeps, surrounded by wilds, and rude uncultivated mountains. The Liris, now Garigliano, winds its peaceful course through wide extensive meadows, scattered over with the remains of aqueducts, and waters the base of the rocks, I have just mentioned. Such a prospect could not fail of bringing Virgil's panegyric of Italy full in my mind:

> Tot congesta manu præruptis oppida saxis,
> Fluminaque antiquos subterlabentia muros.[106]

As soon as we arrived in sight of Capua, the sky darkened, clouds covered the horizon, and presently poured down such deluges of rain, as floated the whole country. The gloom was general;

---

105. Tommaso de Vio Cajetan (1469–1534), theologian. He was called Gaetano (Cajetan) after his place of birth, Gaeta.

106. *Georgics,* bk. II. ll. 156–157. "All the towns were raised with labor upon rocky steeps, with rivers gliding silently beneath their ancient walls."

Vesuvius disappeared, just after we had the pleasure of discovering it. Lightning began to flash with dreadful rapidity, and people to run frightened to their homes. At four o'clock, darkness universally prevailed; except when a livid glare of lightning presented instantaneous glimpses of the bay and mountains. We lighted torches, and forded several torrents, almost at the hazard of our lives. The fields round Naples were filled with herds, lowing most piteously; and yet, not half so much scared as their masters, who ran about, cursing and swearing, like Indians during the eclipse of the moon. I knew Vesuvius had often put their courage to proof, but little thought of an inundation occasioning such commotions. For three hours the storm increased in violence; and, instead of entering Naples on a calm evening, and viewing its delightful shores by moon-light; instead of finding the squares and terraces thronged with people, and animated by music, we advanced with fear and terror, through dark streets, totally deserted, every creature being shut up in their houses; and we heard nothing but driving rain, rushing torrents, and the fall of fragments, beaten down by their violence. Our inn, like every other habitation, was in great disorder, and we waited a long while before we could settle in our apartments, with any comfort. All night, the waves roared round the rocky foundations of a fortress beneath my windows, and the lightning played clear in my eyes. I could not sleep, and was full as disturbed as the elements.

November 4th. Peace was restored to nature in the morning, but every mouth was full of the dreadful accidents which had happened in the night. The sky was cloudless when I awoke, and such was the transparence of the atmosphere, that I could clearly discern the rocks, and even some white buildings on the island of Caprea, though at the distance of several miles. A large window fronts my bed, and, its casements being thrown open, gives me a vast prospect of ocean, uninterrupted, except by the Peaks of Caprea, and the Cape of Sorento. I lay, half an hour, gazing on the smooth level waters, and listening to the confused voices of the fishermen, passing and repassing in light skiffs, which came, and disappeared, in an instant. Running to the balcony the moment my eyes were fairly open (for till then I saw objects, I know not how, as one does in dreams) I leaned over its rails, and viewed Vesuvius, rising distinct into the blue æther, with all that world of gardens and casinos, which are scattered about its base; then, looked down into the street, deep below, thronged with people in holiday garments, and carriages, and soldiers in full parade.

The woody, variegated shore of Posilipo next drew my attention. It was on those very rocks, under those tall pines, Sannazaro[107] was wont to sit by moon-light, or at peep of dawn, holding converse with the Nereids. 'Tis there he still sleeps; and I wished to have gone immediately, and strewed coral over his tomb; but I was obliged to check my impatience, and hurry to the palace, in form and gala. A courtly mob had got thither, upon the same errand, daubed over with lace, and most notably be-perriwigged. Nothing but bows and salutations were going forward on the stair-case, one of the largest I ever beheld, and which a multitude of prelates and friars were ascending, in all the pomp of awkwardness. I jostled along to the presence-chamber, where his majesty was dining, alone, in a circular inclosure of fine cloaths and smirking faces. The moment he had finished, twenty long necks were poked forth, and it was a most glorious struggle, amongst some of the most decorated, who first should kiss his hand. Doing so was the great business of the day, and every body pressed forwards to the best of their abilities. His majesty seemed to eye nothing but the end of his nose, which is doubtless a capital object. Though people have imagined him a weak monarch, I beg leave to differ in opinion; since he has the boldness to prolong his childhood, and be happy, in spite of years and conviction. Give him a boar to stab, and a pigeon to shoot at, a battledore, or an angling-rod, and he is better contented than Solomon in all his glory; and will never discover, like that sapient sovereign, that "all is vanity and vexation of spirit." His courtiers, in general, have rather a barbaric appearance, and differ little, in the character of their physiognomies, from the most savage nations. I should have taken them for Calmucks or Samoieds,[108] had it not been for their dresses, and European finery. You may suppose I was not sorry, after my presentation was over, to return to Sir W.'s, and hear Lady H. play;[109] whose music breathes the most pastoral Sicilian ideas, and

---

107. Jacopo Sannazaro (1458–1530), Italian poet.

108. Mongolian tribesmen. The Kalmucks inhabited a vast area extending from parts of China to southeastern Russia; the Samoyeds inhabited Siberia.

109. Sir William Hamilton (1730–1803), British envoy to the court of Naples from 1764 to 1800. His wife, Catherine Barlow, the first Lady Hamilton, became one of Beckford's closest friends, though the relationship was doomed to be brief with her death in 1782. "Had she lived to a later period," Beckford wrote in the 1834 edition, "her example and influence might probably have gone great lengths towards arresting that tide of corruption and profligacy which swept off this ill-fated court to Sicily, and threatened its total destruction."

The second Lady Hamilton, Emma Lyon, was the notorious mistress of Lord Nelson.

transports me to green meads on the sea-coast, where I wander
with Theocritus. The evening was passing swiftly away in this
delightful excursion of fancy, and I had almost forgotten there
was a grand illumination at the theatre of St. Carlo. After traversing a number of dark streets, we suddenly entered this enormous
edifice, whose six rows of boxes blazed with tapers. I never beheld
such lofty walls of light, nor so pompous a decoration, as covered
the stage. Marchesi[110] was singing, in the midst of all these splendors, some of the poorest music imaginable, with the clearest and
most triumphant voice, perhaps, in the universe. It was some time
before I could look to any purpose around me, or discover what
animals inhabited this glittering world; such was its size and glare.
At last, I perceived vast numbers of ugly beings, in gold and silver
raiment, peeping out of their boxes. The court being present,
a tolerable silence was maintained; but the moment his majesty
withdrew (which great event took place at the beginning of the
second act) every tongue broke loose, and nothing but buz and
hubbub filled up the rest of the entertainment. The last ballet,
formed upon the old story of Le Festin de Pierre,[111] had wonderful effect, and terminated in the most striking perspective of the
infernal region. Picq[112] danced incomparably, and Signora Rossi
led the Fandango, with a grace and activity that pleased me beyond
idea. Music was never more rapturous than that which accompanies this dance. It quite enchanted me, and I longed to have
sprung upon the stage. The cadence is so strongly marked by the
castanets, that it is almost impossible to be out of time; and the
rapidity of steps, and varied movements, scarcely allows a moment,
to think of being tired. I should imagine the eternal dance; with
which certain tribes of American savages fancy they are to be
rewarded in a future existence, might be formed somewhat on
this model. Indeed, the Fandango arrived in Spain with the con-
querors of the other hemisphere; and is far too lively and extatic
to be of European original.

November 6th. Till to-day, we have had nothing but rains; the
sea covered with mists, and Caprea invisible. Would you believe
it? I have not yet been able to mount to St. Elmo, and the Capo
di Monte, in order to take a general view of the town. This
morning, a bright gleam of sunshine roused me from my slumbers,
and summoned me to the broad terrace of Chiaja, directly above

---

110. Luigi Marchesi (1755–1829), popular Italian soprano.
111. A comedy in prose by Molière, produced in 1665; also known as *Don Juan,*
a Spanish story originally dramatized by Gabriel Tellez (1571–1641).
112. Carlo de Picq.

the waves, and commanding the whole coast of Posilipo. Insensibly I drew towards it (and you know the pace I run when out upon discoveries) soon reached the entrance of the coast, which lay in dark shades, whilst the crags that lower over it were brightly illumined. Shrubs and vines grow luxuriantly in the crevices of the rock; and their fresh yellow colours, variegated with ivy, have a beautiful effect. To the right, a grove of pines sprung from the highest pinnacles; on the left, bay and chesnut conceal the tomb of Virgil, placed on the summit of a cliff, which impends over the opening of the grotto, and is fringed with a florid vegetation. Beneath, are several wide apertures, hollowed in the solid stone, which lead to caverns sixty or seventy feet in depth; where a number of peasants, who were employed in quarrying, made such a noise with their tools and their voices, as almost inclined me to wish the Cimmerians would start from their subterraneous habitation, and sacrifice these prophane, to the Manes. Walking out of the sunshine, I set myself on a loose stone, immediately beneath the first gloomy arch of the grotto, and, looking down the vast and solemn perspective, terminated by a speck of grey uncertain light, venerated a work, which some old chroniclers have imagined as antient as the Trojan war. 'Twas here the mysterious race, I have just mentioned, performed their infernal rites; and it was this excavation, perhaps, which led to their abode. The Neapolitans attribute a more modern, though full as problematical an origin to their famous cavern, and most piously believe it to have been formed by the enchantments of Virgil; who, as Mr. Addison very justly observes, is better known as Naples in his magical character, than as the author of the Æneid. This strange infatuation, most probably arose from the vicinity of the tomb, in which his ashes are supposed to have been deposited; and which, according to popular tradition, was guarded by those very spirits who assisted in constructing the cave. But, whatever may have given rise to these ideas, certain it is, they were not confined to the lower ranks alone. King Robert,[113] a wise, though far from poetical monarch, conducted his friend Petrarch with great solemnity to the spot; and, pointing to the entrance of the grotto, very gravely asked him, whether he did not adopt the general belief, and conclude this stupendous passage derived its origin from Virgil's powerful incantations? The answer, I think, may easily be conjectured. When I had sat for some time, contemplating this dusky avenue, and trying to persuade myself it

---

113. [J. F. P. A. de Sade] Mém[oires] pour la vie de Pétrarque, vol. i. p. 439 [Amsterdam, 1764–1767]. [Beckford's note.]

was hewn by the Cimmerians, I retreated, without proceeding any farther, and followed a narrow path, which led me, after some windings and turnings, along the brink of the precipice, across a vineyard, to that retired nook of the rocks, which shelters Virgil's tomb, most venerably mossed over, and more than half concealed by bushes and vegetation. Drops of dew were distilling from the niches of the little chamber which once contained his urn, and heaps of withered leaves had gathered on the pavement. Amongst these I crept, to eat some grapes and biscuit; having duly scattered a few crumbs, as a sort of offering to the invisible guardians of the place. I believe they were sensible of my piety, and, as a reward, kept vagabonds and clowns away. The one who conducted me, remained aloof, at awful distance, whilst I sat commercing with the manes of my beloved Poet, or straggling about the shrubbery which hangs directly above the mouth of the grot. I wonder I did not visit the eternal shades sooner than I expected; for no squirrel ever skipped from bough to bough more ventrously. One instant, I climbed up the branches of a chesnut, and sat almost on its extremity, my feet impending over the chasm below; another, I boldly advanced to the edge of the rock, and saw crouds of people and carriages, diminished by distance, issuing from the bosom of the mountain, and disappearing almost as soon as discovered, in the windings of the road. Having clambered high above the cavern, I hazarded my neck on the top of one of the pines, and looked contemptuously down on the race of pigmies, that were so busily moving to and fro.[114] The sun was fiercer than I could have wished; but the sea-breezes fanned me, in my aerial situation, which commanded the grand sweep of the bay; varied by convents, palaces, and gardens, mixed with huge masses of rock; and crowned by the stately buildings of the Carthusians, and fortress of Saint Elmo. Add a glittering blue sea to this perspective, with Caprea rising from its bosom, and Vesuvius breathing forth a white column of smoke into the æther; you will then have a scene upon which I gazed with delight, for more than an hour; almost forgetting that I was perched upon the head of a pine, with nothing but a frail branch to uphold me. However, I descended alive; as Virgil's Genii, I am resolved to believe, were my protectors.

---

114. When the Caliph Vathek climbs his great tower for the first time, he beholds a similar scene: "men not larger than pismires, mountains than shells, and cities than beehives."

Letter XXIII.

November 8th.

This morning I awoke in the glow of sunshine; the air blew fresh and fragrant: never did I feel more elastic and enlivened. A brisker flow of spirits, than I had for many a day experienced, animated me with a desire of rambling about the shore of Baii, and creeping into caverns and subterraneous chambers. Off I set along Chaija, and up strange paths which impend over the grotto of Posilipo; amongst the thickets, mentioned a letter or two ago: for, in my present lively humour, I disdained ordinary roads, and would take paths and ways of my own. A society of kids did not understand what I meant, by intruding upon their precipices; and, scrambling away, scattered sand and fragments upon the good people, that were trudging along the pavement below. I went on from pine to pine, and thicket to thicket, upon the brink of rapid declivities. My conductor, a shrewd savage Sir William had recommended me, cheered our route with stories that had passed in the neighbourhood, and traditions about the grot over which we were travelling. I wish you had been of the party, and sat down by us on little smooth spots of sward, where I reclined; scarcely knowing which way caprice was leading me. My mind was full of the tales of the place, and glowed with a vehement desire of exploring the world beyond the grot. I longed to ascend the promontory of Misenus, and follow the same dusky route down which the Sybil conducted Æneas. With these dispositions I proceeded; and, soon, the cliffs and copses opened to views of the Baian bay, with the little isles of Niscita and Lazaretto, lifting themselves out of the waters. Procita and Ischia appeared at a distance, invested with that purple bloom so inexpressibly beautiful, and peculiar to this fortunate climate. I hailed the prospect, and blessed the transparent air, that gave me life and vigour to run down the rocks, and hie, as fast as my savage, across the plain to Puzzoli. There we took bark, and rowed out into the blue ocean, by the remains of a sturdy mole: many such, I imagine, adorned the bay in Roman ages, crowned by vast lengths of slender pillars; pavilions at their extremities, and taper cypresses spiring above their ballustrades: this character of villa, occurs very frequently in the paintings of Herculaneum. We had soon crossed over the bay, and landing on a bushy coast, near some fragments of a temple, which they say was raised to Hercules, advanced into the country by narrow tracks, covered with moss, and strewed with shining pebbles; to the right and left, broad masses of luxuriant foliage, chesnut, bay, and ilex, that shelter the ruins of columbariums and sepulchral chambers, where the dead sleep snug, amidst rampant herbage. The region was still, save when a cock crew from the hamlets; which, as well as the tombs, are almost concealed by thickets. No parties of smart Englishmen, and connoisseurs were about. I had all the land to myself, and mounted its steeps, and penetrated into its recesses, with the importance of a discoverer. What a variety of narrow paths, between banks and shades, did I wildly follow! my savage laughing loud at my odd gestures, and useless activity. He wondered I did not scrape the ground for medals, and pocket little bits of plaster, like other plausible young travellers, that had gone before me. After ascending some time, I followed him into the *piscina mirabilis,* the wondrous reservoir which Nero constructed to supply his fleet, when anchored in the neighbouring bay. 'Tis a grand labyrinth of solid vaults and pillars, as you well know; but you cannot conceive the partial gleams of sunshine which played on the arches; nor the variety of roots and ivies trailing from the cove. A noise of trickling waters prevailed, that had almost lulled me to sleep, as I rested myself on the celandine which carpets the floor; but, curiosity urging me forwards, I gained the upper air; walked amongst woods a few minutes; and then, into grots and dismal excavations (prisons they call them) which began to weary me. After having gone up and down, in this manner, for some time, we at last reached an eminence, that looked over the Mare Morto, and Elysian fields trembling with poplars. The Dead lake, a faithful emblem of eternal tranquillity, looked deep and solemn. A few peasants were passing along its margin, their shadows moving on the water: all was serene and peaceful. The meridian sun played on the distant sea. I enjoyed the pearly atmosphere, and basked in the pure beams, like an inhabitant of Elysium. Turning from the lake, I espied a rock, at about a league distant, whose summit was clad with verdure; and, finding this to be the promontory of Misenus, I immediately set my face to that quarter. We passed several dirty villages, inhabited by an ill-favoured generation, infamous for depredations and murders. Their gardens, however, discover some marks of industry; the fields are separated by neat hedges of cane, and corn seemed to flourish in the inclosures. I walked on, with slowness and deliberation; musing at every step, and stopping, ever and anon, to rest myself by springs and tufted bay-trees; when insensibly we began to leave the cultivated lands behind us, and to lose ourselves in shady wilds, which, to all appearance, no mortal had ever trodden. Here, were no paths; no inclosures; a primeval rudeness characterized the whole scene.

> Juvat arva videre,
> Non rastris, hominum non ulli obnoxia curæ.[115]

The idea of going almost out of the world, soothed the tone of mind, into which, a variety of affecting recollections had thrown me. I formed conjectures about the promontory to which we were tending; and, when I cast my eyes around the savage landscape, transported myself four thousand years into antiquity, and half persuaded myself, I was one of Æneas's companions. After forcing our way about a mile, through glades of shrubs and briars, we entered a verdant opening, at the base of the cliff which takes its name from Misenus. The poets of the Augustan age, would have celebrated such a meadow with the warmest raptures: they would have discovered a nymph in every flower, and detected a dryad under every tree. Doubtless, imagination never formed a lovelier prospect. Here were clear streams and grassy hillocks; leafy shrubs, and cypresses spiring out of their bosom:

> Et circum irriguo surgebant lilia prato
> Candida purpureis mista papaveribus.[116]

But, as it is not the lot of human animals to be contented, instead of reposing in the vale, I scaled the rock, and was three parts

---

115. Virgil, *Georgics,* bk. II, ll. 438–439. "It is a profitable thing to look at the fields, where you don't find a trace of man's rake, or any indication of his obnoxious care."

116. Propertius, *Elegies,* bk. I, ll. 37–38. "White lilies mixed with red poppies were springing forth all about the watered meadow."

dissolved in attaining its summit; a flat spot, covered with herbage, where I lay contemplating the ocean, and fanned by its breezes. The sun darted upon my head: I wished to avoid its immediate influence; no tree was near; deep below, lay the pleasant valley; 'twas a long way to descend. Looking round and round, I spied something like a hut, under a crag, on the edge of a dark fissure. Might I avail myself of its covert? My conductor answered in the affirmative; and added, that it was inhabited by a good old woman, who never refused a cup of milk, or slice of bread, to refresh a weary traveller. Thirst and fatigue urged me speedily down an intervening slope of stunted mytle. Though oppressed with heat, I could not help deviating a few steps from the direct way, to notice the uncouth rocks which rose frowning on every quarter. Above the hut, their appearance was truly formidable: dark ivy crept among the crevices, and dwarf aloes with sharp spines, such as Lucifer himself might be supposed to have sown. Indeed, I knew not whether I was not approaching some gate that leads to his abode, as I drew near a gulph (the fissure lately mentioned) and heard the hollow gusts which were imprisoned below. The savage, my guide, shuddered as he passed by, to apprize the old woman of my coming. I felt strangely, and stared around me; and but half liked my situation. To say truth, I wished myself away, and heartily regretted the green vale. In the midst of my doubts, forth tottered the old woman. You are welcome, said she, in a feeble voice, but a better dialect, than I had heard in the neighbourhood. Her look was more humane, and she seemed of a superior race to the inhabitants of the surrounding valleys. My savage treated her with peculiar deference. She had just given him some bread, with which he retired to a respectful distance, bowing to the earth. I caught the mode, and was very obsequious, thinking myself on the point of experiencing a witch's influence, and gaining, perhaps, some insight into the volume of futurity. She smiled at my agitation, and kept beckoning me into the cottage. Now, thought I to myself, I am upon the verge of an adventure. O Quixote! O Sylvio di Rosalva! how would ye have strutted in such a situation! What fair Infantas would ye not have expected to behold, condemned to spinning-wheels, and solitude? I, alas, saw nothing but clay walls, a straw bed, some glazed earthen bowls, and a wooden crucifix. My shoes were loaded with sand: this, my old hostess perceived; and, immediately kindling a fire in an inner part of the hovel, brought out some warm water to refresh my feet, and set some milk and chesnuts before me.

This patriarchal politeness was by no means indifferent, after my tiresome ramble. I sat down opposite to the door which fronted the unfathomable gulph; beyond, appeared the sea, of a deep cerulean, foaming with waves. The sky also, was darkening apace with storms. Sadness came over me like a cloud, and I looked up to the old woman for consolation. "And you too are sorrowful, young stranger," said she, "that come from the gay world! how must I feel, who pass year after year in these lonely mountains?" I answered, that the weather affected me, and my spirits were exhausted by the walk. All the while I spoke, she looked at me with such a melancholy earnestness, that I asked the cause; and began again to imagine myself in some fatal habitation,

> where more is meant than meets the ear.

Said she, "Your features are wonderfully like those of an unfornate young person, who, in this retirement . . . . ." the tears began to fall as she pronounced these words: she seemed older than before, and bent to the ground with sorrow. My curiosity was fired. "Tell me," continued I, "what you mean? who was this youth, for whom you are so interested? and why did he seclude himself in this wild region? Your kindness might no doubt alleviate, in some measure, the horrors of the place; but, may God defend me from passing the night near such a gulph! I would not trust myself in a despairing moment . . . . ." "It is," said she, "a place of horrors. I tremble to relate what has happened on this very spot;[117] but your manner interests me; and, though I am little given to narrations, for once I will unlock my lips, concerning the secrets of yonder fatal chasm. I was born in a distant part of Italy, and have known better days. In my youth, fortune smiled upon my family; but in a few years they withered away; no matter, by what accident: I am not going, however, to talk much of myself. Have patience a few moments! A series of unfortunate events reduced me to indigence, and drove me to this desert, where, from rearing goats, and making their milk into cheese, by a different method than is common in the Neapolitan state, I have, for about thirty years, prolonged a sorrowful existence. My silent grief and constant retirement, had made me

---

117. This passage is echoed in a letter Beckford wrote to Samuel Henley on 29 January 1782: "You are answerable for having set me to work upon a story so horrid that I tremble whilst relating it, and have not a nerve in my frame but vibrates like an Aspen." This resemblance is worth noting since the letter is often mistakenly used to help date the composition of *Vathek.*

appear, to some, a saint; and, to others, a sorceress. The slight
knowledge I have of plants, has been exaggerated; and, some years
back, the hours I gave up to prayer, and the recollection of former
friends, lost to me for ever! were cruelly intruded upon, by the
idle and the ignorant. But soon I sunk into obscurity: my little
recipes were disregarded; and you are the first stranger, who,
for these twelve months past, has visited my abode. Ah, would to
God its solitude had ever remained inviolate! It is now three and
twenty years"—and she looked upon some characters cut on the
planks of the cottage—"since I was sitting by moon-light, under
that cliff you view to the right, my eyes fixed on the ocean; my
mind lost in the memory of my misfortunes; when I heard a step,
and starting up, a figure stood before me. It was a young man, in a
rich habit, with streaming hair, and looks, that bespoke the
utmost terror. I knew not what to think of this sudden apparition.
'Mother,' said he, with faultering accents, 'let me rest under your
roof; and deliver me not up to those, who thirst after my blood.
Take this gold; take all, all!' Surprize held me speechless; the
purse fell to the ground; the youth stared wildly on every side:
I heard many voices beyond the rocks; the wind bore them distinctly; but, presently, they died away. I took courage, and assured
the youth, my cot should shelter him. 'O! thank you; thank you!'
answered he, and pressed my hand. He shared my scanty provision.
Overcome with toil (for I had worked hard in the day) sleep
closed my eyes for a short interval. When I awoke, the moon was
set, but I heard my unhappy guest sobbing in darkness. I disturbed
him not. Morning dawned, and he was fallen into a slumber. The
tears bubbled out of his closed eye-lids, and coursed one another
down his wan cheeks. I had been too wretched myself, not to
respect the sorrows of another: neglecting therefore my accustomed occupations, I drove away the flies that buzzed around
his temples. His breast heaved high with sighs, and he cried
loudly in his sleep, for mercy. The beams of the sun dispelling
his dream, he started up like one that had heard the voice of an
avenging angel, and hid his face with his hands. I poured some
milk down his parched throat. 'Oh, mother!' did he exclaim, 'I
am a wretch unworthy of compassion; the cause of innumerable
sufferings; a murderer! a parricide!' My blood curdled to hear
a stripling utter such dreadful words, and behold such agonizing
sighs swell in so young a bosom: for I marked the sting of conscience, urging him to disclose, what I am going to relate. It seems
he was of high extraction, nursed in the pomps and luxuries of

Naples, the pride and darling of his parents, adorned with a thousand lively talents, which the keenest sensibility conspired to improve. Unable to fix any bounds to whatever became the object of his desires, he passed his first years in roving from one extravagance to another; but, as yet, there was no crime in his caprices. At length, it pleased Heaven to visit his family, and make their idol the slave of an unworthy passion. He had a friend, who from his birth had been devoted to his interest, and placed all his confidence in him. This friend loved to distraction a young creature, the most graceful of her sex (as I can witness) ; and she returned his affection. In the exultation of his heart, he shewed her to the wretch, whose tale I am about to tell. He sickened at her sight. She too, caught fire at his glances. They languished; they consumed away; they conversed, and his persuasive language finished, what his guilty glances had begun. Their flame was soon discovered; for he disdained to conceal a thought, however dishonourable. The parents warned the youth in the tenderest manner; but advice and prudent counsels were to him so loathsome, that, unable to contain his rage, and infatuated with love, he menaced the life of his friend, as the obstacle of his enjoyment. Coolness and moderation were opposed to violence and frenzy, and he found himself treated with a contemptuous gentleness. Stricken to the heart, he wandered about for some time, like one intranced. Meanwhile the nuptials were preparing, and the lovely girl he had perverted, found ways to let him know, she was about to be torn from his embraces. He raved; and, rousing his dire spirit, applied to a malignant dæmon, who sold the most inveterate poisons. These he presented, like a cup of pure iced water, to his friend; and, to his own affectionate father. They drank the draught, and soon began to pine. He marked the progress of their dissolution with a horrid firmness. He let the moment pass, beyond which all antidotes were vain. His friend expired; and the young criminal, though he beheld the dews of death hang on his parent's forehead, yet stretched not forth his hand. In a short space, the miserable father breathed his last, whilst his son was sitting aloof in the same chamber. The sight overcame him. He felt, for the first time, the pangs of remorse. His agitations passed not unnoticed. He was watched: suspicions beginning to unfold, he took alarm, and, one evening, escaped; but not without previously informing the partner of his crimes, which way he intended to flee. Several pursued; but the inscrutable will of Providence blinded their search, and I was doomed to behold the effects of celestial vengeance. Such are the chief circumstances of the tale, I gathered from the youth. I swooned whilst he related it; and could take no sustenance. One whole day afterwards did I pray the Lord, that I might die, rather than be near an incarnate dæmon. With what indignation did I now survey that slender form, and those flowing tresses, which had interested me before, so much in his behalf! No sooner did he perceive the change in my countenance, than sullenly retiring to yonder rock, he sat careless of the sun and scorching winds; for it was now the summer solstice. Equally was he heedless of the unwholesome dews. When midnight came, my horrors were augmented; and I meditated, several times, to abandon my hovel, and fly to the next village; but a power, more than human, chained me to the spot, and fortified my mind. I slept, and it was late next morning, when some one called at the wicket of the little fold, where my goats are penned. I arose, and saw a peasant of my acquaintance, leading a female, strangely muffled up, and casting her eyes on the ground. My heart misgave me. I thought this was the very maid, who had been the cause of such unheard-of wickedness. Nor were my conjectures ill-founded. Regardless of the clown, who stood by in stupid astonishment, she fell to the earth, and bathed my hand with tears. Her large blue eyes gleamed between long eye-lashes, her bosom was more agitated than the waves, and whiter than their foam. Her trembling lips, with difficulty, enquired after the youth; and, as she spoke, a glow of conscious guilt lightened up her pale countenance. The full recollection of her lover's crimes shot through my memory. I was incensed, and would have spurned her away; but she clung to my garments, and seemed to implore my pity, with a look so full of misery, that, relenting, I led her in silence to the extremity of the cliff, where the youth was seated; his feet dangling above the sea. His eye was rolling wildly around, but it soon fixed upon the object, for whose sake he had doomed himself to perdition. I am not inclined to describe their extasies, nor the eagerness with which they sought each other's embraces. I turned indignantly my head; and, driving my goats to a recess amongst the rocks, sat revolving in my mind these strange events. I neglected procuring any provision for my unwelcome guests; and, about midnight, returned homewards by the light of the moon, which shone serenely in the heavens. Almost the first object her beams discovered, was the guilty maid, sustaining the head of her lover; who had fainted, through weakness and want of nourishment. I fetched some dry bread; and, dipping it in milk, laid it before them. Having performed this duty, I set open the door of my hut; and, retiring to a neighbouring cavity, there stretched myself on a heap of leaves, and offered my prayers to Heaven. A thousand fears, till this moment unknown, thronged into my fancy. I mistook the shadow of leaves that chequered the entrance of the grot, for ugly reptiles, and repeatedly shook my garments. The flow of the distant surges, was deepened by my apprehensions into distant groans: in a word, I could not rest; but, issuing from the cavern, as hastily as my trembling knees would allow, paced along the edge of the precipice. An unaccountable impulse hurried my steps. Dark clouds were driving athwart the sky, and the setting moon was flushed with the deepest crimson. A wan gleam coloured the sea. Such was my terror and shivering, that, unable to advance to my hut, or retreat to the cavern, I was about to shield myself from the night in a sandy crevice, when a loud shriek pierced my ear. My fears had confused me: I was in fact hard by my hovel, and scarcely three paces from the brink of the cavern. It was from thence the cries proceeded. Advancing, in a cold shudder, to its edge, part of which was newly crumbled in, I discovered the form of the young man, suspended by one foot to a branch of juniper, that grew ten feet down. Thus dreadfully did he hang over the gulph, from the branch bent with his weight. His features were distorted, his eye-balls glared with agony, and his screams became so shrill and terrible, that I lost all power of assistance. Fixed I stood, with my eyes rivetted upon the criminal; who incessantly cried out, 'O God! O Father! save me, if there be yet mercy! Save me; or I sink into the abyss!' I am convinced he saw me not; for, not once, did he implore my help. My heart was dead within me. I called out upon the Lord. His voice grew faint; and, as I gazed intent upon him, he fell into utter darkness. I sunk to the earth in a trance; during which, a sound, like the rush of pennons, assaulted my ear: methought, the evil spirit was bearing off his soul. I lifted up my eyes, but nothing stirred: the stillness that prevailed was awful. The moon looked stained with streaks of blood: her orb, hanging low over the waves, afforded a sickly light, by which I perceived some one, coming down that white cliff you see before you; and, soon, I heard the voice of the young woman, calling aloud on her guilty lover. She stopped. She repeated, again and again, her exclamation; but there was no reply. Alarmed and frantic, she hurried along the path; and now, I saw her on the promontory; and now, by yonder pine; devouring with her glances every crevice in the rock. At length, perceiving me, she flew to where I stood, by the fatal precipice; and, having noticed the fragments fresh crumbled in, pored importunately on my countenance. I continued pointing to the chasm. She trembled not; her tears could not flow; but she divined my meaning. 'He is lost!' said she; 'the earth has swallowed him! but, as I have shared with him the highest joy, so will I partake his torments. I will follow: dare not to hinder me!' I shrunk back. Like the phantoms I have seen in dreams, she glanced beside me; and, clasping her hands high above her head, lifted a stedfast look on the hemisphere, and viewed the moon with an anxiousness that told me, she was bidding it farewell, for ever. Observing a silken handkerchief on the ground, with which she had, but an hour ago, bound her lover's temples, she snatched it up, and, imprinting it with burning kisses, thrust it into her bosom. Once more, expanding her arms in the last act of despair and miserable passion, she threw herself, with a furious leap, into the gulph. To its margin I crawled on my knees, and, shuddering, looked down into the gloom. There I remained in the most dreadful darkness; for now, the moon was sunk, the sky obscured with storms, and a tempestuous blast ranging the ocean. Showers poured thick upon me, and the lightning, in clear and frequent flashes, gave me terrifying glimpses of yonder accursed chasm."——"Stranger, dost thou believe in the great Being? in our Redeemer? in the tenets of our faith?" I answered with reverence, but said I was no catholic. "Then," continued the aged woman, "I will not declare before an heretic, what were the sacred visions of that night of vengeance." She paused: I was silent. After a short interval, with deep and frequent sighs, she resumed her narration. "Day-light began to dawn, as if with difficulty; and it was late, before its radiance had tinged the watery and tempestuous clouds. I was still kneeling by the gulph, in prayer, when the cliffs began to brighten, and the beams of the morning sun to strike against me. Then did I rejoice. Then, no longer did I think myself of all human beings the most abject and miserable. How different did I feel myself from those, fresh plunged into the abodes of torment, and driven, for ever, from the morning!——Three days elapsed in total solitude: on the fourth, some grave and antient persons arrived from Naples, who questioned me, repeatedly, about the wretched lovers; and to whom I related their fate with every dreadful particular. Soon after I learned, that all discourse concerning them, was expressly stopped; and, that no prayers were offered up for their souls."——With these words, as well as I recollect, the old woman ended her singular narration. My blood thrilled as I walked by the gulph to call my guide, who stood aloof under the cliffs. He seemed to think, from the paleness of my countenance, that I had heard some gloomy prediction; and shook his head, when I turned round to bid my old hostess, adieu! It was a melancholy evening, and I could hardly refrain from tears, as, winding through the defiles of the rocks, the sad scenes which had passed amongst them, recurred to my memory. Traversing a wild thicket, we soon regained the shore; where I rambled a few minutes, whilst the peasant went for the boat-men. The last streaks of light were quivering on the waters, when I stepped into the bark; and, wrapping myself up in an awning, slept, till we reached Puzzoli; some of whose inhabitants came forth with torches, to light us home. I was vexed to be roused from my visions; and had much rather have sunk into some deep cave of the Cimmerians, than returned to Naples.

Letter XXIV.

Naples, November 9th.

We made our excursion to Pompeii, passing through Portici, and over the last lava of Mount Vesuvius. I experienced a strange mixture of sensations, on surveying at once, the mischiefs of the late eruption, in the ruin of villages, farms, and vineyards; and, all around them, the most luxuriant and delightful scenery of nature. It was impossible to resist the impressions of melancholy from viewing the former, or not to admit that gaiety of spirits which was inspired by the sight of the latter. I say nothing of the Museum at Portici, which we saw in our way, on account of the ample descriptions of its contents already given to the public; and, because, it should be described no otherwise, than by an exact catalogue, or by an exhibition of engravings. An hour and half brought us from this celebrated repository to Pompeii. Nothing can be conceived more delightful than the climate and situation of this city. It stands upon a gently-rising hill, which commands the bay of Naples, with the islands of Caprea and Ischia, the rich coasts of Sorento, the tower of Castel a Mare; and, on the other side, Mount Vesuvius, with the lovely country intervening. It is judged to be about an Italian mile long, and three and an half in circuit. We entered the city at the little gate which lies towards Stabiæ. The first object upon entering, is a colonade round a square court, which seems to have formed a place of arms. Behind the colonade, is a series of little rooms, destined for the soldiers barracks. The columns are of stone, plaistered with stucco, and coloured. On several of them we found names, scratched in Greek and Latin; probably, those of the soldiers who had been quartered there. Helmets, and armour for various parts of the body, were discovered, amongst the skeletons of some soldiers, whose hard fate had compelled them to wait on duty, at the perilous moment of the city's approaching destruction. Dolphins and tridents, sculptured in relief on most of these relics of armour, seem to shew they had been fabricated for naval service. Some of the sculptures on the arms, probably, belonging to officers, exhibit a greater variety of ornaments. The taking of Troy, wrought on one of the helmets, is beautifully executed; and much may be said in commendation of the work of several others.

We were next led to the remains of a temple and altar, near these barracks. From thence, to some rooms floored (as indeed were almost all that have been cleared from the rubbish) with tesselated, mosaic pavements; of various patterns, and most of them of very elegant execution. Many of these have been taken up, and now form the floors of the rooms in the Museum at Portici; whose best ornaments of every kind, are furnished from the discoveries at Pompeii. From the rooms just mentioned, we descended into a subterraneous chamber, communicating with a bathing apartment. It appears to have served as a kind of office to the latter. It was, probably, here, that the cloaths, used in bathing, were washed. A fire-place, a capacious caldron of bronze, and earthen vessels proper for that purpose, found here, have given rise to the conjecture. Contiguous to this room, is a small circular one with a fire-place; which was the stove to the bath. I should not forget to tell you, that the skeleton of the poor laundress (for so the antiquaries will have it) who was very diligently washing the bathing cloaths, at the time of the eruption, was found lying in an attitude of the most resigned death, not far from the washing caldron, in the office just mentioned.

We were now conducted to the temple, or rather chapel, of Isis. The chief remains are, a covered cloister; the great altar, on which was, probably, exhibited the statue of the goddess; a little edifice to protect the sacred well; the pediment of the chapel, with a symbolical vase in relief; ornaments in stucco on the front of the main-building, consisting of the lotus, the sistrum, representations of gods, Harpocrates, Anubis, and other objects of Egyptian worship. The figures on one side of this temple, are Perseus with the Gorgon's head; on the other, Mars and Venus, with Cupids bearing the arms of Mars. We next observe three altars of different sizes. On one of them, is said to have been found, the bones of a victim unconsumed; the last sacrifice having, probably, been stopt by the dreadful calamity which had occasioned it. From a niche in the temple, was taken a statue of marble; a woman pressing her lips with her fore-finger. Within the area is a well, where the priest threw the ashes of the sacrifices. We saw, in the Museum at Portici, some lovely arabesque paintings, cut from the walls of the cloister. The foliage, which ran round the whole sweep of the cloister itself, is in the finest taste. A tablet of basalte, with Egyptian hieroglyphics, was transported from hence to Portici, together with the following inscription, taken from the front gate of the chapel:

N. POPIDIUS N. F. CELSINUS.
AEDEM ISIDIS TERRAE MOTU COLLAPSAM
A FUNDAMENTO P. SUA RESTITUIT.
HUNC DECURIONES OB LIBERALITATEM
CUM ESSET ANNORUM SEX ORDINI SUO
GRATIS ADLEGERUNT.

Behind one of the altars we saw a small room, in which our guide informed us a human skeleton was discovered, with some fish-bones on a plate near it, and a number of other culinary utensils. We then passed on to another apartment, almost contiguous; where, nothing more remarkable had been found than an iron crow; an instrument with which, perhaps, the unfortunate wretch, whose skeleton I have mentioned above, had vainly endeavoured to extricate herself; this room being, probably, barricaded by the matter of the eruption. This temple, rebuilt, as the inscription imports, by N. Popidius, had been thrown down by a terrible earthquake, that likewise destroyed a great part of the city (sixteen years before the famous eruption of Vesuvius, described by Pliny, which happened in the first year of Titus, A.D. 79) and buried, at once, both Herculaneum, and Pompeii. As I lingered alone in these environs sacred to Isis, some time after my companions had quitted them, I fell into one of those reveries, which my imagination is so fond of indulging; and, transporting myself seventeen hundred years back, fancied I was sailing with the elder Pliny, on the first day's eruption, from Misenum, towards Retina and Herculaneum; and, afterwards, toward the villa of his friend Pomponianus[118] at Stabiæ. The course of our galley seldom carried us out of sight of Pompeii; and, as often as I could divert my attention from the tremendous spectacle of the eruption, its enormous pillar of smoke standing conically in the air, and tempests

---

118. Pomponius was the subject of a biography by Pliny: *De vita Pomponi Secundi.*

of liquid fire, continually bursting out from the midst of it, then raining down the sides of the mountain, and flooding this beautiful coast with innumerable streams of red-hot lava, methought I turned my eyes upon this fair city, whose houses, villas, and gardens, with their long ranges of columned courts and porticos, were made visible through the universal cloud of ashes, by lightning from the mountain; and saw its distracted inhabitants, men, women, and children, running to and fro in despair. But in one spot, I mean the court and precincts of the temple, glared a continued light. It was the blaze of the altars; towards which I discerned a long-robed train of priests, moving in solemn procession, to supplicate by prayer and sacrifice, at this destructive moment, the intervention of Isis, who had taught the first fathers of mankind the culture of the earth, and other arts of civil life. Methought, I could distinguish in their hands, all those paintings and images sacred to this divinity, brought out, on this portentous occasion, from the subterraneous apartments, and mystic cells of the temple. There was every form of creeping thing, and abominable beast, every Egyptian pollution, which the true Prophet had seen in vision, among the secret idolatries of the temple at Jerusalem. The priests arrived at the altars; I saw them gathered round, and purifying the three, at once, with the sacred meal; then, all moving slowly about them, each with his right hand towards the fire: it was the office of some, to seize the firebrands of the altars, with which they sprinkled holy water on the numberless by-standers. Then, began the prayers, the hymns, and lustrations of the sacrifice. The priests had laid the victims, with their throats downward, upon the altars; were ransacking the baskets of flour and salt, for the knives of slaughter, and proceeding in haste to the accomplishment of their pious ceremonies; when one of our company, who thought me lost, returned with impatience, and, calling me off to some new object, put an end to my strange reverie. We were now summoned to pay some attention to the scene and corridor of a theatre, not far from the temple. Little more of its remains being yet cleared away, we hastened back to a small house and garden, in the neighbourhood of Isis. Sir W. Hamilton (in his account of Pompeii, communicated to the Society of Antiquaries) [119] when speaking of this house, having taken occasion to give a general idea of the private mansions of the antient citizens, I shall take the liberty of transcribing the

---

119. *Account of the Discoveries at Pompeii Communicated to the Society of Antiquaries of London* (1777).

whole passage. "A covered cloister, supported by columns, goes round the house, as was customary in many of the houses at Pompeii. The rooms in general are very small; and, in one, where an iron bedstead was found, the wall had been pared away to make room for this bedstead; so that it was not six feet square, and yet this room was most elegantly painted, and had a tesselated, or mosaic floor. The weight of the matter erupted from Mount Vesuvius, has universally damaged the upper parts of the houses; the lower parts are mostly found as fresh as at the moment they were buried. The plan of most of the houses at Pompeii is a square court, with a fountain in the middle, and small rooms round, communicating with that court. By the construction and distribution of the houses, it seems, the inhabitants of Pompeii were fond of privacy. They had few windows towards the street, except where, from the nature of the plan, they could not avoid it; but, even in that case, the windows were placed too high for any one in the streets to overlook them. Their houses nearly resemble each other, both as to distribution of plan, and in the manner of finishing the apartments. The rooms are in general small, from ten to twelve feet, and from fourteen to eighteen feet; few communications between room and room; almost all without windows, except the apartments situated to the garden, which are thought to have been allotted to the women. Their cortiles, or courts, were often surrounded by porticos, even in very small houses. Not but there were covered galleries before the doors of their apartments, to afford shade and shelter. No timber was used in finishing their apartments, except in doors and windows. The floors were generally laid in mosaic work. One general taste prevailed, of painting the sides and ceilings of the rooms. Small figures, and medallions of low relief, were sometimes introduced. Their great variety consisted in the colours, and in the choice and delicacy of the ornaments, in which they displayed great harmony and taste. Their houses were some two, others three stories high."

We now pursued our way through, what is with some probability thought to have been, the principal street. Its narrowness, however, surprised me. It is scarcely eleven feet wide, clear of the foot-ways raised on each side of it. The pavement is formed of a large sort of flattish-surfaced pebbles; not laid down with the greatest evenness, or regularity. The side-ways may be about a yard wide, each paved, irregularly enough, with small stones. There are guard-stones, at equal intervals, to defend the foot-passengers from carriages and horses. I cannot say I found any thing either elegant or pleasant in the effect of this open street. But, as the houses in general present little more than a dead wall toward it, I do not imagine any views, beyond mere use and convenience, were consulted in the plan. It led us, however, through the principal gate, or entrance, to a sort of Villa Rustica, without the limits of the city; which amply recompensed our curiosity. The arcade, surrounding a square garden, or court-yard, offers itself first to the observer's notice. Into this, open a number of coved rooms, adorned with paintings of figures, and arabesque. These rooms, though small, have a rich and elegant appearance, their ornaments being very well executed, and retaining still their original freshness. On the top of the arcade runs a walk, or open terrace, leading to the larger apartments of the higher story. One of the rooms below, has a capacious bow-window, where several panes of glass, somewhat shattered, were found; but in sufficient preservation to shew, that the antients were not without knowledge of this species of manufacture. As Horace, and most of the old Latin Poets, dwell much on the praises of antient conviviality, and appear to have valued themselves considerably on their connoisseurship in wine, it was with great pleasure I descended into the spacious cellars, sunk and vaulted beneath the arcade abovementioned. Several earthen amphoræ were standing in rows against the walls; but the Massic and Falernian, with which they were once stored, had probably long been totally absorbed by the earth and ashes, which were now the sole contents of these venerable jars. The antients are thought to have used oil instead of corks; and that the stoppers were of some matter that could make but little resistance, seems confirmed by the entrance of that, which now supplied the place of wine. The skeletons of several of the family, who had possessed this villa, were discovered in the cellar; together with brass and silver coins, and many such ornaments of dress as were of more durable materials. On re-ascending, we went to the hot and cold baths; thence, to the back of the villa, separated by a passage from the more elegant parts of the house: we were shewn some rooms which had been occupied by the farmer, and from whence several implements of agriculture had been carried, to enrich the collection at Portici. On the whole, the plan and construction of this villa are extremely curious, and its situation very happily chosen. I could not, however, help feeling some regret, in not having had the good fortune to be present at the first discovery. It must have been highly interesting to see all its antient relics (the greatest part of which are now removed) each in its proper place; or, at least, in the place they had possessed for so long a course of years. His Sicilian majesty has ordered a correct draught of this villa to be taken, which, it is hoped, will one day be published, with a complete account of all the discoveries at Pompeii.

Our next walk was to see the Columbarium, a very solemn-looking edifice, where probably the families of higher rank only at Pompeii, deposited the urns of their deceased kindred. Several of these urns, with their ashes, and one, among the rest, of glass inclosed in another of earth, were dug out of the sepulchral vaults. A quantity of marble statues, of but ordinary execution, and colossal masks of terra cotta, constituted the chief ornaments of the Columbarium. It is situated without the gates, on the same side of the city with the villa, just described. There is something characteristically sad in its aspect. It threw my mind into a melancholy, but not disagreeable, tone. Under the mixed sentiments it inspired, I cast one lingering look back on the whole affecting scene of ruins, over which I had, for several hours, been rambling; and quitted it to return to Naples, not without great reluctance.[120]

---

120. Beckford left Naples about the beginning of December. He arrived in Rome on the 5th of the same month and on the next day he described his journey in a letter to Lady Hamilton in the following manner: "I hardly am yet sensible how I reached Rome. My journey was like a dream. Objects passed swiftly and unnoticed before my eyes. Just now the sun set, and the cliffs of Cajeta were glowing with ruddy light. Next instant Monte Circello presented itself and the moon gleamed upon the tranquil waters. A minute after all was darkness and gloom. Sometimes I heard the roar of distant waves, and sometimes undetermined sounds which seemed to issue from the mountains."

Letter XXV.

Rome, December 9th.

My last letter was dispatched in such a hurry, that I had not time to conclude it. This will be nearly as imperfect; but yet I cannot forbear writing, having the vanity to believe you are pleased with hearing only, that I am well.

Your friend H.[121] walked with me this morning in the Loggios of Raffaele, and we went afterwards to the Capitol. Nothing delighted me more, in the whole treasury of sculptures, than a figure, in alto relievo, of Endymion, reclined on the mountain's brow: his head falls upon his breast with an ease and gracefulness, of which the Greeks alone had ever a true conception. Most of the chambers, if you recollect, are filled with the elegant remains of Adrian's collection. The villa of that classic Emperor at Tivoli, must have been the most charming of structures. Having travelled into various, and remote parts of his empire, he assembled their most valuable ornaments on one spot. Some of his apartments were filled with the mysterious images and symbols of Egypt: others, with eastern tripods, and strange Asiatic wares. Though enraptured with St. Peter's and the Vatican; with the gardens and groves of pine, that surround this interesting city; still I cannot help sighing after my native hills and copses: which look (I know not how it happens) more like the haunts of Pan, than any I have

---

121. A. P. Oppé conjectures that Mr. "H." was Gavin Hamilton (1723–1798), painter, excavator, and steady resident of Rome since 1769. See *Alexander and John Robert Cozens* (Cambridge: Harvard University, 1954), pp. 14–15. This seems to have been the second meeting Beckford had with "H." In a letter to Alexander Cozens from Naples, 7 November 1780, Beckford writes: "I saw your Friend H. at Rome, who seems to have a share of Taste but wants our fiery enthusiasm." The correspondence between these two statements, it should be noted, supports the view that A. Cozens was the person to whom most of the letters of *Dreams* were directed.

seen in Italy. I eagerly anticipate the placid hours we shall pass, perhaps, next summer, on the wild range which belongs to our sylvan deities. In their deep fastnesses, I will hide myself from the world, and never allow its glare to bicker through my foliage. You will follow me, I trust, into retirement, and equally forget the turmoils of mankind. What have we children of the good old Sylvanus to do, with the miseries, or triumphs of the savages that prowl about London? Let us forget there exists such a city; and, when reposing amongst ivy and blossoms of broom, imagine ourselves in the antient dominion of Saturn, and dream that we see him pass along, with his rustic attendants.[122]

---

122. Beckford left Rome on December 11th and headed for the "pestilential air" of Venice. He was in Venice on December 29th and stayed there until 10 January 1781, whereupon he traveled ten days to Augsburg, reaching this city on the 20th.

Letter XXVI.

Augsburg, January 20th, 1781.

For these ten days past, have I been traversing Lapland; winds whistling in my ears, and cones showering down upon my head, from the wilds of pine, through which our route conducted us. Often were we obliged to travel by moon-light; and I leave you to imagine the awful aspect of the Tirol mountains, buried in snow. I scarcely ventured to utter an exclamation of surprize, though prompted by some of the most striking scenes in nature; lest I should interrupt the sacred silence that prevails, during winter, in these boundless solitudes. The streams are frozen, and mankind petrified, for aught I know to the contrary; since whole days have we journeyed on, without perceiving the slightest hint of their existence. I never before felt the pleasure of discovering a smoke rising from a cottage, or of hearing a heifer lowing in its stall; and could not have supposed there was so much satisfaction in perceiving two or three fur-caps, with faces under them, peeping out of their concealments. I wish you had been with me, exploring this savage region. Wrapped up in our bear-skins, we should have followed its secret avenues, and penetrated, perhaps, into some inchanted cave lined with sables, where, like the heroes of northern romances, we should have been waited upon by dwarfs, and sung drowsily to repose. I think it no bad scheme to sleep away five or six years to come; since, every hour, affairs are growing more and more turbulent. Well, let them! provided we may but enjoy, in security, the shades of our thickets.[123]

123. Beckford was in Strasbourg on January 28th and by early February he was in Paris where he resided until his return to England on the 14th of April, thus bringing his Grand Tour to an end.

Reflections on the Economy, Politics, and Fine Arts of Several European Nations[124]
Letter XXVII.

Here, my dear Sir, have I finished my rapid excursion, and marked each part of it with the impression, whether of sentiment or imagination, with which every object struck me, as I passed along. That I have rendered back every impression whilst warm, and, if I may so express it, whilst perfectly alive, I flatter myself, I need not tell you. But I cannot help reflecting, that I may appear to have run over so considerable a tract of country, with as much political indifference, as if I had affected the character of a citizen of the world; to which, however, I pretend no farther, than the rights of humanity oblige me. No: I boast myself an Englishman, amidst all the misfortunes and disgraces of my country. Nor have I hurried up and down Europe, with so total an inattention to its political aspects, as not to have observed some prevalent circumstances, some ruling points of character, particularly in the nations combined against us, which, compared with our own characteristics, forbid me to despair. I confess the lion of England had been lulled too long by that splendid fortune, which, from the late peace, to the present war, has so deeply

124. Editor's title. Writing on a preliminary leaf of a copy of *Italy* given to him by Beckford, Richard Samuel White lamented the omission of this letter, "which was both admirable, & prophetic; which another 10 years proved accurate to a miracle." "It is impossible," he added, "to conceive *why* Mr. Beckford should have chosen to dip his Honors by leaving it out of *Italy*." The observations it contained "would have redounded to the *Name* of the Author, & rescued this publication from the charge of a *too rapid* Sketch." White's copy of *Italy* is part of the Beckford collection housed at Yale's Beinecke Library.

wounded the jealousy of Europe; and, at length, provoked the revenge of a high and mighty republic, and two great monarchies. But, has this triple league, with all its efforts or successes, brought us to the term of our prosperity? Shall England no more lift up her head among the nations? I do not, I say, despair. Since the opportunity I have had of comparing both our political and civil temper, with that of our enemies, hath convinced me of our being so far from disadvantageously opposed to them in these respects, that I am persuaded, were the measures of our ministers, once to inspire such confidence and union, as to bring our discriminative qualities and advantages to their natural operation, some strange reverse would yet dissipate that awful cloud, which hangs over our country. May we sound no hope on our natural impatience, and love of change? or on those fits of enthusiasm, to which we are sometimes wrought up by accidental causes? These qualities and affections seem as inherent in Englishmen, as frigidity, heaviness, and phlegm in the people of Holland; and as naturally dispose men to action, as the others do, to rest. Will not our national generosity, that liberal spirit of contribution, which the ministers of England have hitherto found inexhaustible, produce better effects than may be expected from the mercantile parsimony of the Dutch? Does not our constitution, with all the impediments which a discontented party can at any time hang on the wheels of government, admit a dispatch and vigour, of which the complicated machine of Dutch polity is utterly incapable? Again, are we never to derive any advantage from our unyielding perseverance, sobriety, and strength of spirit, in either fortune; when thrown into the balance against that extreme levity, or dejection, which success on one hand, and misfortune on the other, never fails to produce in the French? Have I not observed too, that universal spirit of philosophy, which was opening the eyes of France to liberty and the rights of mankind, beginning visibly to decline; a spirit, which, perhaps, boded worse to England, than all the ambition, or resources, of this potent neighbour? Her ruling powers are evidently afraid that its influence should go farther than they meant. It has eradicated superstition, and restrained intolerance. Its business is done. By a few steps more it had produced jealousy and alarm; if it were not sufficiently advanced, to have done it already. The wits of France, probably, paid a much sincerer tribute, than her politicians, in their grief for the death of Voltaire. By the operation of some secret encouragement, we now see the *Encyclopedie*[125] gently giving way to the *Bibliotheque des Romans*,[126] and Tressan's *Extraits de Chevalerie;*[127] which are rising every day into consideration and importance, under the fostering wing of fashion. Had France learnt a more general application of her philosophy, the power of the people would have undoubtedly increased, but probably at the monarch's expence; much more, however, had it increased at the expence of her envied rival, Great Britain. Let her then be as obedient as she will to her *Grande Monarque;* but, if reason should once become her sovereign, we should have tenfold more cause to fear her, than at present.

The slow and pompous march of the Spaniard, which way soever he moves, or toward whatever object; a vain parade, much more than real effect, of naval or military force; his inexperience and inability, the inevitable consequences of long cessation from war; his indigence, which a senseless pride of nobility, and contempt of useful industry, when once rooted in a country, never fail to engender; are marks of character so diametrically opposed to the substantial bravery and activity; the warlike habits, naval strength, and adroitness; and, above all, to the rich resources of the agriculture, arts, and commerce of his enemies; that I cannot help presaging, some material advantages to England, must result from the contest of national characters, so different; and of which, the common sense of mankind has ever decidedly preferred our own.

Nothing can more strongly evince the prodigious superiority of England, above any one of her enemies taken singly, than her firm and unremitted resistance to so many united; and that too, whilst more than half the natural advantages of her character and circumstances have, by some strange fatality, been prevented from operating in her favour.

The result of this comparative survey of England, France, Spain, and Holland, will not suffer us to despair, that we may end this unhappy contest, without much more injury, upon the whole, than our enemies themselves must sustain. I shall not pursue the parallel betwixt England and her adversaries any further, as the state of war under which I have travelled through them, has prevented so familiar an inspection into a thousand particulars, as is

---

125. Diderot's *Encyclopédie*, the monumental 18th-century dictionary of the arts, sciences, and the trades, published between the years 1751 and 1780.

126. *Bibliothèque Universelle des Romans* (1775–1778).

127. Louis-Elisabeth de la Vergne's *Corps d'extraits de Romans de Chevalerie* (1782).

necessary to judge with clearness, and impartiality. But I will endeavour to gratify the curiosity you express, to know under what views, and with what results, I have compared our own country with others which I have visited, and with which we have happily no quarrel. The actual state of their agriculture, manufactures, or commerce; together with that of their fine arts, chiefly engaged my attention; but I do not mean to give you an account of each of these objects, under the several countries that made part of my tour; but of one, or more of them, according to the different pretensions of each nation. With respect to Flanders, particularly the Austrian part of it, I need not say, that neither manufactures, nor commerce, form any longer its characteristics. It is long since the fleece of England and of Andalusia, employed the looms of Antwerp and Bruges: the manufactures of brilliant tissues, and tapestries, formed of wool, silk, and gold, which once drew wealth and splendor into these cities, would be lost arts, but for the imitations to which they have given rise at the Gobelins. For their exquisite skill in thread laces, the Flemings may still challenge the world. The noble canals, which intersect their country, (the first works of their kind in Europe) may be considered as monuments of their antient commerce. Though the trade and manufactures of Flanders are, at present, inconsiderable; yet, it cannot be denied, that agriculture appears in a very flourishing state; and, what is much to the credit of government, that the mass of the people seem to be as much at their ease, as those of any country in Europe. The poor are no where better fed, better cloathed, or better lodged. The meanest habitations are neat, and chearful, both within, and without; and their tenants carry all an air of contentment. I saw nothing in their villages of that singular raggedness and dejection, which, in some other countries, tell a reproachful tale of oppression and bad police, on one part; and, of despondency and wretchedness, on the other. Will my own country here stand the comparison, without a blush?—When I say, that her agriculture is not less flourishing, nor less skilfully managed than that of Flanders; and that her manufacture, and commerce have, in some measure, bid defiance to war; what shall I say to that extensive poverty and wretchedness, which the evil genius of our own country seems to delight in contrasting, with our opulence and prosperity? The philosopher, or politician, may search for the cause of this phenomenon; but the most hasty traveller, with his eyes open, will want no proof of its existence. With respect to the fine arts, and particularly Painting, in which Flanders once boasted her school; it is enough to say, that, whatever be the cause of it, she no longer supports any pretensions to them, worth particular consideration.

The standing armies of Germany present a striking appearance to a traveller, who finds the whole country, nevertheless, wrapt in profound peace, from one end to the other. Almost every sovereign prince, (and countless is the number of sovereign princes in Germany) has his battalions drawn out in long array before his palace, with as much order as the parallel rows of beech, or poplar, that form the avenues which conduct us to his capital. But what does all this mean, was I continually asking myself at every post, as I passed through some new dominion? Is there still some unknown continent, for the conquest of which these numerous hosts are by and by to unite? The days of crusading are long gone by; and indeed, into so consumptive a state, are fallen the monastic institutions, since the death of the pious Empress, that, shortly, there will not be left a hermit to preach them. For what purpose then is kept on foot all this armed force, who have turned their plough-shares into swords, and are devouring the fruits of the earth, instead of contributing, as formerly, to their more plentiful production? Is it not possible, they may one day prove an army of locusts, and more than threaten this fair region with famine? A celebrated annalist, from his observation of this phenomenon, has boldly concluded, "that Germany is on the eve of undergoing a change, which, three ages ago, has taken place around her; that she is labouring every instant to accelerate that moment, when the feudal system, which still enervates her, shall disappear before one real monarchy, under which her lay princes will become peers of the imperial court, and her ecclesiastical, the chaplains." Were there only one considerable power in Germany, M. Linguet's[128] conjecture would wear the appearance of greater probability. But, that not being the fact, (another, of greater force, and in a very flourishing state, being established there, jealous and watchful of every motion on the part of that power from whom the politician supposes the change will come) it will admit of much doubt, whether the abolition of the remains of the feudal system in Germany be at all in contemplation. Nothing, however, is likely to effect such an alteration, but, either, a perfect agreement, or, an absolute rupture, betwixt the two rival powers. In the first

---

128. Simon Nicolas Henri Linguet (1736–1794), political journalist and editor. Beckford is referring to Linguet's periodical, *Les Annales politiques, civiles et littéraires du dix-huitième siècle,* which was started in London in 1777.

case, the business might perhaps be managed by the fashionable method of partition; but the result would be different from that which the Annalist supposes, and two monarchies, instead of one, would be fixed on the ruins of the petty sovereignties; and still great enough would either of them be, for the tranquillity of Europe. In the case of an absolute rupture betwixt the rival states, on account of the leading object alluded to, it is most probable, that without a greater disparity of forces, than at present subsists, neither party, at the end of the contest, would find itself so superior to the other, as to bring the little powers under its own dominion; so that at last, the grand point could be no otherwise accomplished, than by partition; and the result will be the same as before. After all, it seems impossible to determine, without more data, that the martial aspect of Germany indicates any such project as has been intimated above. If, however, it should be granted; it will by no means follow, that no other end is proposed. The motives for establishments of such expence, military establishments too, which are ever regarded with an eye of jealousy and distrust, may possibly be many and important. If I may be allowed a conjecture upon this occasion, I should not hesitate to assign, as a principal one, the increase of infidelity and extreme dissolution of modern manners, caused by the Encyclopedic philosophy. The disregard of sanctions, which were wont to influence human conduct, makes the use of other means requisite for that purpose; or civil society must be dissolved. What means, at once cries every sovereign, great or little, so effective, so cogent, so compendious, as the sword? what more conducive to our own dignity, splendor, or security, than military government? I know not whether, in my representation of this matter, I have not given the cause and effect each other's place. The philosophy, as it is called, of the *Encyclopedie* has, doubtless, contributed abundantly to the relaxation of our old obligations, and the licentiousness of manners; so that the suspension of the sword over the head of civil society, has some appearance of being naturally introduced, in consequence of things being in such a state. But, may not the ambition of princes, (which thus very decently steps in with its military apparatus, as if almost appealed to, for the prevention of anarchy and confusion) have been the first moving principle of the whole mischief? and is it not probable, that the love of empire first nursed that philosophic spirit, whose evident tendency, if not design, has been, to strike at the foundations of religion, the grand rule of mankind, in order to make necessary the more immediate rule of the sovereign's sword. The sword, perhaps, may teach mankind better political manners, as far as the sovereign's immediate happiness is concerned, than the gown. But the social conduct of citizen towards citizen, will be much better taught by the free discussion, and candid injunctions, of religious and moral duties, than by the narrow decrees of a despot's will; forced upon slaves, under the terror of the sword. The feudal system, as formerly conditioned, when its thousand little sovereignties knew their respective privileges and interests no better, than to be ever at variance; was undoubtedly a very unhappy situation. The present state of Germany, with all its remains of feudality, presents no such gloomy, political aspect; and it may well be questioned, whether the general happiness of the empire would be better provided for, under the abolition of them, than it is at present. Probably, it would not; when we consider how the jealousy of Europe would be excited by such an event; and, perhaps, the Germans themselves, from the Emperor to the lowest Baron, may be sufficiently convinced of it, neither to wish on his part, nor to dread on theirs, so momentous a change. If this be a true state of the case, whatever other motives there may have been for the enormous military establishments, in these countries; the principal ones, more probably, regard internal government, than either conquest, or defence. Such, at least, are the ideas, which the martial appearance of Germany has suggested to myself; and, I hope, on bringing it home to a comparison with my own country, I have some reason to flatter myself, that, amongst all the untoward circumstances which cloud our political horizon, there are none that bode so ill to the civil liberties of England, as do the standing armies in a time of peace, to those of Germany. After all, it is, with respect to Germany, a very surprising circumstance, that split, as she still is, into electorships, dukedoms, bishopricks, abbacies, landgravates, and baronies, imperial, and hanse towns; computed in all to amount to no less than three hundred distinct sovereignties; sovereignties, too, which owe their origin to a total change in the German constitution; effected by the Popes, in order to lessen the Imperial power, and render the empire elective: it is, I say, a surprising circumstance, that a body, consisting of so many heterogeneous members, each claiming independency within itself, should have braved the political storms of so many ages, and have preserved a form, which, according to all analogy, seems so ill calculated for duration. To develope the causes of so singular a circumstance, you will easily imagine to have made no part of the plan of a hasty traveller; as an object of such extent, would require the minutest investigation, during a long residence in the country; but, whatever they be, I doubt not they would, on discovery, be found such, as to reflect honour on the national character of the Germans.

Many nations surpass Swisserland in riches, splendor, and magnificence; but, in most of those attributes which form the solid basis of civil happiness, it may fairly be questioned, whether she may not dispute the palm with any country in Europe. Liberty, patriotism, toleration, economy, justice, and simplicity of manners, unite to characterise the respectable states, which constitute the Helvetic body. We read their antient love of liberty, in the noble assertions of it, against their surrounding tyrants, the Dukes of Burgundy and Savoy; the Emperor of Germany, and other potentates; of whose disgraces in the contest their annals are full. Nor does their zeal for liberty at this day, want its antient warmth. Their free forms of government are all jealously guarded, and invariably maintained. The patriotism of the Swiss, is eminently displayed in the numerous projects of individuals for the improvement of their country, and, in the encouragement they continually meet with in their societies of agriculture and commerce; in the admirable establishment and regulation of their militia; not to mention their great public works of roads and bridges, to facilitate the communication of the inhabitants through their country of mountains, rivers, and lakes. The liberal spirit of toleration appears no where to greater advantage, than in the constant example of mutual indulgence and concession, and that political harmony resulting from them, exhibited in the cordial confederacy of the Catholic and Protestant states; at the same time that both are attached to their different forms of worship, with as much zeal and sincerity, as any people in Europe.

Their public economy is manifested by the means they use to keep the balance of trade in their own favour. As their woollen and linen manufactures, though considerable, are not able to supply their necessities, without importation, they strictly prohibit, within themselves, the use of those ornaments of gold, of silver lace, and jewellery, in the manufacture of which they excel. The exportation of these articles, much more than pays the cloathing they are obliged to import. The abundance of cattle from their pastures, allows them an overplus for foreign markets; at least, sufficient to answer the importation of corn, of which article, notwithstanding their industry and improvements in tillage, their scanty pittance of arable land does not produce them enough for their common consumption. On the subject of Swiss economy, should not be forgotten their sumptuary laws, their general police, their establishment of public magazines of corn, their wise provisions for the poor, and many other economical regulations; which seem better understood, or at least better executed, in this country, than in others. The primitive simplicity of living, and pastoral habits of the mountainous cantons; the discouragements of luxury, gaming, and ostentation in the rest, arising from the spirit of equality, natural to republics; the want of foreign territory, from whence to draw too copious an influx of wealth; and of those enlarged scenes of commerce, which maritime situations alone can open to a country; conspire to keep the state of property, whether in houses, or lands, much more fixt in Swisserland, than in other nations. It is needless to infer from this circumstance, that the law, finding little to devour, or to feed upon, will not thrive in such a situation; that the points of contention, being few and unimportant, will be left chiefly to the decisions of natural equity, and that justice will consequently have place among the characteristics of the Swiss.

O fortunatos nimium, sua si bona norint![129]

And I know not whether it be not due to this people, to number among their other good qualities, the consciousness of their own happiness. The wise provisions they have, hitherto, made for its preservation, give us no small reason for so honourable a supposition in their behalf. They seem well aware, that their first political interest is to observe a strict neutrality in the quarrels of their neighbours; and to live in perfect peace with them all. These valuable advantages can be no way secured to them, but by their own concord and prudence.

Another interesting object is, their military service. It is of great importance to the security of the Helvetic confederacy, that fortitude and bravery be not extinguished, among the people who compose it; and, since the science of tactics, unhappily so necessary, has undergone such mighty improvements, it much imports to Swiss to be instructed in the new manœuvres of the military art. It is under this point of view, and that of forming auxiliary connections with the great powers, that the cantons con-

---

129. *Georgics*, bk. II, 1. 458. "How blessed will they be if they come to know their fortune."

sider the mercenary service. Without these considerations, the treaties which regulate the conditions of that service, would be more indifferent to the confederacy, than to individuals, who devote themselves to the profession of arms. If the luxury introduced among the military, no longer allows Swisserland to derive all the advantages she might promise herself from a military school, kept up at the expence of foreign powers; yet, her mercenary service, now rendered permanent under the regulation of fixed rules, will no more expose her states to the same fermentations, or the same corruption, of which certain epochs of the fifteenth and sixteenth centuries offered some melancholy instances. If this country can find but means to prevent that state of luxury and refinement, which her officers in foreign service have unfortunately contracted, from spreading into other ranks; if the heights of the Jura could prove a barrier against the contagious politeness of their western neighbours; it might long continue to be, what it still is, the happiest in Europe. I have ventured, in talking of the other countries I have seen, to draw some parallel betwixt them and our own; and shall I confess to you, that I should probably have abstained from it, had I not been convinced, that I could allow her some advantages over them, without risquing any question of my impartiality? Suppose now, in attempting a comparison betwixt Great Britain and Helvetia, I were to pronounce the former infinitely more wealthy, more magnificent, more powerful, it would be saying little, if I must be silent on her political wisdom, or national happiness; or could I, at best, but affirm, that whilst we flourish in our conversation, or in our books, on these important articles, the Swiss, despising insignificant parade, practise the one, and feel the other. In the cursory retrospect I am making of the countries I have travelled through, it being my plan to attend only to such objects as characterise them, in Italy, I must chiefly confine my reflections to their genius for the management of affairs; to their manners; and to their fine arts. The people of this country having always supported pretensions to superior sagacity and address in political arrangements, and a talent for what is called, business; I caught all opportunities of observing them in this point of view. It is at Rome, that one sees this character more frequently, and more conspicuously displayed, than in all the other states together; I shall therefore select the Roman for a portrait of the dextrous man of affairs; and may safely leave the Venetian, the Tuscan, the Neapolitan, or citizen of any other Italian state, in the same predicament (though the features will not be so strongly marked) to be discovered by his family likeness. Dissimulation and secrecy, joined with address to take advantage of any false step in a competitor; intrigues to gain his confidence, and dexterity in using the acquisition, to supplant him; lying à propos to improve a fair occasion; ever affecting an air of business, in the very center of idleness and dissipation; and ostentatious display of one's own credit; a readiness to promise magnificently; an officious intrusion into all affairs that present themselves; and a constant solicitude to impress a great idea of one's own importance; these qualities and practices united, form the principal springs of a policy, so much boasted of for ages, that the court of Rome was considered as the school of the most able and subtle ministers, who have figured in Europe.

Religion, in Italy, being nearly reduced to a shell, the fruit of which has long been given up to nations better disposed to taste its value, and consequently having little or nothing left but exterior, demands no particular consideration apart from the Italian manners; and to them it certainly gives a very strong tincture; their ceremonious practice of it throwing a deep shade of decency and solemnity over their ordinary conduct, and serving, in the eye of the world, as a useful contrast to their natural vivacity, and to irregularities springing from their warmth of temperament. Of their civil morality, if I may so express it, as professedly distinguished from religion, one may judge with tolerable certainty, if we admit this general principle, that to be, and to appear, are two things absolutely different; and that it is seldom men of the world are not obliged, for their own advantage, to shew themselves different from what they really are. From this sort of obligation will result imposing appearances, dissimulation, cunning, and all such dispositions and habits, as are best calculated to conceal the real character, and support the counterfeit. These being admitted as fundamental principles of conduct in the world, we may judge of their influence upon a people accustomed to intrigue, supple and artificial, acquainted with few necessities more powerful than the calls of vanity, and who, to gratify them, are habituated to give, without remorse, into any means that present themselves; and that, commonly, under the mask of benevolence; or, at least, under a very seducing air of politeness. It is observable, however, that when the Italians have to deal with each other, they know pretty well how far their own assurances and pretences will go; and what credit to give to those they mutually receive.

Now, it will be easily imagined, that the practice of dissembling their sentiments, and of continually holding a language that has little to do with their thoughts, must reduce those who, nevertheless, wish to display their wit and parts in conversation, to the necessity of talking much, without saying any thing, and of exhausting the chapter of indifferent trifles, and general observations. This every foreigner must have remarked, particularly at Rome; and cannot but have attributed to it the pompous insipidity of their conversations. Any one, the least used to them, foresees nearly what every man will say, that enters the room. This poverty of conversation, amidst a great deal of talking, is the most striking in those who have rank to support it, and who have their constant assemblies, on certain fixed days. What makes all this the more provoking to a stranger is, that these persons are so far from wanting wit, or talents, that they fall into these habits from having too much of them. The reason is, as already intimated, that every man must have his pretensions; will seem deeply informed of public affairs; and would not, for the world, but appear to labour under a load of importance. This affectation of consequence, marks, in general, the higher orders of society. One of the characteristics of the middle and lower ranks, is their inattention to domestic economy, and their resolution of enjoying, at all events, the present hour; with little regard either to past, or future considerations. This humour is wonderfully encouraged by the voluptuous softness of the climate, which indisposes both body and mind to much exertion; by the happy fertility of a soil, productive with little labour; and, perhaps, most of all, in the lowest station, by the numerous charitable establishments, with which every city and town in Italy abounds; holding out a sure resource to want, sickness, and old age. But the great nursery of indolence and laziness, in this, as well as all other Catholic countries, are the monastic foundations. The habitual neglect of accumulation, the *humour de vivre au jour la journée,* naturally slacken that ardour of gain, which constitutes a specific distinction of the mercantile and manufacturing classes, in most other countries, where the parent refuses himself a thousand comforts and accommodations, to lay up fortunes for his children. The true Italian suffers no inconvenience from any such ambition. Indeed another reason co-operates with their disposition to self-enjoyment in this case; which is, the general infidelity to the marriage-bed. This circumstance, destroying all idea of exclusive property in a man's posterity, must greatly abate

the natural warmth and activity of parental affection. Hence it
is, that a father thinks he has done very handsomely by his
children, when he has fed and cloathed them during their infancy
and youth; and procured them some talent, by which they can
get their own livelihood. People with this way of thinking may
get pleasantly enough through the world, from one generation to
another, in a country, where the succours and resources abovementioned, are so frequently to be found; and where, through
the felicity of climate, there almost always reigns an abundance,
pretty nearly equal. But, from the moment this abundance happens to fail, through some extraordinary intemperature of seasons;
or whatever other cause; the Italians are the most miserable people
in the world; for there being a certain point, beyond which the
established charities can afford no assistance, and that point being
generally reached in common times, the majority of those, who,
in the case supposed, wish to have recourse to this fund, must
necessarily be disappointed; and nothing can then exceed the
wretchedness of such individuals, as have made no provision
against a moment of scarcity. Travellers who have seen the kingdom of Naples a little before harvest, are astonished at the fertility of the lands, and the richness of their produce; and are
unable to conceive how, from this state of abundance, it is
possible to fall into such extreme dearth, that the poor perish
from hunger. This, however, happened in the year 1749.

There is another mark of character in which the Italians, without the exception of a single state, or that of any rank, or class
of people, universally partake; I mean their rage for theatrical
spectacles, and indeed every species of public exhibition, or enter-
taiment. This passion they seem to inherit from the antient
Romans, and the bequest has lost nothing in their hands. In the
fashionable world, the morning is spent in a slovenly dishabille,
that prevents their going out, or receiving frequent visits at home.
Reading, or work takes up a very small portion of this part of
the day; so that it passes away in a yawning sort of nonchalance.
People are scarcely wide awake, till about dinner-time. But, a few
hours after, the important business of the toilette puts them
gently into motion; and, at length, the opera calls them completely
into existence. But it must be understood, that the drama, or the
music, do not form a principal object of theatrical amusement.
Every lady's box is the scene of tea, cards, cavaliers, servantis,
lap-dogs, abbés, scandal, and assignations; attention to the action
of the piece, to the scenes, or even to the actors, male, or female,

is but a secondary affair. If there be some actor, or actress, whose merit, or good fortune, happens to demand the universal homage of fashion, there are pauses of silence, and the favourite airs may be heard. But without this cause, or the presence of the sovereign, all is noise, hubbub, and confusion, in an Italian audience. The hour of the theatre, however, with all its mobbing and disturbance, is the happiest part of the day, to every Italian, of whatever station; and the least affluent will sacrifice some portion of his daily bread, rather than not enjoy it. Those who have not one sous, that can possibly be spared (for life is found preferable to theatric diversions) are however not so forlorn as to be cut off from all opportunities of spectacle. Such never fail to attend the pompous ceremonies of the church, the rites and mummeries of the saints, and to swell the shabby consequence of every farthing-candle procession. Politeness, refinement of manners, and the true spirit of society, (although there are many individuals, especially such as have travelled, very highly accomplished in these respects) not making any distinct characteristic of the Italians, I shall forbear to consider them, under this point of view. But, having observed the very opposite qualities to be generally prevalent in one nation of Italy, and that the last in which I should have expected to find it, so the plan I proposed in this letter, requires from me a particular intimation or two, upon the subject.

The Neapolitans, are by most authors, antient and modern, represented as a soft, effeminate, and voluptuous people. Admitting these attributes, we are apt to conclude, that whatever other imperfections they may stand charged with, we shall, at least, be sure to meet with great gentleness, civility, and, even, refinement of manners in such a nation. I paid my first visit to Naples under this prepossession, and was not a little surprized to perceive how ill it was founded. But my wonder ceased, on being convinced, after no long residence, that I had made my conclusion, with the world in general, upon a false hypothesis. Nothing, I will venture to affirm, is less true than that the Neapolitans are soft and effeminate; nor are they even voluptuous, in the more elegant sense in which that word is usually understood. They are fiery, and sensual, in a high degree, and during the prevalence of the siroc wind, extremely relaxed, and indolent. But, their general tone of character is rough, harsh, and impetuous, even, in higher life; in the lower, gross, barbarous, and violent; choleric and vindictive, in both. What, undiscerning eyes may have mistaken for politeness, is nothing but the habitual cringe of adula-

tion to the iron rod of arbitrary power. But let me do the Neapolitans justice: they want not feeling, nor generosity; and would
but the church and the state emancipate them from that superstition and ignorance; which one hath been no less fond than the
other, of converting into an engine of power; the Neapolitans,
with the genius and sensibility which no person can deny them,
would soon become a gallant and respectable nation.

It is an easy transition from the manners to the fine arts of a
people; and I know you are growing impatient for my strictures
upon the latter. As I by no means am writing you a dissertation,
you must not expect me to enter into any discussion of the long-
agitated question; whether, when the fine arts have once, in any
country, attained their zenith, it be possible for them, during any
considerable course of time, to continue in an unaltered state of
perfection? My business is only to state with impartiality the
matter of fact, as it relates to Italy. You know how it stood with
respect to antient Greece and Rome; the only two countries,
besides modern Italy, where the fine arts can be said to have
grown to maturity. Although modern Italy should be found to
resemble her two great ancestors in this matter; yet, from so scanty
a number of examples, it would be unphilosophical, perhaps, to
attempt the decision: I have, therefore, another good reason for
not meddling with it.

Although Constantine removed a great number of the beautiful
remains of antiquity from Rome, and other parts of Italy, to
adorn his new capital in the East; though the northern barbarians
destroyed a considerable part of those he left; and the nonsensical
zeal of bigots and devotees led them, in after-times, to mutilate
some of the finest models that had escaped the blind fury of the
Goths and Huns, Rome was, nevertheless, fortunate enough to
have preserved in part, and partly to have discovered, a multitude
of inestimable gems, statues, vases, bas-reliefs, and relics of architecture. The Venetians, as the fruit of commerce, or of conquest,
brought home many precious monuments from Greece; and the
Florentines are obliged to the taste and opulence of the Medicis,
for the finest collection of antiques in every kind, that the world
ever saw. But Florence, and indeed all Europe, acknowledges a
still greater obligation to this family, for having placed these
models before the artists of their times; and given the most generous patronage to the successful imitation of them. The eyes of
all Italy were soon opened to works of genius, and the fine arts
made the most rapid progress towards their antient splendor.

Most of the great artists of that age were contented with their near approach to perfection, in producing models, that might be opposed to the antique. Michael Angelo, however, soared still higher; and, perhaps, it may be safely affirmed, that his Moses on the tomb of Julius the Second, has a force and sublimity of expression, beyond any relic of antiquity. Some of his statues, likewise, which adorn the tombs of the Medici, in the church of St. Laurence at Florence, boast the noblest expression. The genius and talents of this wonderful artist, are the more remarkable, inasmuch as most of these statues are not finished. Bandinelli, John of Bologna, and Algardi,[130] have run the same career, with the most conspicuous success. Bernini,[131] in a different stile, less elevated, but always elegant and graceful, is, like them, original in most of his productions. The statue of St. Teresa, in the church of the Vittoria at Rome, is an admirable work, and exhibits every possible charm of expression. Indeed, I know few antique statues which, all considerations being made, can be compared with it.

In the ages of ignorance and barbarity, which preceded that of the Medicis, architecture, at once, the most beautiful, and useful of the fine arts, seemed totally lost. They, from whom alone its patronage and encouragement were to be expected, employed themselves more in destroying the admirable monuments of antiquity, than in imitating them. The palaces of princes and nobles, were then, for the most part, little else than a confusion of towers, united by strong walls, without symmetry, taste, or idea of architecture. These fortresses were asylums, where violence and rapine secured themselves with impunity, and, indeed, were calculated for nothing better. The antient gothic buildings of the same time, dedicated to the service of religion, were nothing but long, dark, and massive vaults, without the least ornament, or beauty; and the same judgment may safely be formed of all their public buildings, from such remains of them as are still subsisting. But, at the period I am speaking of, architecture revived with the other arts. The Popes, and sovereign princes of Florence, Modena, Mantua, Ferrara, not to mention the nobles of the states of Genoa and Venice, left such superb and beautiful edifices behind them, as will, for ages to come, remain indisputable proofs of their taste for antient architecture. As to works of decoration among

---

130. Alessandro Algardi (1602–1654), Italian sculptor.
131. Giovanni Lorenzo Bernini (1598–1680), Italian architect and sculptor. He was responsible for the colonnade of St. Peter's and the façade of the Barberini palace. "Apollo and Daphne" is one of his most famous works of sculpture.

the antients, though, perhaps, much cannot with certainty be said
of their colouring, we are perfectly acquainted with the beauty
of the forms they employed. Their vases still remain the finest
models that can be imitated; nor is any thing to be found com-
parable, in point of form, to their urns. It is needless to mention
the exquisite workmanship of their gems, or the elegant capricios
of their arabesque ornaments. We read with astonishment what
has been written of the perfection of antient painting. It should
seem to have been carried to a degree of expression, scarcely
imaginable. The famous picture of "the sacrifice of Iphigenia," by
Timanthes,[132] was a masterpiece of the art. Pliny speaks of it,
as a work above all praise; and that, without doubt, on the credit
of the Greek authors. It should, however, be remembered, that
the Greeks joined to extreme sensibility of beauty, a great propensity to hyperbole; considerable allowance must, therefore, be
made, for their representations on this subject. It was long before
any antique painting was found, that could give an opportunity
of forming any equitable judgment. Under the pontificate of
Clement the Eighth, toward the end of the sixteenth century, was
at length discovered, in the ruins of the gardens of Mæcenas, a
picture representing a marriage, celebrated under the title of the
"Nôce Aldobrandine," from the name of the Pope. The connoisseurs of the time viewed it with rapture; the antiquaries called
it two thousand years old; and, without hesitation, attributed it to
the pencil of Apelles.[133] A veneration for antiquity, which then
wanted a little philosophical correction, determined them to regard this picture as a wonder of the art, at a time, too, when
they had under their eyes the *chef d'œuvres* of Raffaelle, Corregio,
Titian, and of many other artists; whose most moderate performances were much above this piece. Many of the paintings
found at Herculaneum and Pompeii, may very fairly be brought
into comparison with this; and yet none of them, in respect of
design, colouring, ordonnance, or execution, approach the perfection of the Medicean age, or, even, that of the present. It was
from the antient gems, bas-reliefs, statues, and bronzes, that the
painters of that age caught their first idea of excellence. They then
turned their eyes upon Nature herself; and, soon, raised the art
of painting to that pitch of perfection, which it knew not before,
and has not known since. Among other arts, music owes its happiest cultivation to Italy; and seems, in the earlier part of the

---

132. A Greek painter of the 4th century B.C.

133. Apelles, one of the great painters of antiquity, lived during the 4th
century B.C. and was the official court painter for Philip of Macedon.

present century, to have arrived at its meridian splendor. We still, however, hear admirable music at Venice. It is there, that the professors and the dilettanti best learn grace, intelligence, and beauty of execution: it is there we still hear the finest voices of Italy. Music, of all the arts is that which maintains itself with the greatest honour in Italy: destined in its origin to celebrate the praises of the Supreme Being, and of the most distinguished of mankind, it is the natural expression of gratitude, contentment, and pleasure; nor can it be easily supposed, though it in some measure shares the corruption of the sister arts, to fall into a disgraceful state of decline, amongst a people so peculiarly sensible of its charms, and famous for their love of spectacles, and feasts, of which music is the soul.

Having thus slightly traced out an idea of the revival of the arts in Italy; their resources in the antient models; the high perfection to which painting, sculpture, and architecture attained in the fourteenth and fifteenth centuries; and music in the earlier part of the eighteenth; I know you will not dispense with my drawing some comparison between their present state in this country, and our own. Nothing occasions greater surprise to every intelligent traveller, than to observe that a country, which, for the space of two hundred years, gave birth to the most consummate painters, sculptors, and architects; and, for a considerable period, to the most accomplished musicians; to find an immense quantity of their most celebrated performances dispersed through that country; and, what is stranger, to see the same taste, and love of the fine arts, prevail among its inhabitants, as formerly distinguished them; and, moreover, no disinclination in its princes, and great men, to patronize, and encourage merit,—yet, be absolutely unable to discover throughout that country, where all its arts are still cultivated, one worthy successor of Raffaelle, Titian, the Caraccis,[134] or Guido;[135] one architect, who treads in the steps of Michael Angelo, Leonardo da Vinci, Sansovino, or Palladio; one sculptor, possessed either of the ideas, or the execution of Bernini, Algardi, or Conradi. I will not say, that Geminiani,[136] Tartini,[137] and Pergolese[138] were the last of their musicians. There

---

134. Family name of three influential Italian painters: Agostino (1557–1602), Annibale (1560–1609), and Lodovico (1555–1619).

135. Guido Reni (1575–1642), Italian engraver and painter. One of his famous frescoes, "Phoebus and the Hours, Preceded by Aurora," now hangs in the Palazzo Rospigliosi in Rome.

136. Francesco Geminiani (1687–1762), Italian violinist and composer.

137. Giuseppe Tartini (1692–1770), Italian musical composer and violinist.

138. Giovanni Battista Pergolese (1710–1736), Italian musical composer.

are still living professors of extraordinary talents; but, taking melody and harmony both, into an estimate of their merits, I dare venture to assure you, they follow those great masters *non passibus æquis.*

It was not till the reign of his present majesty, that England discovered her genius for the fine arts. We had produced but one painter[139] in history, in any former reign, whose name is not now forgotten; and the most distinguished of those who flattered the national vanity in portrait-painting, were foreigners. What we had done in sculpture, or architecture, on the Grecian models, shews neither taste, nor intelligence. Music was little more than dry counter-point; without air, or grace. The arts, after their decline in Italy, seemed long wavering where to fix their seat. The French made attempts to allure them, in the last century, without much success. If, however, they have done little worth admiration, in the four great arts, designed under the name of the fine arts, it is but justice to allow, that no nation hath exceeded the French in the manufactures of silk and tapestry, as well as in all those minute ornaments that can contribute to the finery of dress. Every species of trinketry that can give eclat to a lady's toilette, or consequence to the person of a *petit-maitre,* is fabricated at Paris, in the utmost perfection. But my partiality to French taste, is leading me astray.

The solid institution of the English youth in the polite literature of the Greeks and Romans; the improvement of their taste by foreign travel; the unrivalled opulence which Great Britain has derived from her conquests, and commerce, conspiring all together with our native energies; have, under the auspices of an enlightened sovereign, at length, raised the fine arts to a degree of consideration, and excellence in England, which they have not known, since their restoration under the Medicis, in any part of Europe, Italy excepted. And such is the rapid, I may say, astonishing progress, they have made in our own country, within these last twenty years, that I do not hesitate to declare, from an attentive, and, I hope, impartial comparison of their present state in Italy, and in England, the superiority in favour of my own country. I must beg you, however, to understand, that, in this comparison, music is not included; for Italy, though inferior to what she has been in this charming art, still bears the palm of music, from every other nation. A circumstance in favour of my decision,

---

139. Beckford's solicitor, Richard Samuel White, wrote in his copy of *Dreams* that the "painter" referred to here is either Sir James Thornhill or Holbein.

and not a little to our honour, should be mentioned:—that we have artists at Rome, who, in almost every branch, surpass those of all other nations, now resident there; and that the Pope, and the Roman princes often employ them, in preference to their own. At the same time, I assure you of this as a fact; and, further, that the performances of some of our artists, now at Rome, are consecrated to fame in the Vatican itself; you and all the world know, that we can boast many others at home, still equal to them, and some superior. To enter particularly into the merits of individuals, is a very delicate undertaking; and the public at this day, are too much informed, and too well agreed in their sentiments, to leave me any opportunity of gratifying curiosity on this subject, were I less disposed to decline so invidious a talk. But, by this time, I can hardly conceive you to wish for any thing, but the conclusion of so long a letter; and, having exhausted the materials, which the shortness of my tour would allow me to collect, I have only to add, that whatever judgment you may form of the strictures this letter contains, you will not infer from them, that I ran abroad, only to admire other countries, at the expence of my own. I am not conscious of having, on any occasion, overlooked their merits; and, I flatter myself, from a survey of the best countries in Europe, I may justly affirm, that in commerce, arts, and arms, not one of them stands superior to Great Britain.

I am, &c.

ADDITIONAL LETTERS

The following letters, written in a second excursion, which was interrupted by a dangerous illness, are added, on account of their affinity to some of the preceding.

Letter I.

Cologne, May 28th, 1782.

This is the first day of summer; the oak-leaves expand, the roses blow, butterflies are about, and I have spirits enough to write to you.[1] We have had clouded skies this fortnight past, and roads like the slough of Despond. Last Wednesday, we were benighted on a dismal plain, apparently boundless. The moon cast a sickly gleam, and, now and then, a blue meteor glided along the morass, which lay before me. After much difficulty, we gained an avenue, and, in an hour's time, discovered something, like a gateway, shaded by crooked elms, and crowned by a cluster of turrets. Here we paused, and knocked; no one answered. We repeated our knocks; the stout oaken gate returned a hollow sound; the horses coughed; their riders blew their horns. At length, the bars fell, and we entered—by what means, I am ignorant; for no human being appeared. A labyrinth of narrow winding alleys, dark as the vaults of a cathedral, opened to our view. We kept wandering along, at least, twenty minutes, between lofty mansions, with grated windows and strange galleries, projecting one over another; from which depended innumerable uncouth figures and crosses, in iron-work, swinging to and fro with the wind. At the end of this gloomy maze, we found a long street, not fifteen feet wide, I am certain; the houses still loftier than those in the alleys, the windows thicker barred, and the gibbets (for I know not what else to call them) more frequent. Here and there, we saw lights glimmering in the highest stories, and arches on the right and left, which seemed to lead into retired courts, and deeper dark-

---

1. This tour actually began on the 16th of May at which time Beckford set out with his party for Dover. After reaching Dover, they drove on to Ostend and were in Brussels on the 19th before they embarked for Cologne.

ness. Along one of these recesses we were jumbled, over such pavement, as I hope you may never tread upon; and, after parading round it, went out at the same arch, where we came in. This procession seemed at first very mystical; but it was too soon accounted for by our postillions, who confessed they had lost their way. A council was held amongst them in form, and then we struck into another labyrinth of hideous edifices; habitations I will not venture to call them, as not a creature stirred; though the rumbling of our carriages was echoed by all the vaults and arches. Towards midnight we rested a few minutes, and a head poking out of a casement, directed us to the hotel of Der Heilige Geist; where an apartment, thirty feet square, was prepared for our reception.

Letter II.

Inspruck, June 4th.
No sooner had we passed Feuzen, than we entered the Tirol, and the country of wonders. Those lofty peaks, those steeps of wood I delight in, lay before us. Innumerable clear springs gush out on every side, overhung by luxuriant shrubs, in blossom. The day was mild, though overcast, and a soft blue vapour rested upon the hills; above which, rise mountains, that bear plains of snow into the clouds. At night we lay at Nasariet, a village buried amongst savage promontories. The next morning we advanced, in bright sunshine, into smooth lawns on the slopes of mountains, scattered over with larches; whose delicate foliage formed a light-green veil to the azure sky. Flights of birds were merrily travelling from spray to spray. I ran delighted into this world of boughs, whilst C.[2] sat down to draw the huts, which are scattered about for the shelter of herds, and discover themselves amongst the groves in the most picturesque manner. These little edifices are uncommonly neat, and excite those ideas of pastoral life, to which I am so fondly attached. The turf from whence they rise, is enamelled, in the strict sense of the word, with flowers. A sort of blue-bell predominated, brighter than ultramarine; here and there, auriculas looked out of the moss, and I often reposed upon tufts of ranunculus. Bushes of phillerea were very frequent; the sun shining full on their glossy leaves. An hour passed away swiftly, in these pleasant groves, where I lay supine under a lofty fir; a tower of leaves and branches.

---

2. John Robert Cozens (1752–1797), English water-colorist, son of Alexander.

Letter III.

Once more, said I to myself, I shall have the delight of beholding
Venice; so got into an open chaise, the strangest curricle that
ever man was jolted in, and drove furiously along the causeways
by the Brenta, into whose deep waters it is a mercy, methinks,
I was not precipitated. Fiesso, the Dolo, the Mira, with all their
gardens, statues, and palaces, seemed flying after each other; so
rapid was our motion. After a few hours confinement between
close steeps, the scene opened to the wide shore of Fusina. I
looked up (for I had scarcely time to look before) and beheld a
troubled sky, shot with vivid red, the Lagunes tinted like the opal,
and the islands of a glowing flame-colour. The lofty mountains
of the distant continent appeared of a deep, melancholy grey,
and innumerable gondolas were passing to and fro in all their
blackness. The sun, after a long struggle, was swallowed up in
the tempestuous clouds. In an hour, we drew near to Venice,
and saw its world of domes rising out of the waters. A fresh breeze
bore the toll of innumerable bells to my ear. Sadness came over
me as I entered the great canal, and recognized (the scene of many
a strange adventure) those solemn palaces, with their lofty arcades
and gloomy arches, beneath which I had so often sat. The Venetians being mostly at their villas on the Brenta, the town appeared
deserted. I visited, however, all my old haunts in the Place of St.
Mark; ran up the Campanile, and rowed backwards and forwards,
opposite the Ducal Palace, by moon-light. They are building a
spacious quay, near the street of the Sclavonians, fronting the
island of San Giorgio Maggiore; where I remained alone, at least
an hour, following the wanderings of the moon amongst mountainous clouds, and listening to the waters dashing against marble

252

steps. I closed my evening at my friend, M. de R.'s, and sung over the airs I composed in the dawn of our acquaintance. Next morning the wind was uncommonly violent for the mild season of June, and the canals much agitated; but I was determined to visit the Lido once more, and bathe on my accustomed beach. The pines in the garden of the Carthusians were nodding as I passed by in my gondola, which was very poetically buffetted by the waves. Traversing the desart of locusts, I hailed the Adriatic, and plunged into its bosom. The sea, delightfully cool, refreshed me to such a degree, that, upon my return to Venice, I found myself able to thread its labyrinths of streets, canals, and alleys, in search of amber, and oriental curiosities. The variety of exotic merchandize, the perfumes of coffee, the shade of awnings, and sight of Greeks and Asiatics, sitting cross-legged under them, made me think myself in the bazars of Constantinople. 'Tis certain, my beloved town of Venice, ever recalls a series of eastern ideas and adventures. I cannot help thinking St. Mark's a mosque; and the neighbouring palace, some vast seraglio; full of arabesque saloons, embroidered sophas, and voluptuous Circassians.

Letter IV.

Padua, June 19th.

The morning was delightful, and St. Anthony's bells in full chime. A shower, which had fallen in the night, rendered the air so cool and grateful, that Mad. de R. and myself determined to seize the opportunity, and go to Mirabello, a country-house which Algarotti[3] had inhabited, situate amongst the Euganean hills, eight or nine miles from Padua.

Our road lay between poplar alleys, and fields of yellow corn, overhung by garlands of vine, most beautifully green. I soon found myself in the midst of my favorite hills, upon slopes covered with clover, and shaded by cherry-trees. Bending down their boughs, I gathered the fruit, and grew cooler and happier every instant. We dined very comfortably in a strange hall, where I pitched my piano-forte, and sung the voluptuous airs of Bertoni's *Armida*. That enchantress might have raised her palace in this situation; and, had I been Rinaldo, I certainly should not very soon have abandoned it. After dinner we drank coffee under some branching lemons, which sprung from a terrace, commanding a boundless scene of towers and villas; tall cypresses and shrubby hillocks rising, like islands, out of a sea of corn and vine. Evening drawing on, and the breeze blowing fresh from the distant Adriatic, I reclined on a slope, and turned my eyes anxiously towards Venice; then, upon some little fields, hemmed in by chesnuts in blossom, where the peasants were making their hay; and, from thence, to a mountain, crowned by a circular grove of fire and cypress. In the center of these shades, some monks have a comfortable nest; perennial springs, a garden of delicious vegetables, and, I dare say, a thousand

---

3. Francesco Algarotti (1712–1764), Italian philosopher and connoisseur in art and music.

luxuries besides, which the poor mortals below never dream of. Had it not been late, I should certainly have climbed up to the grove, and asked admittance into its recesses; but, having no mind to pass the night in this eyrie, I contented myself with the distant prospect.

Letter V.

Rome, June 29th.

It is needless for me to say I wish you with me: you know I do; you know how delightfully we should ramble about Rome, together. This evening, instead of jiggeting along the Corso, with the puppets in blue and silver coats, and green and gold coaches; instead of bowing to Cardinal this, and dotting my head to Abbé t'other, I strolled to the Coliseo; found out my old haunts amongst its arches, and enjoyed the pure transparent sky, between groves of slender cypress. Then, bending my course to the Palatine Mount, I passed under the arch of Titus, and gained the Capitol, which was quite deserted; the world, thank Heaven, being all slip-slopping in coffee-houses, or staring at a few painted boards, patched up before the Colonna palace, where, by the by, to-night is a grand rinfresco, for all the dolls and doll-fanciers of Rome. I heard their buzz at a distance; that was enough for me! Soothed by the rippling of waters, I descended the capitoline stairs, and leaned several minutes against one of the Egyptian lionesses. This animal has no knack at oracles; or else, it would have murmured out to me the situation of that secret cave, where the wolf suckled Romulus and his brother. About nine, I returned home; and am now writing to you, like a Prophet on the house-top. Behind me rustle the thickets of Villa Medici; before, lies roof beyond roof, and dome beyond dome; these are dimly discovered: but, don't you see the great cupola of cupolas, twinkling with illuminations? The town is real, I am certain; but, surely, that structure of fire must be visionary.

Letter VI.

Rome, June 30th.

As soon as the sun declined, I strolled into the Villa Medici; but finding it haunted by fine pink and yellow people; nay, even by the Spanish ambassador, and several more dignified carcasses, I moved off to the Negroni garden. There I found, what my soul desired, thickets of jasmine, and wild spots overgrown with bay; long alleys of cypress totally neglected, and almost impassable through the luxuriance of the vegetation; on every side, antique fragments, vases, sarcophagi, and altars, sacred to the Manes, in deep, shady recesses; which I am certain the Manes must love. The air was filled with the murmurs of water, trickling down basins of porphyry, and losing itself amongst over-grown weeds and grasses. Above the wood, and between its boughs, appeared several domes, and a strange lofty tower. I will not say they belong to St. Maria Maggiore: no, they are fanes and porticos dedicated to Cybele, who delights in sylvan situations. The forlorn air of this garden, with its high and reverend shades, make me imagine it as old as the baths cf Dioclesian, which peep over one of its walls: yes, I am persuaded some consul, or prætor, dwelt here, only fifty years ago. Would to God, our souls might be transported to such solitary spots! where we might glide along the dark alleys together, when bodies were gone to bed. I discovered a little cave, that would just suit us; celandine, Venus' hair, and a thousand delicate plants growing downwards from the cove; beneath, lies a clear spring. At the close of day, I repaired to the platform before the stately porticos of the Lateran. There, I sat, folded up in myself. Some priests jarred the iron gates behind me. I looked over my shoulder through the portals, into the portico. Night began to fill it with darkness. Shall I confess that I shuddered; and that

257

I thought an avenging angel might, on some future day, bar me up in a similar edifice, far from you? Upon turning round, the sad waste of the Campagna met my eyes, and I wished to go home; but had not the power. A pressure, like that I have felt in horrid dreams, seemed to fix me to the pavement. I was thus, in a manner, forced to view the melancholy scene; the long line of aquæducts, and lonesome towers. Perhaps, the unwholesome vapours, rising like blue mists from the plains, affected me. I know not how it was; but I never experienced such strange, such chilling terrors. About ten o'clock, thank God, the spell dissolved. I found my limbs at liberty, and returned home.

Letter VII.

The sea-breezes restore me to life. I set the heat of mid-day at defiance, and do not believe in the horrors of the Sirocco. Yesterday, I passed at Portici, with Lady H. The morning, refreshing and pleasant, invited us at an early hour into the open air. We drove, in an uncovered chaise, to the royal Bosquetto. No other carriage than Sir W's is allowed to enter its alleys. We breathed a fresh air, untainted by dust or garlick. Every now and then, amidst wild bushes of ilex and myrtle, one finds a graceful antique statue; sometimes, a fountain; and, often, a rude knole, where the rabbits sit undisturbed; contemplating the blue, glittering bay: at least, I should do so, if I were a rabbit. The walls of this shady inclosure are lined with Peruvian aloes, whose white blossoms, scented like those of the magnolia, form the most magnificent clusters. They are plants to salute respectfully, as one passes by: such is their size and dignity. In the midst of the thickets, stands the King's Pagliaro, surrounded by gardens, with hedges of luxuriant jessamine, whose branches are suffered to flaunt, as much as Nature pleases. The morning sun darted his first rays on their flowers, just as I entered this pleasant spot. The hut looks as if erected in the days of fairy-pastoral life: its neatness is quite delightful. Bright tiles compose the floor; straw, nicely platted, covers the walls. In the middle of the room, you see a table spread with a beautiful Persian carpet: at one end, four niches with mattresses of silk, where the king and his favourites repose, after dinner; at the other, a white marble basin. Mount a little staircase, and you find yourself in another apartment, formed by the roof; which, being entirely composed of glistening straw, casts that comfortable yellow glow, I admire. From the windows you look over the gardens, not flourished with parterres; but divided into plats of fragrant herbs and flowers, with, here and there, a little marble table, or basin of the purest water. These sequestered inclosures are cultivated with the greatest care, and so frequently watered, that I observed lettuces, and a variety of other vegetables, as fresh as in our green England.[4]

---

4. An extended illness and the sudden deaths of two friends, Lady Hamilton and the musician John Burton, must have contributed to Beckford's decision to return to England sooner than he had planned. He left Naples on the 10th of September traveling by sea to Leghorn on his way to Paris. It is not known when he reached Leghorn, but he was in Geneva on the 12th of October and in Paris on the 28th. He finally reached England on the 9th of November.

AN EXCURSION TO THE GRAND CHARTREUSE, IN THE YEAR 1778

The Grand Chartreuse has exceeded my expectations; it is more wonderfully wild than I can describe, or even you can imagine. It has possessed me to such a degree, that I can at present neither think, speak, nor write upon any other subject.

June 5th, I left Geneva; and, after passing through a succession of valleys, between innumerable mountains, and after crossing a variety of picturesque bridges, thrown over the streams which water them, arrived at Aix, in Savoy, famous for its baths; which, as disagreeable things are generally the most salutary, ought, doubtless, to be of the greatest efficacy; for more uninviting objects one seldom meets with.

Advancing beneath a little eminence, partly rock, partly wall, we discovered the principal bath, filled with a blue reeking water, whose very steam is sufficient to seethe one, without further assistance.

Scarce had we stood looking on it a minute, before down dashed three or four dirty boys, as copper-coloured as the natives of Bengal; who, by splashing us all over, and swimming about *à la crapaudine,* convinced us, that it was not their fault, if we would not have companions in the delights of bathing. I soon hurried away from this salubrious cauldron; and, stepping into a little chapel hard by, where they were singing vespers, prayed heartily to the Virgin, that I might never need the assistance of those wonder-working waters, over which she presides. As there was but little company in the town, and little amusement, I went to bed at nine, and rose at four the next morning, that I might reach, before sun-set, the celebrated road which Charles Emanuel had cut through a rocky mountain. My plan succeeded; and after dining at Chambery (a place scarce worth speaking of to you) and passing by a cataract that throws itself from a lofty steep, I began to discover a beautiful woody vale, terminated, on one side, by the hallowed cliffs of the Grand Chartreuse; and, on the other, by the mountain, which Charles Emanuel had perforated in so extraordinary a manner. The sun was just sinking in a brilliant cloud, which seemed to repose on a swelling hill covered with cattle, when we quitted the chearful valley, and began to descend between two ridges of precipices, that, at some distance, had the appearance of towering ramparts. Pursuing our route, we found ourselves in a deep cleft, surrounded by caverns, echoing with a thousand rills, which trickle down their sides, and, mingling their murmurs with the rattling of our wheels, and the steps of our horses, infinitely repeated and multiplied, formed all together the strangest combination of sounds that ever reached my ears. The road itself is admirably cut, and hewn with such neatness, that, were it not for the savage and desolate air of its environs, I should have imagined myself approaching some grand castle, or considerable city. Towards the summits of the precipices, that in some places rise to a majestic elevation (the two sides here and there, nearly meeting in an arch) hung light woods of glossy green, which, being agitated by a gentle wind, cast a moving shadow over the cleft beneath; and, at a little distance, gave our road the appearance of a chequered pavement.

Having wound through the bosom of the mountain for some time, I was struck by the unexpected appearance of a grand edifice, resembling a vast portal, supported by doric pilasters, and crowned with an ornamented pediment. Upon my nearer approach, I found a smooth tablet, filling up the space I had allotted for an entrance, on which was engraven a pompous Latin inscription, setting forth, with what incredible labour and perseverance his majesty Charles Emanuel the Second, of Sardinia, Cyprus, and Jerusalem, king, had cut this road through the mountain; which great enterprize, though unattempted by the Romans, and despaired of by other nations, was executed under his auspices. I very sincerely wished him joy; and, as the evening was growing rather cool, was not sorry to perceive, through an opening in the rocks, a wide-extended plain, interspersed with meadows embosomed by woods, in which I distinguished Les Echelles, a village, where we were to lie, with its chimneys smoking, under the base of one of the Carthusian mountains; round which had gathered a concourse of red and greyish clouds.

The twilight was beginning to prevail when we reached our inn, and very glad I was, to leave it all, the first dawn of the next day. We were now obliged to abandon our coach; and, taking horse, proceeded towards the mountains, which, with the valleys between them, form, what is called, the Desert of the Carthusians.

In an hour's time we were drawing near, and could discern the opening of a narrow valley overhung by shaggy precipices, above which rose lofty peaks, covered to their very summits with wood. We could now distinguish the roar of torrents, and a confusion of strange sounds, issuing from dark forests of pine. I confess at this moment I was somewhat startled; I experienced some disagreeable sensations, and it was not without a degree of unwillingness that I left the gay pastures and enlivening sunshine, to throw myself into this gloomy and disturbed region. How dreadful, thought I, must be the despair of those, who enter it, never to return! But after the first impression was worn away, all my curiosity redoubled; and, desiring our guide to put forwards with greater speed, we made such good haste, that the meadows and cottages of the plain were soon left far behind, and we found ourselves on the banks of the torrent, whose agitation answered the ideas, which its sounds had inspired. Into the midst of these troubled waters we were obliged to plunge with our horses, and, when landed on the opposite shore, were by no means displeased to have passed them. We had now closed with the forests, over which the impending rocks diffused an additional gloom.

The day grew obscured by clouds, and the sun no longer enlightened the distant plains, when we began to ascend towards the entrance of the desart, marked by two pinnacles of rock far above us, beyond which, a melancholy twilight prevailed. Every moment, we approached nearer and nearer to the sounds which had alarmed us; and, suddenly emerging from the woods, we discovered several mills and forges, with many complicated machines of iron, hanging over the torrent, that threw itself headlong from a cleft in the precipices; on one side of which I perceived our road winding along, till it was stopped by a venerable gateway. A rock above one of the forges was hollowed into the shape of a round tower, of no great size, but resembling very much an altar in figure; and, what added greatly to the grandeur of the object was, a livid flame continually palpitating upon it, which the gloom of the valley rendered perfectly discernible.

The road, at a small distance from this remarkable scene, was become so narrow, that, had my horse started, I should have been but too well acquainted with the torrent that raged beneath; dismounting, therefore, I walked towards the edge of the great fall, and there, leaning on a fragment of the cliff, looked down into the foaming gulph, where the waters were hurled along over broken pines, pointed rocks, and stakes of iron. Then, lifting up my eyes, I took in the vast extent of the forests, frowning on the brows of the mountains. It was here first, I felt myself seized by the Genius of the place, and penetrated with veneration of its religious gloom; and, I believe, uttered many extravagant exclamations; but, such was the dashing of the wheels, and the rushing of the waters at the bottom of the forges, that what I said was luckily undistinguishable. I was not yet, however, within the consecrated inclosure, and, therefore, not perfectly contented; so, leaving my fragment, I paced in silence up the path, which led to the great portal. When we arrived before it, I rested a moment, and looking against the stout oaken gate, which closed up the entrance to this unknown region, felt at my heart a certain awe, that brought to my mind the sacred terror of those, in antient days, going to be admitted into the Eleusinian mysteries. My guide gave two knocks: after a solemn pause, the gate was slowly opened; and, all our horses having passed through it, was again carefully closed. I now found myself in a narrow dell, surrounded on every side by peaks of the mountains, rising almost beyond my sight, and shelving downwards, till their bases were hidden by the foam and spray of the water; over which hung a thousand withered and distorted trees. The rocks seemed crouding upon me, and, by their particular situation, threatened to obstruct every ray of light; but, notwithstanding the menacing appearance of the prospect, I still kept following my guide, up a craggy ascent, partly hewn through a rock, and bordered by the trunks of antient fir-trees, which formed a fantastic barrier, till we came to a dreary and exposed promontory, impending directly over the dell. The woods are here clouded with darkness, and the torrents rushing with additional violence are lost in the gloom of the caverns below; every object, as I looked downwards from my path, that hung midway between the base and the summit of the cliff, was horrid and woeful. The channel of the torrent sunk deep amidst frightful crags, and, the pale willows and wreathed roots spreading over it, answered my idea of those dismal abodes, where, according to the druidical mythology, the ghosts of conquered warriors were bound. I shivered whilst I was regarding these regions of desolation, and, quickly lifting up my eyes to vary the scene, I perceived a range of whitish cliffs, glistening with the light of the sun, to emerge from these melancholy forests. On a fragment, that projected over the chasm, and concealed for a moment its terrors, I saw a cross, on which was written, VIA COELI. The cliffs being the heaven to which I now aspired, we deserted the edge of the precipice; and, ascending, came to a retired nook of the rocks, in which several copious rills had worn irregular grottos. Here, we reposed an instant, and were enlivened with a few sun-beams, piercing the thickets, and gilding the waters that bubbled from the rock; over which hung another cross, inscribed with this short sentence, which the situation rendered wonderfully pathetic, O SPES UNICA! the fervent exclamation of some wretch disgusted with the world, whose only consolation was found in this retirement.

We quitted this solitary cross, to enter a thick forest of beech-trees, that screened in some measure the precipices on which they grew, catching however, every instant, terrifying glimpses of the torrent below. Streams gushed from every crevice on the cliffs, and, falling over the mossy roots and branches of the beech, hastened to join the great torrent; athwart which I, every now and then, remarked certain tottering bridges; and, sometimes, could distinguish a Carthusian crossing over to his hermitage, that just peeped above the woody labyrinths on the opposite shore. Whilst I was proceeding amongst the innumerable trunks of the beech-trees, my guide pointed out to me a peak rising above the others, which he called the Throne of Moses. If that prophet had received his revelations in this desart, no voice need have declared it holy ground; for every part of it is stamped with such a sublimity of character, as would, alone, be sufficient to impress the idea. Having left these woods behind, and crossing a bridge of many lofty arches, I shuddered once more at the impetuosity of the torrent; and, mounting still higher, came, at length, to a kind of platform, before two cliffs, joined by an arch of rock, under which we were to pursue our road.

Below, we beheld again innumerable streams turbulently precipitating themselves from the woods, and lashing the base of the mountains, mossed over with a dark sea green. In this deep hollow such mists and vapours prevailed, as hindered my prying into its recesses; besides, such was the dampness of the air, that I hastened gladly from its neighbourhood; and, passing under the second portal, beheld, with pleasure, the sun-beams gilding the Throne of Moses.

It was now about ten o'clock, and my guide assured me I should soon discover the convent. Upon this information I took new courage, and continued my route on the edge of the rocks, till we struck into another gloomy grove. After turning about it for some time, we entered again into the glare of daylight and saw a green valley, skirted by ridges of cliffs and sweeps of wood, before us. Towards the farther end of this inclosure, on a gentle acclivity, rose the revered turrets of the Carthusians, which extend in a long line on the brow of the hill: beyond them, a woody amphitheatre majestically presents itself, terminated by spires of rock, and promontories, lost amongst the clouds. The roar of the torrent was now but faintly distinguishable, and all the scenes of horror and confusion, I had passed, were succeeded by a sacred and profound calm. I traversed the valley with a thousand sensations I despair of describing, and stood before the gate of the convent, with as much awe, as some novice, or candidate, newly arrived, to solicit the holy retirement of the order.

As admittance is more readily granted to the English, than to almost any other nation, it was not long before the gates opened; and, whilst the porter ordered our horses to the stable, we entered a court, watered by two fountains, and built round with lofty edifices, characterized by a noble simplicity.

The interior portal opening, discovered an arched aisle, extending till the perspective nearly met, along which, windows, but scantily distributed between the pilasters, admitted a pale, solemn light, just sufficient to distinguish the objects with a picturesque uncertainty. We had scarcely set out feet on the pavement when the monks began to issue from an arch, about half way down; and, passing in a long succession from their chapel, bowed reverently, with much humility and meekness, and dispersed in silence, leaving one of their body, alone in the aile.

The Father Coadjutor (for he only remained) advanced towards us with great courtesy, and welcomed us, in a manner which gave me far more pleasure than all the frivolous salutations, and affected greetings, so common in the world beneath. After asking us a few indifferent questions, he called one of the lay-brothers, who live in the convent, under less severe restrictions than the fathers, whom they serve; and, ordering him to prepare our apartment, conducted us to a large square hall with casement windows, and, what was more comfortable, an enormous chimney, whose hospitable hearth blazed with a fire of dry aromatic fir; on each side of which, were two doors that communicated with the neat little cells destined for our bed-chambers. Whilst he was placing us round the fire, a ceremony by no means unimportant in the cold climate of these upper regions, a bell rung, which summoned him to prayers. After charging the lay-brother to set before us the best fare their desart afforded, he retired, and left us, at full liberty, to examine our chambers.

The weather lowered, and the casements permitted very little light to enter the apartment; but, on the other side, it was amply enlivened by the gleams of the fire, that spread all over a certain comfortable air, which even sunshine, but rarely, diffuses. Whilst the showers descended with great violence, the lay-brother, and another of his companions, were placing an oval table, very neatly carved, and covered with the finest linen, in the middle of the hall; and, before we had examined a number of portraits, which were hung in all the pannels of the wainscot, they called us to a dinner, widely different from what might have been expected, in so dreary a situation. The best fish, the most exquisite fruits, and a variety of dishes, excellent, without the assistance of meat, were served up, with an order and arrangement, that shewed it was not the first time they had entertained in the noblest manner. But I was not more struck with the delicacy of the entertainment, than with the extreme cleanliness, and English-like neatness, of the whole apartment, and its furniture. A marble fountain, particularly, gave it a very agreeable air, and the water that fell from it, into a porphyry shell, was remarkable for its clearness, and purity. Our attendant friar was helping us to some Burgundy, which we pronounced of very respectable antiquity, when the Coadjutor returned, accompanied by two other fathers, the Secretary and Procurator, whom he presented to us.

You would have been both charmed, and surprized, with the chearful resignation that appeared in their countenances, and with the easy turn of their conversation.

The Coadjutor, though equally kind, was as yet more reserved: his countenance, however, spoke for him, without the aid of words; and there was something so interesting in his manner, such a mixture of dignity and humility, as could not fail of inspiring respect and admiration. There were moments when the recollection of some past event seemed to shade his countenance with a melancholy, that rendered it still more affecting. I should suspect, he formerly possessed a great share of natural vivacity (something of it being still, indeed, apparent in his more unguarded moments;) but this spirit is almost entirely subdued by the penitence and mortification of the order. The Secretary displayed some share of knowledge in the political state of Europe, furnished probably by the extensive correspondence these fathers preserve with the three hundred and sixty subordinate convents, dispersed throughout all those countries where the Court of Rome still maintains its influence. In the course of our conversation, they asked me innumerable questions about England, where formerly, they said, many monasteries had belonged to their order; and, principally, that of W.[1] which they had learnt to be now in my possession.

The Secretary, almost with tears in his eyes, beseeched me to revere these consecrated edifices, and to preserve their remains, for the sake of St. Hugo, their canonized Prior. I replied greatly

---

1. Witham Abbey, a monastic ruin on one of Beckford's properties.

to his satisfaction; and then declaimed so much in favour of Saint Bruno, and the holy prior of Whitham, that the good fathers grew exceedingly delighted with the conversation, and made me promise to remain some days with them. I readily complied with their request, and, continuing in the same strain, that had so agreeably affected their ears, was soon presented with the works of Saint Bruno, whom I so zealously admired; and, with the voluminous records of the Abbey of Whitham. After we had sat extoling them, and talking upon much the same sort of subjects, for about an hour, the Coadjutor proposed a walk amongst the cloisters and galleries; as the weather would not admit of any longer excursion. He leading the way, we ascended a flight of steps, which brought us to a gallery; on each side of which, a vast number of pictures, representing the dependent convents, were ranged; for I was now in the capital of the order, where the General resides, and from whence he issues forth his commands to his numerous subjects; who depute the Superiors of their respective convents, whether situated in the wilds of Calabria, the forests of Poland, or, in the remotest districts of Portugal and Spain, to assist at the grand chapter, held annually under him, a week or two after Easter. This reverend Father, Dom Biclét, died about ten days before our arrival; a week ago they elected the Père Robinét, prior of the Carthusian, convent at Paris, in his room; and two fathers were now on their route, to apprize him of their choice, and to salute him General of the Carthusians. During this interregnum the Coadjutor holds the first rank in the temporal, and the Grand Vicaire in the spiritual affairs of the order; both of which are very extensive. If I may judge from the representation of the different convents, which adorn this gallery, there are many highly worthy of notice, for the singularity of their situations, and the wild beauties of the landscapes which surround them. The Venetian Chartreuse, placed in a woody island; and, that of Rome, rising from amongst groups of majestic ruins, struck me as peculiarly pleasing. Views of the English monasteries hung formerly in such a gallery, but had been destroyed by fire, together with the old convent. The list only remains, with a few written particulars concerning them. Having amused myself some time with the pictures, and the descriptions the Coadjutor gave me of them, we quitted the gallery, and entered a kind of chapel; in which were two altars with lamps burning before them, on each side of a lofty portal. This, opened into a grand coved hall, adorned with historical paintings of St. Bruno's life, and the portraits of all the Generals of the order, since the year of the great founder's death (1085) to the present time. Under these portraits, are the stalls for the Superiors, who assist at the grand convocation. In front, appears the General's throne; above, hangs a representation of the canonized Bruno, crowned with stars.

Were I, after walking along the dim cloisters, and passing through the anti-chapel, faintly illuminated by a solitary lamp, suddenly to enter this hall at midnight, when the convocation is assembled, and the synod of venerable fathers, all in solemn order, surrounding the successor of Bruno; it would be a long while, I believe, before I could recover from the surprize of so august a spectacle. It must indeed be a very imposing sight: the gravity they preserve on these occasions, their venerable age (for Superiors cannot be chosen young) and the figures of their deceased Generals, dimly discovered above, may surely be allowed to awe even an heretical spectator into a momentary respect for the order. For my own part, I must confess, that the hall, though divested of all this accompanyment, filled me with a veneration I scarcely knew how to account for; perhaps, the portraits inspired it. They were all well executed, and mostly in attitudes of adoration. The form of Bruno was almost lost in the splendors of the stars which hovered over him. I could, in some moments, fancy myself capable of plunging into the horrors of a desart, and foregoing all the vanities and delights of the world, to secure my memory so sublime a consecration.

The Coadjutor seemed charmed with the respect with which I looked round on these holy objects; and, if the hour of vespers had not been drawing near, we should have spent more time in the contemplation of Bruno's miracles, pourtrayed on the lower pannels of the hall. We left that room, to enter a winding passage (lighted by windows in the roof) that brought us to a cloister, above six hundred feet in length, from which branched off two others, joining a fourth, of the same extraordinary dimensions. Vast ranges of slender pillars extend round the different courts of the edifice, many of which, are thrown into gardens, belonging to particular cells. We entered one of them: its inhabitant received us with much civility, walked before us through a little corridor that looked on his garden, shewed us his narrow dwelling, and, having obtained leave of the Coadjutor to speak, gave us his benediction, and beheld us depart with concern. Nature has given this poor monk very considerable talents for painting. He has drawn the portrait of the late General, in a manner, that discovers great facility of execution; but, he is not allowed to exercise his pencil on any other subject, lest he should be amused; and amusement, in this rigid order, is a crime. He had so subdued, so mortified an appearance, that I was not sorry to hear the bell, which summoned the Coadjutor to prayers, and prevented my entering any more of the cells. We continued straying from cloister to cloister, and wandering along the winding passages and intricate galleries of this immense edifice, whilst the Coadjutor was assisting at vespers.

In every part of the structure reigned the most death-like calm; no sound reached my ears, but the "minute drops from off the eaves." I sat down in a niche of the cloister, and fell into a profound reverie; from which I was recalled by the return of our conductor; who, I believe, was almost tempted to imagine, from the cast of my countenance, that I was deliberating, whether I should not remain with them for ever. But I soon roused myself, and testified some impatience, to see the great chapel; at which we at length arrived, after traversing another labyrinth of cloisters. The gallery, immediately before its entrance, appeared quite gay, in comparison with the others I had passed, and owes its chearfulness to a large window (ornamented with slabs of polished marble) that admits the view of a lovely wood. Being neatly glazed, and free from paintings, or gothic ornaments, it allows a full blaze of light to dart on the chapel door; which is also adorned with marble, in a plain, but noble stile of architecture. The father sacristan stood ready, on the steps of the portal, to grant us admittance; and, throwing open the valves, we entered the chapel, and were struck by the justness of its proportions, the simple majesty of the arched roof, and the mild solemn light, equally diffused over every part of the edifice. No tawdry ornaments, no glaring pictures, disgraced the sanctity of the place. The high altar standing distinct from the walls, which were hung with a rich velvet, was the only object on which many ornaments were lavished; and, even there, the elegance of the workmanship concealed the glare of the materials, which were silver, solid gold, and the most costly gems. It being Whitsunday, this altar was covered with statues of gold, shrines, and candelabrums of the stateliest shape, and most delicate execution. Four of the latter, of a gigantic size, were placed on the steps; which, together with part of the inlaid floor within the choir, were spread with beautiful carpets. The illumination of so many tapers, striking on the shrines, censers, and pillars of polished jasper, sustaining the canopy of the altar, produced a wonderful effect; and, as the rest of the chapel was visible only by the faint external light admitted from above, the splendor and dignity of the altar was inconceivable. I retired a moment from it, and, seating myself in one of the furthermost stalls of the choir, looked towards it, and fancied, it had risen like an exhalation. Here I remained several minutes, breathing nothing but incence, with which the air of the whole chapel was impregnated; and, I believe, should not have quitted my station soon, had I not been apprehensive of disturbing the devotions of two aged fathers, who had just entered, and were prostrating themselves before the steps of the altar. These venerable figures added greatly to the solemnity of the scene; which, as the day declined, increased every moment in splendor; for the sparkling of several lamps of chased silver, that hung from the roofs, and the gleaming of nine huge tapers, which I had not before noticed, began to be visible, just as I left the chapel. Passing through the sacristy, where lay several piles of rich, embroidered vestments, purposely displayed for our inspection; we regained the cloister, which led to our apartment, where the supper was ready prepared. We had scarcely finished it, when the Coadjutor, and the fathers who had accompanied us before, returned, and, ranging themselves round the fire, resumed the conversation about St. Bruno. Finding me very piously disposed, by the wonders I had seen in the day, to listen to things of a miraculous nature, they began to relate the inspirations they had received from him; and his mysterious apparitions. I was all attention, respect, and credulity. The old Secretary worked himself up to such a pitch of enthusiasm, that, I am very much inclined to imagine, he believed, in these moments, all the miracles he told. The Coadjutor, being less violent in his pretensions to St. Bruno's modern miracles and inspirations, contented himself with relating the noble works he had done in the days of his fathers, and, in the old time, before them. It grew rather late, before my kind hosts had finished their narrations, and I was not sorry, after all the exercise I had taken, to return to my cell, where every thing invited to repose. I was charmed with the neatness and oddity of my little apartment; its cabin-like bed, oratory, and ebony crucifix; in short, every thing it contained; not forgetting the aromatic odour of the pine, with which it was roofed, floored, and wainscotted. The night was luckily dark. Had the moon appeared, I could not have prevailed upon myself to have quitted her till very late; but, as it happened, I crept into my cabin, and was by "whispering winds soon lulled asleep." Eight o'clock struck the next morning before I awoke; when, to my great sorrow, I found the peaks, which rose above the convent, veiled in vapours, and the rain descending with violence. After we had breakfasted by the light of our fire (for the casements admitted but a very feeble gleam) I sat down to the works of St. Bruno; of all medleys, the strangest. Allegories without end,—a theologico-natural history of birds, beasts, and fishes; several chapters on paradise; the delights of solitude; the glory of Solomon's temple; the new Jerusalem; and, numberless other wonderful subjects, full of enthusiasm and superstition.

Saint Bruno was certainly a mighty genius: I admire the motives which drew him to this desart; but, perhaps, before we come to that part of the story, you will like to know what preceded it.

My Saint (for Bruno has succeeded Thomas of Canterbury) was of noble descent, and possessed considerable wealth. He was not less remarkable for the qualities of his mind, and his talents gained him the degree of Master of the great Sciences, in the university of Rheims: here, he contracted a friendship with Odo, afterwards, Urban the Second. Being always poetical, singular, and visionary, he soon grew disgusted with the world, and began, early in life, to sigh after retirement. His residence at Grenoble, where he was invited by Hugo, its bishop, determined him to the monastic state.

This venerable prelate imparted to him a vision, in which he seemed to behold the desert, and mountain beyond his city, visible in the dead of night, by the streaming of seven lucid stars, that hung directly over them.

Whilst he was ardently gazing at this wonder, a still voice was heard, declaring it, the future abode of Bruno; by him to be consecrated, as a retirement for holy men, desirous of holding converse with their God. No shepherd's pipe was to be heard within these precincts: no huntsman's prophane feet to tread these silent regions, which were to be dedicated, solely, to their Creator: no woman was to ascend this mountain, nor violate, by her allurements, the sacred repose of its inhabitants. Such were the first institutions of the order, as the inspired bishop of Grenoble delivered them to Bruno; who, selecting a few persons, that, like himself, contemned the splendors of the world, and the charms of society, repaired with them to this spot; and, in the darkest part of the forests, which shade the most gloomy recesses of the mountains, founded the first convent of Carthusians, long since destroyed. Several years passed away, whilst Bruno was employed in actions of the most exalted piety; and, the fame of his exemplary conduct reaching Rome, (where his friend had been lately invested with the papal tiara) the whole conclave was desirous of seeing him, and intreated Urban to invite him to Rome. The request of Christ's vicegerent was not to be refused; and Bruno quitted his beloved solitude, leaving some of his disciples behind, who propagated his doctrines, and tended zealously the infant order.

The pomp of the Roman court soon disgusted the saintly Bruno, who had weaned himself entirely from worldly affections.

Being wholly intent on futurity, the bustle and tumults of a busy metropolis became so irksome, that he supplicated Urban for leave to retire; and, having obtained it, left Rome, and immediately seeking the wilds of Calabria, there sequestered himself in a lonely hermitage, calmly expecting his last moments. Many are the miracles which he wrought, and which his canonized bones have since effected: angels (it is said) hovered round him in his departing hour, and bore him on their wings to heaven. The different accounts of his translation are almost endless; and, as they are all, nearly, in the same style, it will be needless to recite them. I had scarcely finished taking extracts from the life and writings of St. Bruno, when the dinner appeared, consisting of every thing most delicate, which a strict adherence to the rules of meagre could allow. The good fathers returned, as usual, with the desert, and served up an admirable dish of miracles, well-seasoned with the devil, and prettily garnished with angels and moon-beams.[2]

Our conversation was interrupted very agreeably, by the sudden intrusion of the sun; which, escaping from the clouds, shone in full splendor above the highest peak of the mountains; and the vapours, fleeting by degrees, discovered the woods in all the freshness of their verdure. The pleasure I received from seeing this new creation rising to view, was very lively; and, as the fathers assured me the humidity of their walks did not often continue longer than the showers, I left my hall. Crossing the court, I hastened out of the gates, and, running swiftly along a winding path, in the side of the meadow bordered by the forests, enjoyed the charms of the prospect, inhaled the perfume of the woodlands; and, now, turning towards the summits of the precipices that

---

2. Angels are frequently represented, in legendary tales, as riding on the beams of the moon. [Beckford's note.]

encircled this sacred inclosure, admired the glowing colours, they borrowed from the sun, contrasted by the dark hues of the forest. Now, casting my eyes below, I suffered them to roam from valley to valley, and from one stream (beset with tall pines and tufted beech-trees) to another. The purity of the air in these exalted regions, and the lightness of my own spirits, almost seized me with the idea of treading in that element.

Not content with the distant beauties of the hanging rocks and falling waters, I still kept running wildly along, with an eagerness and rapidity, that, to a sober spectator, would have given me the appearance of one possessed; and, with reason; for I was affected with the scene, to a degree I despair of expressing. Whilst I was continuing my course, pursued by a thousand strange ideas, a father, who was returning from some distant hermitage, stopped my career, and made signs for me to repose myself, on a bench erected under a neighbouring shed; and, perceiving my agitation and disordered looks, fancied, I believe, that one of the bears, which lurk near the snows of the mountains, had alarmed me by his sudden appearance.

The good old man, expressing by his gestures that he wished me to recover myself in quiet on the bench, hastened, with as much alacrity as his age permitted, to a cottage adjoining the shed; and, returning in a few moments, presented me some water in a maple cup, into which he let fall several drops of an elixir, composed of innumerable herbs; and, having performed this deed of charity, signified to me by a look, in which benevolence, compassion, and, perhaps, some little remains of curiosity were strongly painted, how sorry he was to be restrained, by his vow of silence, from enquiring into the cause of my imaginary evil, and giving me further assistance. I answered also by signs, on purpose to carry on the adventure, and suffered him to depart with all his conjectures unsatisfied. No sooner had I lost sight of the benevolent hermit, than I started up, and pursued my path with my former agility, till I came to the edge of a woody dell, that divided the meadow, on which I was running, from the opposite promontory. Here I paused; and, looking up at the cliffs, now but faintly illumined by the sun, which had been some time sinking on our narrow horizon, reflected, that it would be madness to bewilder myself, at so late an hour, in the mazes of the forest. Being thus determined, I abandoned, with regret, the idea of penetrating into the lovely region before me, and contented myself, for some moments, with marking the pale tints of the

evening gradually overspreading the cliffs, so lately flushed with
the gleams of the setting sun: but my eyes were soon diverted
from contemplating these objects, by a red light streaming over
the northern sky, which attracted my notice, as I sat on the brow
of a sloping hill, looking down a steep, hollow vale, surrounded
by the forests; above which, rose majestically the varied peaks
and promontories of the mountains.

The upland lawns, which hang far above the vale, next caught
my attention. I was gazing alternately, at them, and the valley,
when a long succession of light, misty clouds, of strange, fantastic
shapes, issuing from a narrow gully between the rocks, passed on,
like a solemn procession, over the hollow dale, midway between
the stream that watered it below, and the summits of the cliffs on
high. The tranquillity of the region, the verdure of the lawn
environed by girdles of flourishing wood, and the lowing of the
distant herds, filled me with the most pleasing sensations. But
when I lifted up my eyes to the towering cliffs, beheld the northern sky streaming with ruddy light, and the long succession of
misty forms hovering over the space beneath, they became sublime
and awful. The dews which began to descend, and the vapours
which were rising from every dell, reminded me of the lateness of
the hour; and, it was with great reluctance that I turned from the
scene, which had so long engaged my contemplations, and traversed, slowly and silently, the solitary meadows, over which I had
hurried, with such eagerness, an hour ago. Hill appeared after
hill, and hillock succeeded hillock, which I had passed unnoticed
before. Sometimes, I imagined myself following a different path
from that, which had brought me to the edge of the deep valley.
Another moment, descending into the hollows between the hillocks that concealed the distant prospects from my sight, I fancied
I had entirely mistaken my route, and expected, every moment,
to be lost amongst the rude brakes and tangled thickets, that
skirted the eminences around. As the darkness increased, my
situation became still more and more forlorn. I had, almost,
abandoned the idea of reaching the convent; and, whenever I
gained any swelling ground, looked above, below, and on every
side of me, in hopes of discovering some glimmering lamp, which
might indicate a hermitage, whose charitable possessor, I flattered
myself, would direct me to the monastery. At length, after a
tedious wandering along the hills, I found myself, unexpectedly,
under the convent walls; and, as I was looking for the gate, the
porter and his attendants came out with lights, in order to search

for me: scarcely had I joined them, when the Coadjutor and the Secretary came forwards, with the kindest anxiety expressed their uneasiness at my long absence, and conducted me to my apartment, where Mr. ——[3] was waiting, with no small degree of impatience; but I found not a word had been mentioned of my adventure with the hermit; so that, I believe, he strictly kept his vow, till the day when the Carthusians are allowed to speak, and which happened after my departure. We had hardly supped, before the gates of the convent were shut; a circumstance, which disconcerted me not a little, as the full moon gleamed through the casements, and the stars, sparkling above the forests of pines, invited me to leave my apartment again, and to give myself up entirely to the spectacle they offered.

The Coadjutor, perceiving that I was often looking earnestly through the windows, guessed my wishes; and, calling the porter, ordered him to open the gates, and wait at them till my return. It was not long before I took the advantage of this obliging permission; and, escaping from the courts and cloisters of the monastery, all hushed in stillness, ascended a green knoll, which several antient pines marked with their fantastic shadows: there, leaning against one of their trunks, I lifted up my eyes to the awful barrier of surrounding mountains, discovered by the trembling silver light of the moon, shooting directly on the woods which fringed their acclivities. The lawns, the vast woods, the steep descents, the precipices, the torrents, lay all extended beneath, softened by a pale blueish haze, that alleviated, in some measure, the stern prospect of the rocky promontories above, wrapped in dark shadows. The sky was of the deepest azure; innumerable stars were distinguished with unusual clearness from this elevation, many of which twinkled behind the fir-trees edging the promontories. White, grey, and darkish clouds came marching towards the moon, that shone full against a range of cliffs, which lift themselves far above the others. The hoarse murmur of the torrent, throwing itself from the distant wildernesses into the gloomy vales, was mingled with the blast that blew from the mountains.

It increased. The forests began to wave, black clouds rose from the north, and, as they fleeted along, approached the moon, whose light they shortly extinguished. A moment of darkness succeeded: the gust was chill and melancholy; it swept along the desart, and then subsiding, the vapours began to pass away, and the moon

---

3. Lettice.

returned: the grandeur of the scene was renewed, and its imposing solemnity was increased by her presence. Inspiration was in
every wind: I followed some impulse, which drove me to the
summit of the mountains before me; and there, casting a look
on the whole extent of wild woods and romantic precipices,
thought of the days of St. Bruno: I eagerly contemplated every
rock, that formerly might have met his eyes; drank of the spring
which tradition says he was wont to drink of; and ran to every
withered pine, whose appearance bespoke a remote antiquity, and
beneath which, perhaps, the Saint had reposed himself, when
worn with vigils, or possessed with the sacred spirit of his institutions. It was midnight: the convent bell tolled; for the most solemn hour of prayer was arrived. I cannot, nor would I, attempt
to unfold to you, in prose, half the strange things, of which I
thought; and which, I seemed to see, during this wild excursion.
However, I owe to it the poetical humour in which I composed
the following lines, written, immediately on my return, in the
Album of the fathers, during the stillest watch of night.

O D E.[4]

> To orisons, the midnight bell
> Had toll'd each silent inmate from his cell:
> The hour was come to muse, or pray,
> Or work mysterious rites that shun the day:
> My steps some whisp'ring influence led,
> Up to yon pine-clad mountain's gloomy head:
> Hollow and deep the gust did blow,
> And torrents dash'd into the vales below:
> At length, the toilsome height attain'd,
> Quick fled the moon, the sudden stillness reign'd.
> As fearful turn'd my searching eye,
> Glanc'd near a shadowy form, and fleeted by;
> Anon, before me full it stood;
> A saintly figure, pale, in pensive mood.
> Damp horror thrill'd me till he spoke,
> And accents faint the charm-bound silence broke:
> "Long, trav'ller! ere this region near,
> "Say did not whisp'rings strange arrest thine ear?
> "My summons 'twas to bid thee come,

4. Cyrus Redding, Beckford's friend and earliest biographer, wrote that Beckford
did not compose the whole of the "Ode" but that Rev. Lettice had a hand in its
composition: "Strangers being desired to write their names in the album of the
monastery with anything they chose to add regarding the place and their reception,
the visitors left the following lines, the larger portion being those of the tutor,
Dr. Lettice, the pupil being, perhaps, not at the moment duly inspired." See
Memoirs of William Beckford of Fonthill (London: Charles Skeet, 1859), I, 135.

"Where sole the friend of Nature loves to roam.
  "Ages long past, this drear abode
"To solitude, I sanctified, and God:
    " 'Twas here, by love of Wisdom brought,
"Her truest lore, self-knowledge, first I sought;
  "Devoted here my worldly wealth,
"To win my chosen sons immortal health.
  "Midst these dun woods and mountains steep,
"Midst the wild horrors of yon desart deep,
  "Midst yawning caverns, wat'ry dells,
"Midst long, sequester'd ailes, and peaceful cells,
  "No passions fell distract the mind,
"To Nature, Silence, and Herself consign'd.
  "In these still mansions who shall bide,
" 'Tis mine, with Heaven's appointment, to decide;
  "But, hither, I invite not all:
"Some want the will to come, and more the call;
  "But all, mark well my parting voice!
"Led, or by chance, necessity, or choice,
  " (Ah! with our Genius dread to sport)
"Sage lessons here may learn of high import.
  "Know! Silence is the nurse of Truth:
"Know! Temperance long retards the flight of Youth:
  "Learn here, how penitence and pray'r
"Man's fallen race for happier worlds prepare:
  "Learn mild demeanor, void of art,
"And bear, amidst the world, the hermit's heart.
  "Fix, trav'ller! deep this heaven-taught lore:
"Know, Bruno brings it, and returns no more."
  (Half sighed, half smiled his long farewell)
He turn'd, and vanish'd in the bright'ning dell.

My imagination was too much disturbed, and my spirits far too active, to allow me any rest for some time; and I had not long been quieted by sleep, when I was suddenly awakened by a furious blast, that drove open my casement, and let in the roar of the tempest; for the night was troubled. In the intervals of the storm, in those moments when the winds seemed to pause, the faint sounds of the choir stole upon my ear; but were swallowed up, the next instant, by the redoubled fury of the gust, which was still increased by the roar of the waters.

I started from my bed, closed the casement, and composed myself as well as I was able; but no sooner had the sun-beams entered my window than I arose, and, gladly leaving my cell, breakfasted in haste, and hurried to the same knoll, where I had stood the night before. The storm was dissipated, and the pure morning air, delightfully refreshing; every tree, every shrub glistened with dew. A gentle wind breathed upon the woods, and waved the fir-trees on the cliffs; which, free from clouds, rose distinctly into the clear blue sky. I strayed from the knoll, into the valley between the steeps of wood and the turrets of the convent, and passed the different buildings, destined for the manufacture of the articles necessary to the fathers; for nothing is worn, or used, within this inclosure, which comes from the profane world. Traversing the meadows, and a succession of little dells, where I was so lately bewildered, I came to a bridge thrown over the torrent, which I crossed; and, here, followed a slight path, that brought me to an eminence, covered with a hanging wood of beech-trees, feathered to the ground; from whence I looked down the narrow pass, towards Grenoble. Perceiving a smoke to arise from the groves which nodded over the eminence, I climbed up a rocky steep; and, after struggling through a thicket of shrubs, entered a smooth, sloping lawn, framed in by woody precipices; at one extremity of which, I discovered the cottage, whose smoke had directed me to this sequestered spot; and, at the other, a numerous group of cattle, lying under the shade of some beech-trees; whilst several friars, with long beards and russet garments, were employed in milking them. The luxuriant foliage of the woods, clinging round the steeps, that skirted the lawn; its gay, sunny exposition; the groups of sleek, dappled cows; and the odd employment of the friars, so little consonant with their venerable beards, formed one of the most singular, and, at the same time, one of the most picturesque spectacles, that had, perhaps, ever offered itself to my sight. I, who had been accustomed to behold "milk-maids singing blithe," and tripping lightly along, with their pails, was not a little surprized at the silent gravity with which these venerable figures shifted their trivets from cow to cow; and it was curious to see, with what adroitness they performed their functions; managing their long beards, with a facility, and cleanliness, equally admirable. I watched all their motions, for some time, concealed by the trees, before I made myself visible; but no sooner did I appear on the lawn, than one of the friars quitted his trivet, very methodically set down his pail, and, coming towards me with an open, smiling countenance, desired me, by signs, to refresh myself with some bread and milk. A second, observing this motion, was resolved not to be exceeded in an hospitable act; and, quitting his pail too, hastened into the woods, from whence he returned, in a few minutes, with some strawberries very neatly enveloped in fresh leaves. These hospitable, milking fathers, next invited me to the cottage; whither I declined going, as I preferred the shade of the spreading beeches; so, reclining myself on the soft herbage, I enjoyed the scene and its productions with all possible glee.

Not a cloud darkened the heavens; every object smiled: innumerable gaudy flies glanced in the sun-beams, that played in a clear spring by the cottage: I saw with pleasure the sultry glow of the distant cliffs and forests, whilst indolently reclined in the shade, listening to the summer hum; one hour passed after another neglected away, during my repose in this most delightful of valleys. The cattle were all slunk into the recesses of the woods, and were drinking at the streams which flow along their shades, before I could prevail on myself to quit the turf, and the beech-trees. Never shall I cease regretting the peaceful moments I spent in Valombré, as, never perhaps, were I even to return to it, may so many circumstances unite to render it pleasing.

When I returned, unwillingly, to the convent, the only topic on which I could converse, was the charms of Valombré; but, notwithstanding the indifference with which I now regarded the prospects, that surrounded the monastery, I could not disdain an offer, made by one of the friars, of conducting me to the summit of the highest peak of the desert. Pretty late in the afternoon, I set out with my guide, and, following his steps, through many forests of pine, and wild apertures among them, strewed with fragments, arrived at a chapel, built on a mossy rock, and dedicated to St. Bruno.

Having once more drank of the spring, that issues from the rock on which this edifice is raised, I moved forwards, keeping my eyes fixed on a lofty green mountain, from whence rises a vast cliff, spiring up to a surprising elevation; and which (owing to the sun's reflection on a transparent mist hovering around it) was tinged with a pale, visionary light. This object was the goal to which I aspired; and, redoubling my activity, made the best of my way over rude ledges of rocks, and crumbled fragments of the mountain, interspersed with firs, till I came to the green steeps I had surveyed at a distance: these I ascended with some difficulty, and, leaving a few scattered beech-trees behind, in full leaf, shortly bid adieu to summer, and entered the regions of spring; for, as I approached that part of the mountain next the summit, the trees, which I found there rooted in the crevices, were but just beginning to unfold their leaves, and every spot of the greensward was covered with cowslips and violets. After taking a few moments repose, my guide prepared to clamber amongst the rocks, and I followed him with as much alertness as I was able, till, laying hold of the trunk of a withered pine, we sprung upon a small, level space, where I seated myself, and beheld, far beneath me, the vast desart and dreary solitudes, amongst which appeared, thinly scattered, the green meadows and hanging lawns. The eye, next overlooking the barrier of mountains, ranged through vast tracts of distant countries; the plains where Lyons is situated; the woodlands and lakes of Savoy; amongst which, that of Bourget was near enough to discover its beauties, all glowing with the warm haze of the setting sun.

My situation was too dizzy to allow a long survey; so, turning my eyes from the extensive scene, I beheld an opening in the rocks, through which we passed into a little irregular glen of the smoothest greensward, closed in, on one side, by the great peak, and, on the others, by a ridge of sharp pinnacles, which crown the range of white cliffs, I had so much admired the night before, when brightened by the moon.

The singular situation of this romantic spot invited me to remain in it, till the sun was about to sink on the horizon; during which time, I visited every little cave delved in the ridges of rock, and gathered large sprigs of the mezereon and rododendron in full bloom, which, with a surprising variety of other plants, carpeted this lovely glen. A luxuriant vegetation,

> That on the green turf suck'd the honey'd showers,
> And purpled all the ground with vernal flow'rs.

My guide, perceiving I was ready to mount still higher, told me it would be in vain; as the beds of snow, that lie eternally in some fissures of the mountain, must necessarily impede my progress; but, finding I was very unwilling to abandon the enterprize, he shewed me a few notches in the peak, by which we might ascend, though not without danger.

This prospect rather abated my courage, and the wind, rising, drove several thick clouds round the bottom of the peak, which encreasing every minute, shortly screened the green mountain, and all the forests from our sight. A sea of vapours soon undulated beneath my feet, and lightning began to flash from a dark, angry cloud, that hung over the vallies, and, probably, deluged them with storms, whilst I was securely standing under the clear expanse of æther. But the hour did not admit of my remaining long in this proud station; so, descending, I was soon obliged to pass through the vapours, and, carefully following my guide (for a false step might have caused my destruction) wound amongst the declivities, till we left the peak behind; and, just as we reached the green mountain, which was moistened with the late storm, the clouds fleeted and the evening recovered its serenity. Leaving the chapel of St. Bruno on the right, we entered the woods; and soon emerged from them, into a large pasture, under the grand amphitheatre of mountains, having a gentle ascent before us, beyond which appeared the neat blue roofs and glittering spires of the convent; where we arrived, as the moon was beginning to assume her empire.

I need not say I rested well after the pleasing fatigues of the day. The next morning early, I quitted my kind hosts with great reluctance. The Coadjutor and two other fathers accompanied me to the outward gate; and, there, within the solemn circle of their desart, bestowed on me their benediction.

It seemed indeed to come from their hearts. They were not even contented with going thus far, they would not leave me till I was an hundred paces from the convent; and then, laying their hands on their breasts, declared that, if ever I was disgusted with the world, here was an asylum. I was in a melancholy mood, when I traced back all the windings of my road; and when I found myself beyond the last gate, in the midst of the wide world again, it increased.

We returned to Les Eschelles; from thence, to Chamberry; and, instead of going through Aix, passed by Amecy; but nothing in all the route engaged my attention, nor had I any pleasing sensations, till I beheld the glassy lake of Geneva, and its lovely environs.

I rejoiced then, because I knew of a retirement on its banks, where I could sit and think of Valombré.

THE END.

Appendix

Textual Variations Between Dreams (1783) and Italy (1834)

In an appendix to Guy Chapman's edition of *Dreams, Waking Thoughts and Incidents,* Hamish Miles prepared a list of the "chief alterations" Beckford had made when he revised *Dreams* (1783) for publication as the first volume of *Italy; with Sketches of Spain and Portugal* (1834). Following Miles's lead, I performed the same arduous task, making a line-by-line comparison of the two editions. Upon completing my collation, I felt that, in addition to a number of errors Miles committed, the principal textual variations he omitted were numerous enough to warrant the preparation of a new list. The fact that Miles noted changes in the Lucca, "September 16" letter (*Travel-Diaries,* I, 337) also indicated to me that he was using the second edition of 1834 instead of the first for his collation. The first 1834 edition of *Italy* did not incorporate any part of that particular letter.

In general, I have adopted Miles's format in the list that follows. However, I have added parenthetical page references to the first edition of *Italy* to facilitate any detailed examination of the variations by the specialist.

The 1834 edition opens with the "Advertisement" which reads as follows:

Some justly admired Authors having condescended to glean a few stray thoughts from these Letters, which have remained dormant a great many years; I have been at length emboldened to lay them before the public. Perhaps, as they happen to contain passages which persons of acknowledged taste have honoured with their notice, they may possibly be less unworthy of emerging from the shade into daylight than I imagined.

285

Most of these Letters were written in the bloom and hey-day of youthful spirits and youthful confidence, at a period when the old order of things existed with all its picturesque pomps and absurdities; when Venice enjoyed her piombi and submarine dungeons; France her bastile; the Peninsula her holy Inquisition. To look back upon what is beginning to appear almost a fabulous era in the eyes of the modern children of light, is not unamusing or uninstructive; for, still better to appreciate the present, we should be led not unfrequently to recall the intellectual muzziness of the past.

But happily these pages are not crowded with such records: they are chiefly filled with delineations of landscape and those effects of natural phenomena which it is not in the power of revolutions or constitutions to alter or destroy.

A few moments snatched from the contemplation of political crimes, bloodshed, and treachery, are a few moments gained to all lovers of innocent illusion. Nor need the statesman or the scholar despise the occasional relaxation of light reading. When Jupiter and the great deities are represented by Homer as retiring from scenes of havoc and carnage to visit the blameless and quiet Ethiopians, who were the farthest removed of all nations, the Lord knows whither, at the very extremities of the ocean,—would they have given ear to manifestos or protocols? No, they would much rather have listened to the Tales of Mother Goose.

LONDON, *June 12th*, 1834.

(1834) divides Beckford's first European tour into two sections, the first is entitled "The Low Countries and Germany," (I, 3–86), the second, "Italy." (I, 89–281)

p. 53 (1834) deletes Letter I.

Letter I (1834) begins "Ostend, 21st June, 1780. We had a rough passage, and arrived at this imperial haven in a piteous condition. Notwithstanding its renown and importance, it is but a scurvy place—preposterous Flemish roofs disgust your eyes when cast upwards—swaggering Dutch skippers and mongrel smugglers are the principal objects they meet with below; and then the whole atmosphere is impregnated with the fumes of tobacco, burnt peat, and garlick. I should esteem myself in luck . . ." etc. (I, 3–4)

p. 55 (1834) deletes "Am I not an object of pity . . . tired with my passage". (I, 4)

p. 55 After "here again was I disappointed" (1834) reads "There happened to be an exposition of the holy wafer with ten thousand candles; and whilst half-a-dozen . . ." etc. (I, 4)

p. 56 For "joined to the desire . . . over the ocean" (1834) substitutes "for the black huddle of clouds, which the late storms had accumulated, were all melted away". (I, 4)

p. 56 For "I fell into a slumber . . . meadows of Enna" (1834) reads "I fell into a slumber. My dreams anticipated the classic scenes of Italy, the proposed term of my excursion." (I, 5)

p. 56 For "I arose quite refreshed . . . Trinacria and Naples suggested" (1834) reads "I arose refreshed with these agreeable impressions. No ideas, but such as Nemi and Albano suggested . . ." etc. (I, 5)

p. 56 (1834) alters passage "In the great church . . . Olympian Jupiter" to read "In the great church were several pictures by Rubens, so striking, so masterly, as to hold me broad awake; though, I must own, there are moments when I could contentedly fall asleep in a Flemish cathedral, for the mere chance of beholding in vision the temple of Olympian Jupiter." (I, 6)

p. 57 (1834) deletes "as it is now three or four years . . . necromancer". (I, 7)

p. 57 (1834) deletes "when capacious paunches . . ." to end of paragraph. (I, 8)

p. 57 For "to leave our swinish moralities behind us, and jog on" (1834) substitutes "to lead". (I, 8)

p. 58 For "some famous artist" (1834) reads "Cortels of Malines" and adds the following footnote: "This crucifix was made of the bronze which had formed the statue of the terrible Duke of Alva, swept in its first form from the citadel where it was proudly stationed, in a moment of popular fury." (I, 9)

p. 59 (1834) deletes "I longed to ascend . . . influence of the planets". (I, 12)

p. 60 (1834) deletes "Were I not still fatigued . . ." to the end of the letter. (I, 13)

p. 61 Letter II (1834) deletes opening of Letter III (1783) down to "would greatly improve your pencil". After "June 23" (1834) adds "1780". (I, 14)

pp. 61-2 For "Chanoin Knyfe" (1834) reads "Canon Knyff"; for "Polemburg" (1834) reads "Polemberg". (I, 15)

p. 62 For "revenue of about five thousand pounds sterling" (1834) reads "a spanking revenue". (I, 16)

p. 63 (1834) deletes "As I had seen cabinets . . . judgment of

Flemish painting" and "to hear a little . . . disposed to harmony." (I, 17–18)

p. 63 For "which has ever been esteemed . . . forty thousand florins" (1834) substitutes "which, large as it is, they pretend here that Old Lewis Baboon offered to cover with gold", and adds the following footnote: "The History of John Bull explains this ridiculous appellation." (I, 18)

p. 63 (1834) deletes "The principal figure . . . tittle of commendation." (I, 18)

p. 63 For "gigantic coarseness of his pencil" (1834) substitutes "gigantic boldness of his pencil." (I, 18)

pp. 63–4 (1834) deletes "Had this powerful artist . . . withhold my adoration." (I, 19)

p. 64 (1834) deletes "but an heretical wind . . . grandeur of the spectacle." (I, 19)

p. 64 (1834) deletes "Several of its marble altars . . . style of Corelli" and then adds "A motet, in the lofty style of Jomelli, performed . . ." etc. (I, 19)

p. 64 (1834) deletes "where my spirit had so long taken up its abode" and "in the Place de Mer . . ." down to the end of the paragraph. (I, 19)

p. 65 (1834) deletes " 'tis but a very scurvy topic." (I, 21)

p. 65 (1834) deletes "It was fresh and pleasant . . . labyrinths of Nemi." (I, 21)

p. 66 For the second parenthetical statement (1834) reads "not ill clad". (I, 23)

p. 67 Letter III (1834) begins at Letter IV (1783). (I, 24)

p. 67 After "June 30" (1834) adds "1780". (I, 24)

p. 67 For "is a St. Anthony" (1834) reads "is a temptation of the holy hermit St. Anthony". (I, 24)

p. 67 "Soorflect" is changed to "Sorgvliet" in (1834). (I, 26)

p. 68 (1834) deletes "and so fragrant . . . this inelegant nation." (I, 26)

p. 68 For "Calvin or Dr. Faustus" (1834) reads "Luther, that disputatious heresiarch." (I, 27)

p. 68 For "Quang-Tong" (1834) reads "Canton." (I, 27)

p. 69 (1834) deletes "The Hague . . . the most agreeable" and substitutes the following anecdote: "Amongst the company were two honourable boobies and their governor, all from Ireland. The youngest, after plying me with a succession of innocent questions, wished to be informed where I proposed spending the carnival. 'At Tunis,' was my answer. The questioner not in the least surprised, then asked who was to sing there? To which I replied, 'Farinelli.' This settled the business to our mutual satisfaction." (I, 28–9)

p. 70 (1834) deletes "To-morrow I bid it adieu . . ." to the end of the paragraph. (I, 31)

p. 71 Letter IV (1834) begins at Letter V (1783). (I, 32)

p. 71 After "July 1st" (1834) adds "1780". (I, 32)

p. 71 For "but when I approached the nymphs . . . Low countries returned" (1834) reads "but instead of nymphs dispersed over the meadows, I met a gang of waddling fishermen." (I, 33)

p. 72 (1834) deletes "Mynheers very busy . . . Netherlands", substitutes "mine hostess" for "prudish dames", and omits "darkness and complaisance . . ." to end of letter. (I, 34)

p. 73 Letter V (1834) begins at Letter VI (1783). (I, 35)

p. 73 After "July 2d" (1834) adds "1780". (I, 35)

p. 73 For "a vast number of round, unmeaning faces" (1834) reads "a vast number of consequential personages". (I, 36)

p. 74 (1834) changes "incorrect a narrative" to "hasty a narrative" and deletes last sentence of the letter. (I, 38)

pp. 75–9 Letter VI (1834) deletes opening of Letter VII (1783) down to "tell your postillions to drive off as fast as their horses will carry them" and begins "We arrived at Aix-la-Chapelle about ten at night . . ." etc. (I, 39)

p. 79 For "found myself . . . banks of the Rhine" (1834) reads "crossed the Rhine and travelled on to Dusseldorf." (I, 40)

pp. 79–80 (1834) deletes "Many wild ideas . . . travelled forwards to the town." (I, 40)

p. 81 For "Lady M." (1834) reads "Lady Miller". (I, 42)

p. 81 For "Mr. Salmon himself" (1834) reads "the most courteous compiler of geographical dictionaries". (I, 42)

p. 82 For "It seems, the holy Empress . . . prophane curiosities" (1834) reads "It seems that great collectress of relics, the holy Empress Helena, first routed . . ." etc. (I, 43)

p. 83 For "Mounted on these fantastic quadrupeds . . . their pinnacles" (1834) reads "Under their capricious influence my fancy built castles and capitols in the clouds with all the extravaganza of Piranesi." (I, 45)

p. 83 For "to one just returned from the courts of fancy" (1834) reads "to me just returned from palaces bedecked with all the pomp of visionary splendour." (I, 46)

pp. 83–4 (1834) deletes "their pediments and capitals . . ." to end of letter. (I, 46)

p. 85 Letter VII (1834) begins at Letter VIII (1783). (I, 47)

p. 85 After "July 11th" (1834) adds "1780". (I, 47)

p. 86 (1834) deletes "there, reposing beneath . . . with great satisfaction." (I, 49)

p. 86 For "Lune" (1834) substitutes "Lahn". (I, 50)

p. 86 (1834) deletes "upon my return . . . its luminaries." (I, 51)

p. 87 (1834) deletes footnote. (I, 52)

p. 87 Letter VIII (1834) begins at "July 14th". (I, 53)

p. 87 (1834) deletes "where they hop and fidget from ball to ball". (I, 53)

p. 88 In (1834) Monsieur l'Administrateur's French is Germanized: *"avec sa crande maidresse, son shamperlan, et guelgues tames donneur"*. (I, 54)

p. 88 (1834) deletes "Unable to stay . . . falling waters." (I, 55)

p. 88 For "took shelter . . . immediately into conversation" (1834) reads "bounced into the room". (I, 55)

p. 89 (1834) deletes "I own, I felt rather intimidated . . . dejection it occasioned." (I, 56)

p. 89 (1834) deletes "and, after tossing and tumbling . . ." to end of paragraph, and adds in its place the following: "Early in the morning we set forward; and proceeding along the edge of the precipices I had been forewarned of, journeyed through the forest which had so recently been the scene of murders and depredations. At length, after winding several hours amongst its dreary avenues, we emerged into open daylight. A few minutes more brought us safe to the village of Weisbaden, where we slept in peace and tranquillity." (I, 57)

p. 90 (1834) deletes "and it was by the mild gleams . . ." to the end of paragraph. (I, 57)

pp. 90–2 (1834) deletes entire letter of "July 17th". (I, 58)

p. 92 (1834) deletes "I almost envied the merchants . . . the whole evening." (I, 58)

p. 92 (1834) deletes "The air was impregnated with the perfume of clover" and "enamelled with flowers". Also "that distance and the evening tinged with an interesting azure." (I, 58)

p. 92 For "meads" (1834) reads "Savannahs". (I, 58)

p. 92 For "Aneantsic" (1834) reads "Ateantsic". (I, 59)

pp. 93–4 (1834) deletes "The dusky hour . . ." to the end of paragraph, and adds "and so fully abandoned was I to the illusion of the moment, that I did not for several minutes perceive our arrival at Günzberg; whence we proceeded the next morning (July 21) to Augsburg . . ." etc. (I, 60)

p. 94 (1834) deletes "under whose auspices the colony was formed." (I, 60)

p. 94 (1834) deletes "as if a triumphal car waited at their feet; or". (I, 62)

p. 94. For "saint's day" (1834) reads "high festival". After "execrable" (1834) adds "sourcroutish". (I, 62)

p. 95 Letter IX (1834) begins at "July 22d". (I, 63)

p. 95 After "the grand fair" (1834) adds "at Munich". (I, 64)

p. 96 For "Mr. and Mrs. T." (1834) reads "Mr. and Mrs. Trevor". (I, 65)

p. 96 For "Madame de ———" (1834) reads "Madame de Baumgarten". (I, 65)

p. 96 For "represented in a coloured print" (1834) reads "represented on Dresden porcelain." (I, 66)

p. 96 For "valz" (1834) reads "waltz". (I, 66)

p. 96 After "dishes changing" (1834) adds "at the risk of showering down upon you their savoury contents". (I, 66)

p. 96 After "grunting" (1834) adds "and whining". (1834) also deletes "though at the expence of toes and noses . . ." to end of paragraph. (I, 66–7)

p. 97 For "and cut velvet" (1834) reads "and furbelowed flounces of cut velvet, most sumptuously fringed and spangled." (I, 67)

p. 97 After "Apuleius" (1834) appends a footnote:
> "* Apuleius Met: Lib. 5
> Vehementer iterum ac sæpius beatos illos qui
> Super gemmas et monilia calcant!" (I, 67)

p. 97 For "Sleitzom" (1834) reads "Elector's". (I, 68)

p. 97 (1834) deletes "Just now, as I have lain by a long while . . ." to end of paragraph. (I, 69)

p. 98 For "all the energetic vehemence of the German tongue" (1834) reads "all the guttural hoarseness of the Bavarian dialect." (I, 69)

p. 98 For "bottle-noses" (1834) reads "honied gingerbread." (I, 69)

p. 98 For "simple edifices" (1834) reads "complicated edifices". (I, 70)

p. 98 For "who remember the Emperor, Lewis of Bavaria" (1834) reads "coeval with their mansions." (I, 70)

p. 98 (1834) deletes "for I can hardly . . . Damascus." (I, 70)

p. 99 (1834) deletes "How we got over . . . must needs have been stranded." (I, 71)

p. 99 For "till this apparition was lost, and confounded with the shades of night" (1834) reads "till this apparition faded away." (I, 72)

p. 99 For "Wallersee" (1834) reads "Walchen-see." (I, 72)

pp. 99–100 (1834) deletes "Great praise is due . . ." to end of paragraph, including footnote, and adds "At length, after some perils but no adventure, we saw lights gleam upon the shore of the Walchen Lake, which served to direct us to a cottage, where we passed the night, and were soon lulled to sleep by the fall of distant waters." (I, 72)

p. 100 Letter X (1834) begins at "July 26th". (I, 73)

p. 100 (1834) deletes "I could contentedly have passed . . . fished for sustenance." (I, 73)

p. 100 For "spurge-laurel" (1834) reads "daphnes of various species". (I, 74)

p. 101 (1834) deletes "I can imagine . . . their cones below." (I, 75)

p. 101 For "Boidou" (1834) reads "Walgau". (I, 76)

p. 102 For "caper-plant" (1834) reads "rhododendron". (I, 79)

p. 103 For "collecting the wild pinks . . . strewed in profusion, (1834) reads "collecting dianthi freaked with beautifully varied colours". (I, 80)

p. 103 For "Ambras" (1834) reads "Embras". (I, 81)

p. 104 (1834) deletes "the shades of evening . . . a vivid red" and adds the following footnote: "Schönberg, beautiful mountain." (I, 82)

p. 104. Letter XI (1834) begins at "July 28th". (I, 84)

p. 105 (1834) deletes "At present, I must confess . . . we shall sink into oblivion and tranquility." (I, 86)

p. 105 The sentence ending with "the moment I awoke next morning" marks the conclusion in (1834) of the section designated "The Low Countries and Germany" and the beginning of a new section entitled "Italy". Letter I (1834) of new section, hereafter called Part II, begins at "July 29th" (1783). (I, 89)

p. 107 After Italian quotation, (1834) adds a footnote: "Ariosto Orlando Furioso——*Canto* 7, *stanza* 32." (I, 91)

p. 108 For "by the interposition of a polite Venetian . . . was introduced" (1834) reads "thanks to a warm-hearted old Venetian (the Senator Querini) was introduced . . ." etc. (I, 95)

p. 108 For "a country house" (1834) reads "at the villa of La Contessa Roberti". (I, 95)

p. 109 Letter II (Part II, 1834) begins at "August 1st". (I, 97)

p. 109 After "August 1st (1834) adds "1780". (I, 97)

p. 109 (1834) deletes "Behind the villa . . . continued garlands." (I, 98)

p. 110 (1834) deletes "and that I could hear . . . breathless for several moments". (I, 98)

p. 110 (1834) deletes "Stretched beneath . . . sight of the waters." (I, 99)

pp. 110–11 (1834) deletes "Here, meditation . . . haze of the horizon." (I, 100)

p. 112 (1834) deletes "I gazed, delighted . . . the most elaborate description." (I, 104)

p. 112 (1834) deletes "by far the most perfect . . . my eyes ever beheld" and adds in its place "one of the most celebrated works of Palladio." (I, 104)

p. 113 (1834) deletes "reclining under its shade . . . over the waters". (I, 104)

p. 113 For "nef" (1834) reads "nave" and deletes "and applauded the genius of Palladio." (I, 106)

p. 114 (1834) deletes "awake from its ignoble slumber", "of idle tears", "Scarce a sovereign supports . . . witness great events", and footnote. (I, 108)

p. 115 For "fancied myself hearing . . . relate their adventures" (1834) reads "a thousand agreeable associations excited my Grecian fancies". (I, 110)

p. 115 Letter III (Part II, 1834) opens with "The rustling of the pines . . ." etc. (I, 111)

p. 116 (1834) deletes "like the hues of the declining sun." (I, 113)

p. 117 For "purity of Sansovino" (1834) reads "elegance of Sansovino". (I, 114)

p. 117 For "adored the tutelary divinities" (1834) reads "contemplated the tutelary divinities." (1834) also reduces "My devotions were" to "My admiration was" and deletes "half my vows unpaid and". (I, 115)

p. 119 For "Mad. de R." (1834) reads "Madame de Rosenberg". (I, 120)

p. 120 (1834) deletes "but mentioned not a syllable . . . upon any subject in the universe?" (I, 120)

p. 120 (1834) deletes "disease and the consequence of". (I, 121)

pp. 120–1 For "and am apt to imagine . . . perpetual doze" (1834) reads "who, thanks to their opium and their harems, pass their lives in one perpetual doze." (I, 122)

p. 121 Letter IV (Part II, 1834) begins at "August 4th". (I, 123)

p. 121 After "August 4th" (1834) adds "1780". (I, 123)

p. 121 For "Chartreuse" (1834) reads "Carthusian". (I, 124)

p. 123 For "and invoked it" (1834) reads "whom twenty ages ago I should have invoked". (I, 128)

p. 123 (1834) deletes "My supplications . . . heroic liberty." (I, 129)

p. 124 For "M. de B." (1834) reads "M. de Benincasa". (I, 130)

p. 124 (1834) deletes "excluded the glow of the western sky, and". (I, 131)

p. 124 For "English churches" (1834) reads "English tabernacles". (I, 131)

p. 125 Letter V (Part II, 1834) begins at "August 18th". (I, 132)

p. 125 After "August 18th" (1834) adds "1780". (I, 132)

p. 125 For "Damascus and Sunristan" (1834) reads "Cairo and Damascus." (I, 133)

p. 126 For "Monsieur de V." (1834) reads "Monsieur de Viloison". (I, 134)

p. 126 For "The martyrdom of St. Peter" (1834) reads "the martyrdom of the hermits St. Paul and St. Peter." (I, 136)

pp. 126–7 (1834) deletes "It being a festival . . . lengthening across the waves, I rowed out" and adds "In the evening I rowed out as usual". (I, 136)

p. 127 (1834) deletes footnotes 49 and 50 and "The form of the hillocks . . ." to the end of the paragraph. (I, 136)

p. 128 Letter VI (Part II, 1834) begins at Letter IX (1783). (I, 137)

p. 128 (1834) deletes footnote 52. (I, 137)

p. 128 (1834) deletes "concealed halls, and". (I, 138)

p. 129 (1834) deletes "The waves coursed . . . smoothly wafted." (I, 138)

p. 129 (1834) deletes footnote. (I, 139)

p. 130 For "I longed to have filled it with bats' blood . . . honour to their witcheries" (1834) reads "filled with bats' blood it would have been an admirable present to the sabbath of witches and have cut a capital figure in their orgies." (I, 141)

p. 131 (1834) deletes "so fatal was the sound . . . conduct of the harmony." (I, 143)

p. 131 For "Bertoni's" (1834) reads "Paesiello's". (I, 143)

p. 131 For "these same Amazons" (1834) reads "this angelic choir", and deletes "which seems to be some of the most picturesque . . . an Italian ever produced." (I, 144)

p. 132 (1834) adds "Bertoni's" before "opera of Quinto Fabio" and deletes "of all operas . . ." to end of paragraph. (I, 144)

p. 133 Letter VII (Part II, 1834) begins at Letter X (1783). (I, 145)

p. 133 (1834) deletes "when the Euganean . . . across the waters." (I, 145)

p. 133 After "my departure" (1834) inserts "the sun was concealed in clouds". (I, 145)

p. 133 For passage "Beds of mint and flowers . . . to the breezes" (1834) reads "Beds of mint and iris clothe the brink of the stream, except where interrupted by a tall growth of reeds and osiers." (I, 145–6)

p. 133 (1834) deletes "I heard their whispers . . . approached in solitude." (I, 146)

pp. 133–4 (1834) deletes "met my eyes wherever . . ." etc. down to "I staid so long amidst the vines that". (I, 146)

p. 134 For "That, where we supped" (1834) reads "That of Cornaro, where we were engaged to sup". (I, 146)

p. 134 For "with a fire, an energy . . . dissolved me in tears" (1834) reads "with surprising energy". (I, 147)

p. 135 For "breathing forth such celestial harmony" (1834) reads "singing". (I, 147)

p. 135 For "The C." (1834) reads "Marietta Cornaro, whose lively talents are the boast of the Venetians". (I, 147)

p. 135 (1834) deletes "I loathed the light . . ." to end of paragraph, and substitutes for it "to wake was painful, and it was not without much lingering reluctance I left these scenes of enchantment and fascination, repeating with melancholy earnestness that pathetic sonnet of Petrarch's

O giorno, o ora, o ultimo momento,
O stelle congiurate a' impoverirme!
O fido sguardo, or che volei to dirme,
Partend' io, per non esser mai contento?" (I, 148)

p. 136 Letter VIII (Part II, 1834) begins at Letter XI (1783). (I, 149)

p. 136 (1834) deletes "who betook himself . . . no ear to his discourses" and adds in its place "one of whose most eloquent sermons the great Addison has translated *con amore*, and in his very best manner." (I, 149–50)

p. 136 (1834) deletes "and offered up my little orizons before it." (I, 150)

p. 137 (1834) deletes "and fell down . . . before the shrine." (I, 150)

p. 137 For "A lofty altar . . . holy pile from prophane glances" (1834) reads "A lofty altar, decked with the most lavish magnificence supports the shrine." (I, 151)

p. 137 (1834) deletes "and rub their rosaries . . . bones of St. Anthony". (I, 151)

p. 137 For "the best artists" (1834) reads "other renowned artists". (I, 151)

p. 137 (1834) deletes "and acted . . . amongst the devotees". (I, 151)

p. 137 For "the coving of the roof . . . for the feathered race" (1834) reads "the arching of the roof, with enormous rafters". (I, 152)

p. 137 For "Scheutzer's Physica Sacra" (1834) reads "many an old Dutch Bible". (I, 152)

pp. 137–8 For "How willingly . . . upon the waves" (1834) reads "Could I but choose my companions, I should have no great objection to encounter a deluge, and to float away a few months upon the waves!" (I, 152)

p. 138 (1834) deletes "till the twilight faded into total darkness." (I, 152)

pp. 139–42 (1834) deletes the whole of Letter XII (1783). (I, 152)

p. 143 Letter IX (Part II, 1834) begins at Letter XIII (1783). (I, 153)

p. 143 (1834) deletes "a noble temple . . . beautiful symmetry of the building." (I, 153)

p. 143 (1834) footnote reads "A nephew of Bertoni, the celebrated composer." (I, 154)

pp. 143–4 (1834) deletes "and makes his slave . . . some time a dying." (I, 154)

p. 144 For "the C." (1834) reads "the Cornaro". (I, 155)

p. 144 For "till the moon tempted . . . to stray on" (1834) reads "till the fineness of the weather tempted us to quit the palace for". (I, 155)

p. 144 (1834) deletes "We listened to the faint . . . the same objects." (I, 155)

p. 144 (1834) deletes "It was evening . . . fantastic visions" and "that was alone to be subdued by harmony." (I, 155)

p. 145 (1834) deletes "Had I but enjoyed . . . Zuccarelli loved to paint!" (I, 156)

p. 145 (1834) deletes "Nothing more remains . . . for their former existence." (I, 157)

p. 146 (1834) deletes "To produce such a revolution . . ." to end of paragraph. (I, 158)

p. 146 For paragraph beginning "September 9th" (1834) substitutes "You may imagine how I felt when the hour of leaving Padua drew near. It happened to be a festival, and high mass was celebrated at the great church of Saint Anthony in all its splendour. The ceremony was about half over when such a peal of thunder reverberated through the vaults and cupolas, as I expected would have shaken them to their foundations. The principal dome appeared invested with a sheet of fire; and the effect of terror produced upon the majority of the congregation, by this sudden lighting up of the most gloomy recesses of the edifice, was so violent that they rushed out in the wildest confusion. Had my faith been less lively, I should have followed their example, but, absorbed in the thought of a separation from those to whom I felt fondly attached, I remained till the ceremony ended; then took leave of Madame de R. with heartfelt regret, and was driven away to Vicenza." (I, 158–9)

p. 146 For "The morning being overcast . . . verses of his furies" (1834) reads "The morning being overcast, I went to Palladio's theatre." (I, 159)

pp. 146–7 (1834) deletes "The august front . . . had remained undiscovered." (I, 159)

p. 147 (1834) deletes "You can enter . . . the most flattering reward" and then alters the text to read "After I had mused a long while in the most retired recess of the edifice, fancying I had penetrated into a real and perfect monument of antiquity, which till this moment had remained undiscovered, we set out for Verona." (I, 160)

p. 147 For "awful assembly of mountains" (1834) reads "group of mountains". (I, 160)

p. 147 (1834) deletes "grapes worthy of Canaan . . . gloried in producing." (I, 161)

pp. 148–9 (1834) deletes "I like the idea of being . . ." to end of paragraph, and substitutes the following: "Throwing myself upon the grass in the middle of the arena, I enjoyed the freedom of my situation, its profound stillness and solitude. How long I remained shut in by endless gradines on every side, wrapped as it were in the recollections of perished ages, is not worth noting down; but when I passed from the amphitheatre to the opening before it, night was drawing on, and the grand outline of a terrific feudal fortress, once inhabited by the Scaligeri, alone dimly visible." (I, 163)

p. 149 (1834) deletes "amongst which start . . . barren hills" and "diversify their craggy summits". (I, 164)

p. 149 (1834) deletes "For my own part . . . the city in despair,"

(I, 164)
p. 149 (1834) deletes "I don't recollect . . . artist to copy them."
(I, 164)
p. 150 (1834) deletes "I gathered a tuberose . . ." to end of paragraph. (I, 165)
p. 150 Letter X (Part II, 1834) begins at "September 12th" (1783). (I, 166)
p. 150 After "September 12th" (1834) adds "1780". (I, 166)
p. 151 (1834) deletes Latin verse. (I, 167)
p. 151 For "I fixed my eyes . . . contented and unknown" (1834) reads "I fixed my eyes on the chain of distant mountains, and indulged a thousand romantic conjectures of what was passing in their recesses—hermits absorbed in prayer—beautiful Contadine fetching water from springs, and banditti conveying their victims, perhaps at this very moment, to caves and fastnesses." (I, 168)
p. 151 (1834) deletes "Her soft light . . . cast aslant them." (I, 168)
p. 151 (1834) deletes "During an hour . . . opposed my progress." (I, 168)
p. 151 For "ten and eleven" (1834) reads "twelve and one at Modena". (I, 168)
p. 151–2 (1834) deletes "Having but a moment . . ." down to "and left Modena." (I, 169)
p. 152 (1834) deletes "almost everyone of which has its grove of chestnuts and cypresses." (I, 169)
p. 152 For "At present, I thought of little else . . . humour at this present moment" (1834) reads "At present I have very little indeed to say about Bologna (where I passed only two hours) except that it is sadly out of humour". (I, 169)
p. 152 (1834) deletes "ran up a tall, slender tower . . . way of exercise". (I, 170)
p. 153 For "Jerusalem" (1834) reads "Loretto." (I, 170)
p. 153 (1834) deletes "but I was not to be frightened . . . their caperings." (I, 171)
pp. 153–4 (1834) deletes "The rocks here formed . . . to meditate upon revenge." (I, 172)
p. 154 (1834) deletes "inspiring evil". (I, 172)
p. 154 For "I never heard such fatal . . . whole nations into dismay" (1834) reads "Walking out of the sound of the carriage, I began interpreting the language of the leaves, not greatly to my own advantage or that of any being in the universe. I was no prophet of good, and had I but com-

manded an oracle, as ancient visionaries were wont, I should have flung mischief about me." (I, 172)

p. 154 For "the huts of Lognone" (1834) reads "an assemblage of miserable huts". (I, 172)

p. 154 (1834) deletes "Its blaze gave me . . . in the crevices; and". (I, 173)

p. 154 Letter XI (Part II, 1834) begins at "Sept. 14th". (I, 174)

p. 154 After "Sept. 14th" (1834) adds "1780". (I, 174)

pp. 154–5 For "basked in the sunshine . . . lavender in full bloom" (1834) substitutes "in the midst of lavender bushes in full bloom." (I, 175)

p. 155 (1834) deletes "the peasants singing . . . as I ascended a hill, and" and substitutes "between groves of poplars and cypress, till late in the evening. Upon winding a hill we discovered . . ." etc. (I, 175)

p. 155 (1834) deletes "I never beheld so mild a sky . . ." down to "I returned to Vaninis" and substitutes "and I was sorry when I found myself excluded from it by the gates of Florence." (I, 175)

p. 156 For "I bowed low . . . immediately up to it" (1834) reads "Having regarded these powers with due veneration, I next cast my eyes upon a black figure, whose attitude seemed to announce the deity of sleep." (I, 176)

p. 156 For "such high ideas of the god as live in my bosom" (1834) reads "very poetical ideas of the god". (I, 177)

p. 156 (1834) deletes "To one who can never . . . must have communicated." (I, 177)

p. 157 For "by remaining much longer . . . drawers of his cabinet" (1834) reads "by lingering to admire the column and cabinets." (I, 178)

p. 157 (1834) deletes "that surprizing genius". (I, 179)

p. 157 (1834) deletes "The colouring of these . . . to the sight alone." (I, 179)

p. 158 For "the execution, as to become remarkable" (1834) reads "the painter's choice". (I, 180)

p. 158 (1834) deletes "I dare engage . . . circle of celestials." (I, 180)

p. 158 (1834) deletes "Their symmetry . . . a breathing divinity." (I, 180)

p. 158 For "the companion of his grave" (1834) reads "just yielding to his influence." (I, 181)

p. 158 (1834) deletes "I contemplated the God . . . hours by his side." (I, 181)

p. 158 (1834) deletes " (to whom the Lord give a fair seat in paradise!) ". (I, 181)

p. 158 (1834) deletes "I easily persuade . . . with complacency." (I, 181)

p. 159 (1834) deletes "and ask, when will they perform . . . but never with pleasure" and substitutes "and view such wearisome attitudes with infinitely more admiration than pleasure." (I, 181)

p. 159 (1834) deletes "The wrestlers . . . formidable of animals." (I, 181)

p. 159 (1834) deletes "and surveyed the hills . . . gleams tempted me" and substitutes "and from thence". (I, 182)

p. 159 For "the Palazzo Pitti" (1834) reads "the Grand Duke's palace". (I, 182)

p. 160 (1834) deletes "where I lingered . . . die gradually away." (I, 184)

p. 160 After "full into my mind" (1834) adds "that, lost in the train of recollections this idea excited". (I, 184)

pp. 160–1 (1834) deletes entire letter dated "Friday, September 16th." (I, 184) This letter with some modifications was included in the second edition of 1834.

p. 162 Letter XII (Part II, 1834) begins at Letter XIV (1783). (I, 185)

p. 162 After "Sept. 25th" (1834) adds "1780". (I, 185)

p. 162 (1834) deletes "Billingsgate never produced such furious orators." (I, 186)

p. 163 (1834) deletes "upon our gross planet." (I, 187)

p. 163 (1834) deletes "here and there, some vines . . . their clusters." (I, 187)

p. 164 (1834) deletes "almost without interruption." (I, 190)

p. 164 For "defied Constantia and the Cape" (1834) reads "defied the richest wines of Constantia". (I, 191)

p. 165 (1834) deletes "I think now I have detained . . ." to end of paragraph. (I, 191)

p. 166 Letter XIII (Part II, 1834) begins at Letter XV (1783). (I, 192)

p. 166 For "Livourno, October 2d" (1834) reads "Leghorn, October 2nd, 1780". (I, 192)

p. 166 Letter XIII (1834) opens "This morning we set out for Pisa. No sooner had we passed the highly cultivated garden-grounds about Lucca than we found ourselves . . ." etc. (I, 192)

p. 166 For "verdant opening" (1834) reads "vast green area".

(I, 193)

p. 166 (1834) deletes "The capitals of the columns . . . but Gothic proportions." (I, 193)

p. 167 (1834) deletes "Many palm-trees . . . Pisanese with Palestine." (I, 194)

p. 167 (1834) deletes "have the cleanliest effect imaginable." (I, 194)

p. 168 (1834) deletes "to act a visionary part". (I, 196)

p. 168 (1834) deletes "It was between ten . . . drove me away" and continues "The heat . . ." etc. (I, 196)

p. 168 For "Livourno" (1834) reads "Leghorn". (I, 196)

p. 168 (1834) deletes "listlessly surveyed . . . bounded the view." (I, 197)

p. 169 (1834) deletes "On the contrary . . . Let us drive away." (I, 198)

p. 169 For "the Fanalè you have", (1834) reads "the very tower you have". (I, 198)

p. 170 Letter XIV (Part II, 1834) begins at Letter XVI (1783). (I, 199)

p. 170 After "October 3d" (1834) adds "1780". (I, 199)

p. 171 (1834) deletes "filled it with jasmine". (I, 201)

p. 171 (1834) deletes "after taking . . . and pomegranate-seeds" and "and gave myself up to Q. Fabio." (I, 201)

p. 171 (1834) deletes "Next day (October 4th) . . . the opera began." (I, 201)

p. 172 Letter XV (Part II, 1834) begins at Letter XVII (1783). (I, 202)

p. 172 After "Florence, October 5th" (1834) adds "1780". (I, 202)

p. 172 (1834) deletes "and cast . . . wave with cypress." (I, 203)

p. 172 (1834) deletes "Its sullen sound . . . Jomelli's Miserere" and substitutes "Its mournful sound filled me with gloomy recollections. I closed the casements, and read till midnight some dismal memoir of conspiracies and assassinations, Guelphs and Ghibelines, the black story of ancient Florence." I, 203)

p. 172 (1834) deletes "Such was the clearness . . . were distinguishable." (I, 203)

p. 173 For "venerable terms" (1834) reads "Trophies badly carved in the true spirit of the antique". (I, 203–4)

p. 173 (1834) deletes "so admirably wrought . . . in astonishment." (I, 204)

p. 173 (1834) changes "Gothic arches" to "pointed arches" and deletes "raised on a pedestal . . . kalendar of genius." (I, 204)

p. 173 For "but exposed . . . Tuscany to public sale" (1834) reads "and not yet entirely frittered away and disposed of by public sale." (I, 204)

p. 173 (1834) deletes "read over your letters". (I, 205)

pp. 173–4 (1834) deletes "From this high . . . grotesque in its neighbourhood" and substitutes "took a sketch of the huge mountainous cupola of the Duomo, the adjoining lovely tower and one more massive in its neighbourhood". (I, 205)

p. 174 (1834) deletes "After I had marked . . . round with ivy" and substitutes "Having marked the sun's going down and all the soothing effects cast by his declining rays on every object, I went through a plot of vines to a favourite haunt of mine:—a little garden of the most fragrant roses, with a spring under a rustic arch of grotto work fringed with ivy." (I, 206)

p. 174 For "Millions" (1834) reads "Thousands". (I, 206)

p. 174 For "a statue of Ganymede, sitting reclined upon the eagle" (1834) reads "an antique statue". (I, 206)

p. 174 (1834) deletes "Her silver brightness . . . holm-oak and bay, amongst". (I, 206)

p. 174 For "everybody was jumbling" (1834) reads "all the world were going". (I, 206)

p. 174 (1834) deletes "However, it being addressed . . . Bedini". (I, 207)

p. 175 (1834) deletes "This, you will say . . ." to end of paragraph. (I, 207)

p. 176 Letter XVI (Part II, 1834) begins at Letter XVIII (1783). (I, 208)

p. 176 After "October 22d" (1834) adds "1780". (I, 208)

p. 176 (1834) deletes "hear, without feeling . . . groves of cypress inclose." (I, 208)

p. 176 (1834) deletes "and marking the golden . . . their leaves." (I, 209)

p. 176 (1834) deletes footnote and adds "celebrated by Dante" after "pleasant hills". (I, 209)

p. 176 For "lost in immensity" (1834) reads "lost in the haze of the horizon." (I, 209)

p. 177 (1834) deletes " (Giesu . . . Madre) ". (I, 209)

p. 177 (1834) deletes "with infinite taste, and simple elegance". (I, 209)

p. 177 (1834) deletes "in the corrupt Greek . . . primitive Christians". (I, 209)

p. 177 (1834) deletes "I thought of the Zancaroon . . . verses of the Koran." (I, 210)

p. 177 (1834) deletes "I staid till sun-set . . . waving of their boughs." (I, 210)

p. 177 For "Her R. H. the G." (1834) reads "Her Royal Highness the Grand". (I, 210)

p. 177 For "began his business" (1834) reads "began the ceremony". (I, 211)

p. 178 For "full gallop" (1834) reads "with thoughtless expedition." (I, 211)

p. 178 For "Lord Tilney's", (1834) reads "Lord T——'s" (I, 211)

p. 178 (1834) deletes last sentence of letter. (I, 212)

p. 179 Letter XVII (Part II, 1834) begins at Letter XIX (1783). (I, 213)

p. 179 After "October 23d" (1834) adds "1780". (I, 213)

p. 179 For "upon the hill of pines . . . in the twilight" (1834) reads "in the valley at F——, under the hill of pines?" (I, 213)

p. 180 (1834) deletes "which shade their acclivities." (I, 215)

p. 181 (1834) deletes "then, springing up . . . its hollow trunk." (I, 217)

p. 181 (1834) deletes "Pardon me . . . still as Gualbertus." (I, 218)

p. 181 (1834) "being troubled with . . . ashamed of inspiring." (I, 218)

p. 181 (1834) deletes "muddled, I conjecture". (I, 218)

pp. 181–2 (1834) deletes "rare stories . . . pass away the evening." (I, 218)

p. 182 For "but where the wild scenery . . . nodding precipices" (1834) reads "had not the wild and mountainous forest". (I, 220)

p. 182 (1834) deletes "and swelling into gentle . . . contrast with its tender green." (I, 220)

p. 183 For "high mountain of Radicofani" (1834) reads "black mountain of Radicofani." (I, 221)

p. 183 (1834) deletes "A sadness . . . with superstitious terrors." (I, 221)

p. 183 (1834) deletes "The music partook of the sadness of the scene." (I, 222)

p. 184 Letter XVIII (Part II, 1834) begins at Letter XX (1783). (I, 223)

p. 184 (1834) deletes "Sienna Oct. 26th" down to "till we entered

Sienna" and begins Letter XVIII with "Sienna, October 27th, 1780". (I, 223)

p. 184 For "which may certainly be esteemed" (1834) reads "which, by many of the Italian devotees to a purer style of architecture, is esteemed". (I, 223)

p. 185 For "but it is so lost . . . part of its effect" (1834) reads "but it wants effect, as seeming out of place in this chaos of caprice and finery." (I, 225)

p. 186 For "the sudden glare . . . mysteries of the place" (1834) reads "I know not what terrible initiation into the mysteries of the place." (I, 226)

p. 186 (1834) deletes "suspecting they would soon turn wizards". (I, 227)

p. 187 Letter XIX (Part II, 1834) begins at Letter XXI (1783). (I, 228)

p. 187 After "Oct. 28th" (1834) adds "1780". (I, 228)

p. 187 For "Peter de Laer" (1834) reads "Bamboche". (I, 229)

p. 187 (1834) deletes "The crackling of flames . . . due to sacrilege." (I, 229)

p. 188 (1834) deletes "My heart . . . approaching Rome." (I, 229)

p. 189 Letter XX (Part II, 1834) begins at Letter XXII (1783). (I, 230)

p. 189 After "Oct. 29th" (1834) adds "1780". (I, 230)

p. 190 For "Heath and furze" (1834) reads "Heath and a greyish kind of moss". (I, 232)

p. 191 (1834) deletes "A spring flowed . . . looked into futurity?" (I, 234)

p. 191 (1834) deletes "and fixed me . . . lost in wonder." (I, 235)

p. 192 (1834) deletes "It was a clear . . . then repaired". (I, 236)

p. 192 For "under the dome" (1834) reads "within this glorious temple." (I, 236)

p. 192 (1834) deletes "for us to read, or draw by." (I, 237)

p. 192 For "to such creatures too as resemble us" (1834) reads "to beings of our own visionary persuasion." (I, 237)

pp. 192–3 (1834) deletes "The windows I should shade . . . to rise and set, at pleasure." (I, 237)

p. 193 After "The whiteness of the dome offending me" (1834) adds "for, alas! this venerable temple has been whitewashed." (I, 237–8)

p. 193 (1834) deletes "But, though it is not so immense . . . sorrowful kind." (I, 238)

p. 193 For "mystic substances beaming" (1834) reads "mystic beings streaming". (I, 238)

p. 193 For "to distinguish me, being . . . supreme degree" (1834) reads "to enliven me" and adds "My spirits were not mended upon returning home." (I, 239)

p. 194 For "which I am half inclined to imagine" (1834) reads "which I try lustily to persuade myself". (I, 239)

p. 194 After "should I lose sight of you" (1834) adds "for ever?" (I, 239)

pp. 194–6 (1834) deletes "October 31st" down to "some compact from Lucifer." (I, 240)

p. 196 Letter XXI (Part II, 1834) begins at "November 1st". (I, 240)

p. 196 After "November 1st" (1834) adds "1780". (I, 240)

p. 197 (1834) deletes "The mountains were covered . . . till the chaise came up." (I, 242)

p. 197 (1834) deletes "I never felt my spirits . . . enchantments of Circe." (I, 243)

p. 197 For "All day were we approaching her rock" (1834) reads "All day we kept winding through this enchanted country." (I, 243)

p. 198 (1834) deletes "found a spring . . . edge of the precipice, and". (I, 244)

pp. 198–9 (1834) deletes "Who knows, but Circe . . ." down to "compound virtues of every flower." (I, 244)

p. 199 For "had sailed, in search of fate . . . those illustrious wanderers" (1834) reads "had sailed to fulfill their mystic destinies." (I, 245)

p. 199 (1834) deletes "some of which I obtained leave to gather." (I, 245)

p. 199 (1834) deletes "catching fresh gales . . . fields on the shore." (I, 245)

p. 200 (1834) deletes "Lightning began to flash . . . frightened to their homes." (I, 246)

p. 200 For "The fields round Naples" (1834) reads "The plains of Aversa". (I, 246)

p. 200 For "cussing and swearing" (1834) reads "ranting and raving". (I, 246)

p. 200 (1834) deletes "I could not sleep . . . disturbed as the elements." (I, 247)

p. 201 After "drew my attention" (1834) adds "to the opposite side of the bay." (I, 248)

p. 201 For "holding converse with the Nereids" (1834) reads "composing his marine eclogues." (I, 248)

pp. 201–2 For "You may suppose . . . wander with Theocritus" (1834) reads "You may suppose I was not sorry after my presentation was over, to return to Sir W. H.'s, where an interesting group of lovely women, literati and artists, were assembled—Gagliani and Cyrillo, Aprile, Milico, and Deamicis—the determined Santo Marco, and the more nymph-like modest-looking, though not less dangerous, Belmonte. Gagliani happened to be in full story, and vied with his countryman Polichinello, not only in gesticulations and loquacity, but in the excessive licentiousness of his narrations. He was proceeding beyond all bounds of decency and decorum, at least according to English notion, when Lady H.* sat down to the pianoforte. Her plaintive modulations breathed a far different language. No performer that ever I heard produced such soothing effects; they seemed the emanations of a pure, uncontaminated mind, at peace with itself and benevolently desirous of diffusing that happy tranquility around it; these were modes a Grecian legislature would have encouraged to further the triumph over vice of the most amiable virtue."

p. 202 (1834) deletes "in this delightful excursion of fancy". (I, 251)

p. 202 For "six rows of boxes" (1834) reads "seven rows of boxes one above the other". (I, 251)

p. 202 For "ugly beings" (1834) reads "swarthy ill-favoured beings". (I, 251)

p. 202 (1834) deletes "The last ballet . . ." to end of paragraph. (I, 252)

p. 202 Letter XXII (Part II, 1834) begins at "November 6th". (I, 253)

p. 202 After "November 6th" (1834) adds "1780". (I, 253)

p. 203 For "made such a noise . . . to the Manes" (1834) reads "made a strange but not absolutely unharmonious din with their tools and their voices." (I, 254)

p. 204 (1834) deletes "drops of dew . . . and clowns away." (I, 256)

p. 204 (1834) deletes "I wonder I did not visit . . . the chasm below; another". (I, 256)

"*This excellent and highly cultivated woman died at Naples in August 1782. Had she lived to a later period her example and influence might probably have gone great length towards arresting that tide of corruption and profligacy which swept off this ill-fated court at Sicily, and threatened its total destruction." (I, 250-1)

p. 205 Letter XXIII (Part II, 1834) begins at Letter XXIII (1783). (I, 258)

p. 205 After "November 8th" (1834) adds "1780". (I, 258)

p. 206 For "Puzzoli" (1834) reads "Pozzuoli." (I, 260)

p. 206 (1834) deletes "columbariums and". (I, 260)

p. 206 (1834) deletes "where the dead sleep . . . concealed by thickets." (I, 260)

p. 206 For "plausible young travellers" (1834) reads "inquisitive young travellers." (I, 261)

p. 206 (1834) deletes " 'Tis a grand labyrinth . . . trailing from the cove"; and after "A noise of trickling waters prevailed", adds "throughout this grand labyrinth of solid vaults and arches". (I, 261)

p. 206 For "were passing along its margin" (1834) reads "seemed fixed on its margin". (I, 261)

p. 207 (1834) deletes "all was serene . . . inhabitant of Elysium." (I, 262)

p. 207 After "hedges of cane" (1834) adds "and a variety of herbs and pulses and Indian corn". (I, 262)

p. 207 (1834) deletes "I walked on . . . tufted bay-trees". (I, 262)

p. 207 (1834) deletes "*Juvat arva videre* . . . one of Æneas's companions." (I, 262)

p. 207 For "they would have discovered . . . out of their bosom" (1834) reads "and peopled its green expanse with all the sylvan demigods of their beautiful mythology. Here were springs issuing from rocks of pumice, and grassy hillocks partially concealed by thickets of bay." (I, 262–3)

p. 208 (1834) deletes "a flat spot . . . fanned by its breezes." (I, 263)

p. 208 For "dark ivy crept among . . . sharp spines" (1834) reads "bristled over with sharp-spired dwarf aloes". (I, 263–4)

p. 208 (1834) deletes "To say truth . . . green vale." (I, 264)

p. 208 (1834) deletes "O Quixote! Quixote! . . . spinning-wheels, and solitude?" (I, 265)

p. 209 (1834) deletes "she seemed older . . . ground with sorrow." (I, 266)

p. 209 After "your kindness" (1834) adds "to him". (I, 266)

p. 212 (1834) deletes "Her large blue . . . whiter than their foam." (I, 273)

p. 213 (1834) deletes "Dark clouds . . . gleam coloured the sea." (I, 274)

p. 213 For "grew ten feet down" (1834) reads "grew several feet down". (I, 275)

p. 213 (1834) deletes "My heart was dead within me. I called upon the Lord" and continues "His voice grew faint, and as I gazed intent upon him, the loose thong of leather, which had entangled itself in the branches by which he hung suspended, gave way, and he fell into utter darkness." (I, 275)

p. 213 (1834) deletes "looked stained with streaks of blood; her orb". (I, 276)

p. 214 (1834) deletes "I shrunk back." (I, 276)

p. 214 (1834) deletes "shuddering, looked down into the gloom." (I, 277)

p. 214 (1834) deletes "in the great Being"; and after "in our Redeemer", adds "in his most holy mother?" Also, for "I answered with reverence . . . no Catholic" (1834) reads "I answered with reverence, but said her faith and mine were different." (I, 277)

p. 215 (1834) deletes "I was vexed . . . returned to Naples." (I, 279)

pp. 216–22 (1834) deletes Letter XXIV (1783) in its entirety.

pp. 223–4 (1834) deletes Letter XXV (1783) in its entirety.

p. 225 Letter XXIV (Part II, 1834) begins at Letter XXVI (1783). (I, 280)

pp. 226–45 (1834) deletes Letter XXVII (1783) in its entirety.

p. 247 The "Additional Letters" are entitled "Second Visit to Italy" in the 1834 edition. (I, 283)

p. 247 In the note prefacing this section (1834) deletes "which was interrupted by a dangerous illness". (I, 284)

p. 251 After "June 4th" (1834) adds "1782". (I, 288)

p. 251 For "Feuzen" (1834) reads "Fuessen". (I, 288)

p. 251 For "Nasariet" (1834) reads "Nasseriet". (I, 288)

p. 251 For "C." (1834) reads "Cozens". (I, 289)

p. 251 For "A sort of blue-bell" (1834) reads "Gentians". (I, 289)

p. 252 After "June 14th (1834) adds "1782". (I, 290)

p. 253 (1834) deletes "and sung over the airs . . . dawn of our acquaintance" and adds "where I met Cesarotti, who read to us some of the most affecting passages in his Fingal, with all the intensity of a poet, thoroughly persuaded that into his own bosom the very soul of Ossian had been transfused." (I, 292)

p. 253 After "Traversing the desart of locusts" (1834) adds the following footnote: "See Letter VII." (I, 292)

p. 253 For "bosom" (1834) reads "agitated waters." (I, 292)

p. 254 After "June 19th" (1834) adds "1782". (I, 297)

p. 254 For "where I pitched my piano-forte" (1834) reads "where

my friend's little wild-looking niece pitched her pianoforte".
(I, 295)

p. 255 After "June 29th" (1834) adds "1782". (I, 297)

p. 256 For "jiggeting along" (1834) reads "parading". (I, 297)

p. 256 (1834) deletes "found out my old haunts" and "and enjoyed the pure transparent sky, between groves of slender
cypress." After "Coliseo" (1834) adds "and scrambled". (I,
297)

p. 257 After "June 30th" (1834) adds "1782". (I, 299)

p. 257 For "fine pink and yellow people" (1834) reads "pompous
people". (I, 299)

p. 257 For "dignified carcases" (1834) reads "red-legged Cardinals". (I, 299)

p. 257 (1834) deletes "Yes, I am persuaded some consul . . . lies
a clear spring." (I, 300)

pp. 257–8 (1834) deletes "Shall I confess . . . similar edifice, far
from you?" (I, 300)

p. 259 After "July 8th" (1834) adds "1782". (I, 302)

p. 259 For "No other carriage than Sir W's" (1834) reads "No
other unroyal carriage except Sir W.'s". (I, 302)

p. 259 (1834) deletes "at least, I should do so, if I were a rabbit."
(I, 302)

p. 261 (1834) entitles new section "Grande Chartreuse." (I, 305)

pp. 263–4 (1834) deletes "The Grand Chartreuse has exceeded
my expectations . . ." down to "first dawn of the next day"
and adds in its place the following:

Letter I

Gray's sublime Ode on the Grande Chartreuse had sunk
so deeply into my spirit that I could not rest in peace on the
banks of the Leman Lake till I had visited the scene from
whence he caught inspiration. I longed to penetrate these
sacred precincts, to hear the language of their falling waters,
and throw myself into the gloom of their forests: no object
of a worldly nature did I allow to divert my thoughts, neither
the baths of Aix, nor the habitation of the too indulgent
Madame de Warens (held so holy by Rousseau's worshippers),
nor the magnificent road cut by Charles Emanuel of Savoy
through the heart of a rocky mountain. All these points of
attraction so interesting to general travellers, were lost upon
me, so totally was I absorbed in the anticipation of the pil-

grimage I had undertaken.

Mr. Lettice, who shared all my sentiments of admiration for Gray, and eagerness to explore the region he had described in his short and masterly letters with such energy, felt the same indifference as myself to commonplace scenery.

The twilight was beginning to prevail when we reached Les Echelles, a miserable village, with but few of its chimneys smoking, situated at the base of a mountain, round which had gathered a concourse of red and greyish clouds. I was heartily glad to leave these forlorn and wretched quarters at the first dawn of the next day." (I, 307–8)

p. 267 Letter II (1834) of "Grand Chartreuse" begins at "We quitted this solitary cross . . ." etc. (I, 314)

p. 269 (1834) deletes "The best fish . . . for its clearness and purity." (I, 319)

p. 269 For "which we pronounced of very respectable antiquity" (1834) reads "of the happiest growth and vintage". (I, 319)

p. 269 For "W." (1834) reads "Witham". (I, 320)

p. 270 (1834) deletes "and, with the voluminous records of the Abbey of Whitham." (I, 321)

p. 270 (1834) deletes "Dom Biclét" and "Père Robinét". (I, 321)

p. 271 (1834) deletes "Were I, after walking along . . . so sublime a consecration." (I, 323)

p. 271 Letter III (1834) of "Grand Chartreuse" begins at "The Coadjutor seemed charmed with the respect . . ." etc. (I, 324)

p. 272 (1834) deletes "Being neatly glazed, and free from paintings, or Gothic ornaments, it". (I, 326)

p. 272 (1834) deletes "even there, the elegance . . . most costly gems." (I, 327)

p. 272 For "Whitsunday" (1834) reads "a high festival". (I, 327)

p. 273 For "inconceivable" (1834) reads "enhanced by contrast." (I, 327)

p. 273 For "it had risen like an exhalation" (1834) reads "the whole structure had risen by 'subtle magic,' like an exhalation." (I, 327)

p. 273 (1834) deletes "very piously". (I, 328)

p. 274 For "enthusiasm and superstition" (1834) reads "the loftiest enthusiasm." (I, 330)

p. 274 (1834) deletes "Saint Bruno was certainly . . . to know what preceded it." (I, 330)

p. 274 Passage beginning "My Saint (for Bruno has succeeded Thomas of Canterbury) . . ." down to "the future abode of Bruno" has been altered in the 1834 edition to read as follows:

"The revered author of this strangely abstruse and mystic volume was certainly a being of no common order, nor do we find in the wide circle of legendary traditions an event recorded, better calculated to inspire the utmost degree of religious terror than that which determined him to the monastic state.

St. Bruno was of noble descent, and possessed considerable wealth. Not less remarkable for the qualities of his mind, their assiduous cultivation obtained for him the chair of master of the great sciences in the University of Rheims, where he contracted an intimate friendship with Odo, afterwards Pope Urban II. Though it appears that a very cheering degree of public approbation, and all the blandishments of a society highly polished for the period, contributed, not unprofitably one should think, to fill up his time, always singular, always visionary, he began early in life to loathe the world, and sigh after retirement.

But a most appalling occurrence converted these sighs into the deepest groans. A man, who had borne the highest character for the exercise of every virtue, died, and was being carried to the grave. The procession, of which Bruno formed a part, was moving slowly on when a low, mournful sound issued from the bier. The corpse was distinctly seen to lift up its ghastly countenance, and as distinctly heard to articulate these words—'*I am summoned to trial.*' After an agonizing pause, the same terrific voice declared—'*I stand before the tribunal.*' Some further moments of amazement and horror having elapsed, the dead body lifted itself up a third time, and moving its livid lips uttered forth this dreadful sentence—'*I am condemned by the just judgment of God.*' 'Alas! alas!' exclaimed Bruno—'of how little avail are apparent good works, or the favourable opinion of mankind!

Ubi fugiam nisi ad te?—

Thy mercies alone can save, and it is not in the frivolous and seductive intercourse of a worldly life those mercies can be obtained.'

Stricken to the heart by these reflections, he hurried in a fever of terror and alarm (the sepulchral voice still ringing in his ears) to Grenoble, of which see one of his dearest friends, the venerable Hugo, had lately been appointed bishop.

This saintly prelate soothed the dreadful agitation of his

spirits by relating to him a revelation he had just received in a dream.

'As I slept,' said Hugo, 'methought the desert mountains beyond Grenoble became suddenly visible in the dead of night which hung directly over them. Whilst I remained absorbed in the contemplation of this wonder, an awful voice seemed to break the nocturnal silence, declaring their dreary solitudes thy future abode, O Bruno!' " (I, 330–2)

p. 274 For "to tread these silent regions" (1834) reads "ever invade their fastnesses" and deletes "which were to be dedicated, solely, to their Creator". (I, 332)

p. 275 (1834) deletes "Many are the miracles . . . needless to recite them" and adds the following paragraph:

"In his death there was no bitterness. A celestial radiance shone around him even before he closed his eyes upon his frail existence, and many a venerable witness has testified that the voices of angelic beings were heard calling him to come and receive his reward; but as the different accounts of his translation are not essentially varied, it would be tedious to recite them." (I, 334)

p. 275 Letter IV (1834) of "Grande Chartreuse" begins at "I had scarcely finished taking extracts . . ." etc. (I, 335)

p. 275 (1834) deletes "The good fathers returned . . . with angels and moonbeams" and the footnote, and substitutes "The good fathers returned as usual before our repast was over, and resumed as usual their mystic discourse, looking all the time rather earnestly into my countenance to observe the sort of effect their most marvellous narrations produced upon it." (I, 335)

p. 275 After "Our conversation" (1834) adds "which was beginning to take a gloomy and serious turn". (I, 335)

p. 276 For "maple cup" (1834) reads "wooden bowl". (I, 337)

p. 277 For "looking down a steep, hollow vale, surrounded by the forests" (1834) reads "looking down what appeared to be a fathomless ravine blackened by the shade of impervious forests". (I, 339)

p. 278 For "Mr. ——" (1834) reads "Mr. Lettice". (I, 341)

p. 278 Letter V (1834) of "Grande Chartreuse" begins at "We had hardly supped . . ." etc. (I, 342)

pp. 279–80 (1834) deletes "It was midnight; the convent . . . the stillest watch of night" and the entire "Ode." It continues "It was midnight before I returned to the convent and retired to my quiet chamber, but my imagination . . ." etc. (I, 344)

p. 280 (1834) deletes "breakfasted in haste, and". (I, 345)

p. 282 (1834) deletes "The cattle were all slunk . . . unite to render it pleasing." (I, 348)

p. 282 After "Valombré" (1834) adds "for so is this beautifully wooded region most appropriately called." (I, 348)

p. 284 (1834) deletes "They were not even contented with going thus far". (I, 352)

p. 284 For "Amecy" (1834) reads "Annecy". (I, 353)

p. 284 (1834) concludes with two letters in a section entitled "Saleve." They are as follows:

Letter I.

I had long wished to revisit the holt of trees so conspicuous on the summit of Saleve, and set forth this morning to accomplish that purpose. Brandoin an artist, once the delight of our travelling lords and ladies, accompanied me. We rode pleasantly and sketchingly along through Carouge to the base of the mountain, taking views every now and then of picturesque stumps and cottages.

At length, after a good deal of lackadaisical loitering on the banks of the Arve, we reached a sort of goats' path, leading to some steps cut in the rock, and justly called the Pas d'Echelle. I need not say we were obliged to dismount and toil up this ladder, beyond which rise steeps of verdure shaded by walnuts.

These brought us to Moneti, a rude straggling village, with its church tower embosomed in gigantic limes. We availed ourselves of their deep cool shade to dine as comfortably as a whole posse of withered hags, who seemed to have been just alighted from their broomsticks, would allow us.

About half past three, a sledge drawn by four oxen was got ready to drag us up to the holt of trees, the goal to which we were tending: stretching ourselves on the straw spread over our vehicle, we set off along a rugged path, conducted aslant the steep slope of the mountain, vast prospects opening as we ascended; to our right the crags of the little Saleve—the variegated plains of Gex and Chablais, separated by the lake; below, Moneti, almost concealed in wood; behind, the mole, lifting up its pyramidical summit amidst the wild amphitheatre of glaciers, which lay this evening in dismal shadow, the sun being overcast, the Jura half lost in rainy mists, and a heavy storm darkening the Fort de l'Ecluse. Except a sickly

gleam cast on the snows of the Buet, not a ray of sunshine enlivened our landscape.

This sorrowful colouring agreed but too well with the dejection of my spirits. I suffered melancholy recollections to
tage full possession of me, and glancing my eyes over the vast
map below, sought out those spots where I had lived so happy
with my lovely Margaret. On them did I eagerly gaze—absorbed in the consciousness of a fatal, irreparable loss, I little
noticed the transports expressed by my companion at the
grand effects of light and shade, which obeyed the movements
of the clouds; nor was I more attentive to the route of our
oxen, which, perfectly familiarized with precipices, preferred
their edge to the bank on the other side, and by this choice
gave us an opportunity of looking down more than a thousand
feet perpendicularly on the wild shrubberies and shattered
rocks deep below, at the base of the mountain. In general I
shrink back from such bird's-eye prospects with my head in
a whirl, and yet, by a most unaccountable fascination, feel a
feverish impulse to throw myself into the very gulph I abhor;
but today I lay in passive indifference, listlessly extended on
our moving bed.

Its progress being extremely deliberate, we had leisure to
observe, as we crept along, a profusion of Alpine flowers; but
none of these gorgeous insects mentioned by Saussure as
abounding on Saleve were fluttering about them. This was no
favourable day for butterfly excursions; the flowers laden with
heavy drops, the forerunners of still heavier rain, hung down
their heads. We passed several chalets, formed of mud and
stone, instead of the neat timber, with which those on the
Swiss mountains are constructed. Meagre peasants, whose sal-
low countenances looked quite of a piece with the sandy hue
of their habitations, kept staring at us from crevices and
hollow places: the fresh roses of a garden are not more different from the rank weeds of an unhealthy swamp, than these
wretched objects from the ruddy inhabitants of Switzerland.

My heart sank as we were driven alongside of one of these
squalid groups, huddled together under a blasted beech in expectation of a storm. The wind drove the smoke and sparks of
a fire just kindled at the root of the tree, full in the face of
an infant, whose mother had abandoned it to implore our
charity with outstretched withered hands. The poor helpless
being filled the air with wailings, and being tightly swaddled
up in yellow rags, according to Savoyarde custom, exhibited

an appearance in form and colour not unlike that of an over-grown pumpkin thrown on the ground out of the way. How should I have enjoyed setting its limbs at liberty, and transporting it to the swelling bosom of a Bernese peasant! such as I have seen in untaxed garments, red, blue and green, with hair falling in braids mixed with flowers and silver trinkets, hurrying along to some wake or wedding, with that firm step and smiling hilarity which the consciousness of freedom inspires.

A few minutes dragging beyond the tree just mentioned, we reached the bold verdant slopes of delicate short herbage which crown the crags of the mountain. We now moved smoothly along the turf, brushing it with our hands to extract its aromatic fragrance, and having no longer rough stones to encounter, our conveyance became so agreeable that we regretted our arrival before a chalet, under a clump of weather-beaten beech. These are the identical trees, so far and widely discovered, on the summit of Saleve, and the point to which we had been tending.

Seating ourselves on the very edge of a rocky cornice, we surveyed the busy crowded territory of Geneva, the vast reach of the lake, its coast, thickset with castles, towns, and villages, and the long line of the Jura protecting these richly cultivated possessions. Turning round, we traced the course of the Arve up to its awful sanctuary, the Alps of Savoy, above which rose the Mont-Blanc in deadly paleness, backed by a gloomy sky; nothing could form a stronger contrast to the populous and fertile plains in front of the mountain than this chaos of snowy peaks and melancholy deserts, the loftiest in the old world, held up in the air, and beaten, in spite of summer, with wintry storms.

I know not how long we should have remained examining the prospect had the weather been favourable, and had we enjoyed one of those serene evenings to be expected in the month of July. Many such have I passed in my careless childish days, stretched out on the brow of this very mountain, contemplating the heavenly azure of the lake, the innumerable windows of the villas below blazing in the setting sun, and the glaciers suffused by its last ray with a blushing pink. How often, giving way to a youthful enthusiasm, have I peopled these singularly varied peaks with gnomes and fairies, the distributors of gold and crystal to those who adventurously scaled their lofty abode.

This evening my fancy was led to no such gay aërial excursions; sad realities chained it to the earth, and to the scene before my eyes, which in lowering, somber hue, corresponded with my interior gloom. A rude blast driving us off the margin of the precipices, we returned to the shelter of the beech. There we found some disappointed butterfly catchers, probably of the watch-making tribe, and a silly boy gaping after them with a lank net and empty boxes. This being Monday, I thought the Saleve had been delivered from such intruders; but it seems that the rage for natural history has so victoriously pervaded all ranks of people in the republic, that almost every day in the week sends forth some of its journeymen to ransack the neighbouring cliffs, and transfix unhappy butterflies.

Silversmiths and toymen, possessed by the spirit of De Luc and De Saussure's lucubrations, throw away the light implements of their trade, and sally forth with hammer and pickaxe to pound pebbles and knock at the door of every mountain for information. Instead of furbishing up teaspoons and sorting watch-chains, they talk of nothing but quartz and feldspath. One flourishes away on the durability of granite, whilst another treats calcareous rocks with contempt; but as human pleasures are seldom perfect and permanent, acrimonious disputes too frequently interrupt the calm of the philosophic excursion. Squabbles arise about the genus of a coralite, or concerning that element which has borne the greatest part in the convulsion of nature. The advocate of water too often sneaks home to his wife with a tattered collar, whilst the partisan of fire and volcanoes lies vanquished in a puddle, or winding up the clue of his argument in a solitary ditch. I cannot help thinking so diffused a taste for fossils and petrifactions of no very particular benefit to the artisans of Geneva, and that watches would go as well, though their makers were less enlightened.

Letter II.

It began to rain just as we entered the chalet under the beech-trees, and one of the dirtiest I ever crept into—it would have been uncharitable not to have regretted the absence of swine, for here was mud and filth enough to have insured their felicity. A woman, whose teeth of a shining whiteness were the only clean objects I could discover, brought us foaming bowls of cream and milk, with which we regaled ourselves, and then got into our vehicle. We but too soon left the smooth herbage behind, and passed about an hour in rambling down the mountain pelted by the showers, from which we took shelter under the limes at Moneti.

Here we should have drunk our tea in peace and quietness, had it not been for the incursion of a gang of bandylegged watchmakers, smoking their pipes, and scraping their fiddles, and snapping their fingers, with all that insolent vulgarity so characteristic of the Rue-basse portion of the Genevese community. We got out of their way, you may easily imagine, as fast as we were able, and descending a rough road, most abominably strewn with rolling pebbles, arrived at the bridge d'Etrombieres just as it fell dark. The mouldering planks with which the bridge is awkwardly put together, sounded suspiciously hollow under the feet of our horses, and had it not been for the friendly light of a pine torch which a peasant brought forth, we might have been tumbled into the Arve.

It was a mild solemn night, the rainy clouds were dissolving away with a murmur of distant thunder so faint as to be scarcely heard. From time to time a flash of summer lightning discovered the lonely tower of Moneti on the edge of the lesser Saleve. The ghostly tales, which the old curè of the mountains had told me at a period when I hungered and thirsted after supernatural narrations, recurred to my memory, in all their variety of horrors, and kept it fully employed till I found myself under the walls of Geneva. The gates were shut, but I knew they were to be opened again at ten o'clock for the convenience of those returning from the *Comedie*.

The *Comedie* is become of wonderful importance; but a few years ago the very name of a play was held in such abhorrence by the spiritual consistory of Geneva and its obsequious servants, which then included the best part of the republic, that the partakers and abettors of such diversions were esteemed on the high road to eternal perdition. Though, God knows, I am unconscious of any extreme partiality for Calvin, I cannot help thinking his severe discipline wisely adapted to the moral constitution of this starch bit of a republic which he took to his grim embraces. But these days of rigidity and plainness are completely gone by; the soft spirit of toleration, so eloquently insinuated by Voltaire, has removed all thorny fences, familiarized his numerous admirers with every innovation, and laughed scruples of every nature to scorn. Voltaire, indeed, may justly be styled the architect of that gay well-ornamented bridge, by which freethinking and immorality have been smuggled into the republic under the mask of philosophy and liberality and sentiment. These monsters, like the Sin and Death of Milton, have made speedy and irreparable havoc. To facilitate their operations, rose the genius of "Rentes Viagères" at his bidding, tawdry villas with their little pert groves of poplar and horse-chesnut start up—his power enables Madame C. D. the bookseller's lady to amuse the D. of G. with assemblies, sets parisian cabriolets and English phaetons rolling from one faro table to another, and launches innumerable pleasure parties with banners and popguns on the lake, drumming and trumpeting away their time from morn till evening. I recollect, not many years past, how seldom the echoes of the mountains were profaned by such noises, and how rarely the drones of Geneva, if any there were in that once industrious city, had opportunities of displaying their idleness; but now Dissipation reigns triumphant, and to pay the tribute she exacts, every fool runs headlong to throw his scrapings into the voracious whirlpool of annuities; little caring, provided he feeds high and lolls in his carriage, what becomes of his posterity. I had ample time to make these reflections, as the *Comedie* lasted longer that usual.

Luckily the night improved, the storms had rolled away, and the moon rising from behind the crags of the lesser Saleve cast a pleasant gleam on the smooth turf of plain-palais, where we walked to and fro above half an hour. We had this extensive level almost entirely to ourselves, no light glimmered in any window, no sound broke the general stillness, except a low murmur proceeding from a group of chesnut trees. There, snug under a garden wall on a sequestered bench, sat two or three Genevois of the old stamp, chewing the cud of sober sermons—men who receive not more than seven or eight per cent for their money; there sat they waiting for their young ones, who had been seduced to the theatre.

A loud hubbub and glare of flambeaus proclaiming the end of the play, we left these good folks to their rumination, and regaining our carriage rattled furiously through the streets of Geneva, once so quiet, so silent at these hours, to the no small terror and annoyance of those whom Rentes Viagères had not yet provided with a speedier conveyance than their own legs, or a brighter satellite than an old cook-maid with a candle and lantern.

It was eleven o'clock before we reached home, and near two before I retired to rest, having sat down immediately to write this letter whilst the impressions of the day were fresh in my memory. (I, 357–71)

Selected Bibliography

I. Editions of Dreams and Italy:

A. DREAMS, WAKING THOUGHTS, AND INCIDENTS

Dreams, Waking Thoughts, and Incidents: in a series of Letters, from various parts of Europe. London: Printed for J. Johnson, St. Paul's Church Yard: and P. Elmsly, in the Strand. M.DCC. LXXXIII.

The History of the Caliph Vathek; and European Travels. By William Beckford: With a Portrait, Full-Page Illustrations, and Biographical Introduction. Ward, Lock and Co., London, New York, and Melbourne. 1891.

Besides *Vathek*, pp. 3–92, this volume contains *Dreams, Waking Thoughts, and Incidents,* pp. 95–269, *An Excursion to the Grand Chartreuse in the Year 1778,* pp. 270–293, *Sketches of Spain and Portugal,* pp. 303–465, and *Recollections of an Excursion to the Monasteries of Alcobaça and Batalha,* pp. 466–549.

The Travel-Diaries of William Beckford of Fonthill. Edited with a Memoir and Notes by Guy Chapman. In Two Volumes with Illustrations. Printed at the University Press, Cambridge, for Constable and Company Limited &. Houghton Mifflin Company, 1928.

Volume I contains the original text of *Dreams, Waking Thoughts, and Incidents* with an appendix listing the principal variations in the 1834 edition. Volume II contains *Sketches of Spain and Portugal* and *Recollections of an Excursion to the Monasteries of Alcobaça and Batalha.*

B. ITALY; WITH SKETCHES OF SPAIN AND PORTUGAL

Italy; with Sketches of Spain and Portugal. By the Author of

"Vathek." In Two Volumes. London: Richard Bentley, New Burlington Street, Publisher in Ordinary to His Majesty. 1834.

Italy; with Sketches of Spain and Portugal. By the Author of "Vathek." In Two Volumes. Second edition, revised. London: Richard Bentley, New Burlington Street, Publisher in Ordinary to His Majesty. 1834.

Italy; with Sketches of Spain and Portugal. By William Beckford, Esq. Paris, Baudry's European Library, Rue du Coq, near the Louvre. Sold also by Amyot, Rue de la Paiz; Truchy, Boulevard des Italiens; Theophile Barrois, Jun., Rue Richelieu: Libraire des Etrangers, Rue Neuv-Saint-Augustin; and French and English Library, Rue Vivienne. 1834.

Italy; with Sketches of Spain and Portugal. By the Author of "Vathek." In Two Volumes. Philadelphia: Key and Biddle, 1834.

First American edition.

Italy; with Sketches of Spain and Portugal. By the Author of "Vathek" in *Waldie's Select Circulating Library,* Part II, Sept. 2, 9, 16, 23, 1834, pp. 152–207.

Italy; with Sketches of Spain and Portugal. By the Author of "Vathek." In Two Volumes. Third edition. London: Richard Bentley, New Burlington Street, Publisher in Ordinary to His Majesty. 1835.

Italy; with Sketches of Spain and Portugal. By the Author of "Vathek." Paris-Lyons; Cormon and Blanc. 1835.

Includes only a portion of *Italy*.

Italy, Spain, and Portugal, with an Excursion to the Monasteries of Alcobaça and Batalha. By the Author of "Vathek." A New Edition. London: Richard Bentley, New Burlington Street. 1840.

This is vol. VI of Bentley's Standard Library of Popular Modern Literature.

Sketches of Italy, by Mrs. Jameson. *Italy,* by William Beckford, Esq., in one volume. Frankfort a.m., Charles Jugel, 1841.

Italy appears on pp. 1–202 in English.

Italy, Spain, and Portugal, with an Excursion to the Monasteries of Alcobaça and Batalha. By the Author of "Vathek." New York: Wiley and Putnam, 1845.

II. Works Relating to Dreams and Italy:

A. BIBLIOGRAPHY:

Chapman, Guy and John Hodgkin. *A Bibliography of William*

Beckford of Fonthill. London: Constable and Co., 1930.

Gemmett, Robert J. "An Annotated Checklist of the Works of William Beckford," *Papers of the Bibliographical Society of America,* LXI (Third Quarter, 1967), 243–258.

Gotlieb, Howard B. *William Beckford of Fonthill.* New Haven: Yale University Library, 1960.

B. OTHER:

Bullough, Geoffrey. "Beckford's Early Travels and his 'Dream of Delusion,'" in *William Beckford of Fonthill, Bicentenary Essays.* ed. Fatma Mahmoud. Cairo, 1960.

Chapman, Guy. *Beckford.* 2nd ed. London: Rupert Hart-Davis, 1952.

Garnett, Richard. "Beckford's *Dreams,*" *Universal Review,* VIII (September, 1890), 112–126.

Grimsditch, Herbert B. "William Beckford's Minor Works," *London Mercury,* XIV (1926), 599–605.

[Lockhart, John Gibson.] "Italy; with Sketches of Spain and Portugal," Rev. art., *Quarterly Review,* LI (June, 1834), 426–456.

Melville, Lewis. *The Life and Letters of William Beckford of Fonthill.* London: William Heinemann, 1910.

[Mitford, John.] "Italy, with Sketches of Spain and Portugal," Rev. art., *Gentleman's Magazine,* New Ser., II (August, September, 1834), 115–121; 234–241.

Oliver, J. W. *The Life of William Beckford.* London: Oxford University Press, 1937.

Parreaux, André. "Beckford en Italie Rêve et Voyage au XVIIIᵉ siècle," *Revue de Littérature Comparée,* XXXIII (1959), 321–347.

Redding, Cyrus. *Memoirs of William Beckford of Fonthill.* 2 vols. London: Charles Skeet, 1859.

Tuckerman, H. T. "William Beckford and the Literature of Travel," *Southern Literary Messenger,* XVI (January, 1850), 7–14.

"Vathek's Grand Tour," (London) *Times Literary Supplement,* Rev. art. May 3, 1928, p. 331.

Index

326   *Dreams, Waking Thoughts and Incidents*